Telecommunications Regulatory Reform in Small Island Developing States: The Impact of the WTO's Telecommunications Commitment

Telecommunications Regulatory Reform in Small Island Developing States: The Impact of the WTO's Telecommunications Commitment

By

Siope Vakataki 'Ofa

CAMBRIDGE SCHOLARS

PUBLISHING

Telecommunications Regulatory Reform in Small Island Developing States:
The Impact of the WTO's Telecommunications Commitment,
by Siope Vakataki 'Ofa

This book first published 2012

Cambridge Scholars Publishing

12 Back Chapman Street, Newcastle upon Tyne, NE6 2XX, UK

British Library Cataloguing in Publication Data
A catalogue record for this book is available from the British Library

ISBN (10): 1-4438-3523-4, ISBN (13): 978-1-4438-3523-7

This Book is dedicated to my wife, Tu'ipulotu,
and daughters, Luseane Salaevalu, Mele Fataimoeloa and Ma'ukakala.

CONTENTS

LIST OF FIGURES

LIST OF TABLES

PREFACE

Why does the government of one small island developing state produce credible telecommunications reform policies while another cannot? While telecommunications reform (competition, privatization and establishment of an independent regulator) is found to enhance the sector's performance and eventual economic growth in developing countries, it is not clear why several small island developing state governments have hindered, amended or reversed pre-announced telecommunications reform policies. The credibility of telecommunications reform therefore demands an in-depth examination, in particular, to examine the impact of the multilateral trade agreement (World Trade Organization, WTO), bilateral investment treaties and independent regulators on the credibility of domestic telecommunications reform in small island developing states.

A mixed-method research design was adopted through comparative case study analyses of Fiji, Papua New Guinea, Samoa, Tonga and Vanuatu. Sixty-four semi-structured interviews of key telecommunications stakeholders were conducted in the capital city of each case study from June to December 2008. Further, multiple regression analyses based on a panel data of 160 developing countries (including 26 small island developing states) covering the period 1995-2006 were undertaken to triangulate the evidence from the fieldwork.

Contrary to conventional findings from the telecommunications and bilateral investment treaty literatures in developing countries, the research found that the establishment of an independent regulator and signatory to Bilateral Investment Treaties instills less pronounced credibility for telecommunications reform in small island developing states, while WTO telecommunications commitment instill stronger credibility. The recent telecommunications reform in the Pacific showed the vulnerability of independent regulators to regulatory capture. The main findings of the research emphasize the importance of considering the disadvantages of smallness when adopting the successful telecommunications policy experiences from larger developing economies into the context of a small island developing state.

ACKNOWLEDGMENTS

This book is based on my PhD research at the Crawford School of Economics and Government, the Australian National University, Canberra, Australia from 2007 to 2010. My PhD journey would not have been possible without the intellectual guidance and moral support of numerous individuals. I extend my sincere thanks to my principal supervisor, Peter Larmour who agreed to supervise this research ensuring a life-long dream to materialize. It was his constant guidance to look "outside the box" and flexible approach to learning that proved invaluable for this research. I am also indebted to my other two supervisors, Chunlai Chen and Satish Chand who have offered profound advice and constructive comments on earlier drafts during the writing stage of this thesis. Further, I owe a great debt to Carsten Fink, Ronald Duncan, Yusaku Horiuchi, Edwini Kessie, Rudolf Adlung, John Uhr, Natasha Beschomer, Malcolm Bosworth and Wendy Noble who provided valuable suggestions and comments at different stages of my research.

My sincere gratitude is extended to many scholars at the Crawford School of Economics and Government who have enhanced this research with their suggestions, ideas and information. In particular, I wish to thank Emma Aisbett, Maree Tait, Anthony Yauieb, Shabaz Nasir, Mia Amalia, Evi Fitriani, Qian Jiang, Huong Dinh and Jared Dent. A special thank you is due to all the friendly and helpful people in Fiji, Papua New Guinea, Samoa, Tonga and Vanuatu who gave precious time to support this research project in various capacities. I especially wish to thank Tevita Veituna and Kulu 'Anisi Bloomfield for assisting in the Fiji fieldwork. Appreciation is also extended to Fonua and Piula Fukofuka for Papua New Guinea; Petaia Leavai for Samoa; Vaimoana Taukolo and Tu'italikitahi 'Anau for Tonga; and Roy Mickey Joy for Vanuatu. In addition, I thank John Delves, Waikato Lefale, Susan Hugget, Timote Katoanga, Alfred Soakai, John Crook, Dionisia Taburecugi, Wayne Golding, Ari Jenshel, Douveri Henao, Samson Rowaro, Michele Marius, Margaret Malua, Tima Leavai, Timothy Sisi, Lora Lini, Tuaimalo Ah Sam, Kolone Vaai and many others who cannot be named in this limited space.

I acknowledge with thanks the financial support from the Australian Aid for International Development (AusAID) funding the research. The Government of the Kingdom of Tonga is also acknowledged for assisting this research in various capacities. Also, to Judy Bell for the professional editing of the PhD thesis. Finally, I am deeply grateful to my late father, Sanilaiti and mother, Luseane for their encouragement and commitment to higher education as a way of improving life in the islands. Last but not the least, to my wife, Tu'ipulotu, and daughters Luseane Salaevalu, Mele Fataimoeloa and Ma'ukakala Tautala ki Mamana, whose love, patience and faith gave me resilience to overcome this challenging journey.

ABBREVIATIONS AND ACRONYMS

ACCC	Australian Competition and Consumer Commission
ADB	Asian Development Bank
ATH	Amalgamated Telecommunications Holdings Limited
AusAID	Australian Agency for International Development
BITs	Bilateral Investment Treaties
CEO	Chief Executive Officer
CPI	Corruption Perception Index
DPEIDC	Department of Public Enterprises, Information and Development Cooperation
DSL	Digital Subscriber Line
ECTEL	Eastern Caribbean Telecommunications Authority
EDC	Export Development Canada
EU	European Union
FDI	Foreign Direct Investment
FINTEL	Fiji International Telecommunications
FITA	Friendly Islands Teachers Associations
FNPF	Fiji National Provident Fund
FPTL	Fiji Posts and Telecommunications Limited
GATS	General Agreement on Trade in Services
GDP	Gross Domestic Product
GLS	Generalized Least Square (method)
GSM	Global System for Mobile Communications
ICCC	Independent Consumer and Competition Commission
ICT	Information Communication Technology
IFC	International Funding Corporation
IMF	International Monetary Fund
IML	Intercai Mondiale Limited
IPBC	Independent Public Business Commission
ITU	International Telecommunications Union
MA	Market Access
MFN	Most-favored Nations (principle)
MP	Member of Parliament
NEC	National Executive Council
NETCO	Network Company
NFPF	Fiji's National Provident Fund
NGO	Non-government Organization
NICTA	National Information and Communication Technology Authority
NPIC	PNG's National Policy on Information and Communication

NT	National Treatment
OECD	Organization of Economic Cooperation and Development
OLS	Ordinary Least Square (method)
PANGTEL	Papua New Guinea Radiocommunications and Telecommunication Technical Authority
PNG	Papua New Guinea
PTD	Posts and Telecommunications Decree 1989
SERVCO	Service Company
SIDs	Small island developing states
TAF	Telecommunications Authority of Fiji
TCC	Tonga Communications Corporations
TFL	Telecom Fiji Limited
TONFON	Tongan Mobile Phone Operator
TPL	Telikom Papua New Guinea Limited
TSC	Telecom Samoa Cellular
TSL	Telecom Samoa Limited
TTIL	Tonga Telecommunications International Limited
TVL	Telecom Vanuatu Limited
TWAC	Tongan Women's Action for Change
UK	United Kingdom
VIF	Variance Inflation Factor
coup d'etat	The sudden overthrow of a government, sometimes with violence, by a small group of people with political or military power.
ceteris paribus	Assuming all else is held constant
sene	Cent
status quo	The existing state of affairs at a particular time

CHAPTER ONE

INTRODUCTION

The global financial crisis that began in 2008 has reignited debate on how to regulate financial and banking sectors across the globe. In particular, the policy debate on fixed over discretionary regulation has been hotly contested. Discretionary regulation originated from the financial and banking sectors. Governments delegate powers to regulate an industry sector to an independent authority—for example, national reserve banks in the case of the banking sector—to instill long-term regulatory credibility from changes in governments and policies. Fixed regulations, on the other hand, are regulatory policies legislated by Government—for example, domestic legislation or legally binding international treaties—which are often predictable but less responsive to immediate regulatory challenges. The proponents of discretionary policies have argued that delegating power to independent authorities provided the flexibility to make decisions based on the situation at hand. The global financial crisis however, has brought into question the effectiveness of these legal entities and the rules they adhere to which can be influenced by profit driven corporate pressures.

The renewed policy debate on fixed over discretion regulation is increasingly relevant not only in the banking sector but also in other industry sectors including telecommunications. Many developing countries undertook telecommunications reform in the 1990s with varying success. Telecommunications reform is, however, a recent phenomenon in small island developing states (SIDS). Small island developing states comprise a group of sovereign island states with natural characteristics—geographical isolation, high susceptibility to natural disasters and micro-size—hamper their development prospects. The Caribbean region first liberalized its telecommunications market with Jamaica in 2001 and soon, other Caribbean island states followed through. The comparator region, the Pacific island states, began its telecommunications reform with Tonga in 2003, followed by Samoa, Papua New Guinea, Vanuatu and Fiji.

While early signs show a positive relationship between telecommunications reform—commonly understood as the introduction of competition policy, privatization policy and the establishment of an independent regulator—and the sector's performance in small island developing states, regulatory capture may have undermined the credibility of the reforms. What is puzzling is that, if telecommunications reform improves sector performance, it is not clear why small island developing state governments tend to hinder, amend or reverse pre-announced reform policies on telecommunications. Some island states' telecommunications sectors perform better than the sectors in other island states. The underperformance may not be explained by natural disadvantages alone, but also by poor institutions and poor policy (World Bank 2006:24-30).

This puzzling question guides the general path of the research in this book. The research proposes that discretionary policies commonly operationalized by independent entities are vulnerable to regulatory capture and therefore provide limited credibility. Telecommunications regulators in the Pacific case studies were found to be subjected to: heavy political influence from governments (as shown by the regulatory experience from Fiji and Papua New Guinea); frequent amendments to national information and communications technology (ICT) policies (as shown by the regulatory experience of Papua New Guinea); legislation amendment (Samoa); and a general lack of human and financial capacity of Pacific case studies' independent regulators, undermining their overall effectiveness and integrity.

A case is made, therefore, for the role of a fixed-rule policy (WTO telecommunications commitment) to instill credibility which is relatively immune to domestic capture. WTO trade rules can only be amended through negotiations by all members and agreed by consensus. A multilateral consensus around a particular member's interest—for instance, to renege a WTO telecommunications commitment for liberalization—could be costly and time consuming. Further, the financial costs of reneging commitments at the WTO are considerably higher for small island developing states. Possible economic sanctions by the WTO members could affect the economic development of small island economies. In addition, other related costs such as the negative effect to a small island state's international reputation could hinder development assistance and aid programs—something that small island developing states are heavily reliant upon. The comparative case studies from Papua New Guinea and Tonga shed evidence on the crucial role of their WTO telecommunications commitments in limiting policy reversals on telecommunications by strengthening their unilateral reform policy initiatives.

Pacific island case studies

There is perhaps nowhere better to examine the impact of international trade policy[1] on telecommunications regulatory reform in small island developing states than the smallest, most disadvantaged and remote island states of the South Pacific. The recent telecommunications reform in the Pacific therefore provides extremely useful case studies resonating small island developing states' socio-economic and natural characteristics. The timing of this research is equally crucial in rendering an early stock-take analysis of the process and outcome of the impact of an international trade policy mechanism—WTO's telecommunications commitments under the General Agreement on Trade in Services Agreement, (GATS)—on the credibility of telecommunications reform in Pacific islands states.

The credibility of telecommunications reform in small island developing states

The motivation to study the credibility of telecommunications reform in small island developing states is threefold. First, this is a timely study to be conducted in the early phases of telecommunications reform in the Pacific and therefore considered important for recording specific international trade policy initiatives and effects on telecommunications reform in a small island developing states context.

The second issue stems from the policy debate in the telecommunications policy on the limited effectiveness of the discretionary-rules policy mechanism (independent regulator) to instill credibility in telecommunications reforms. It is therefore necessary to examine alternative policy initiatives that may equally or better instill telecommunications reform credibility. Further, the literature on telecommunications policy provides an extremely narrow interpretation

[1] For the purpose of this research, it is understood as the General Agreement on Trade in Services Agreement (GATS) of the WTO.

and academic scholarship in the policy options[2] for instilling credibility in telecommunications reforms (Bertelli and Whitford 2009; Lee and Levendis 2006; Stern and Trillas 2003; Wallsten 2003; Noll 1999; Ros 1997; Melody 1997; Levy & Spiller 1994). Most of these studies focused on domestic regulatory mechanisms including independent regulators and their role on the certainty of telecommunications reform, while no study examines the specific role and effects of external regulatory mechanisms (such as the WTO and Bilateral Investment Treaty) on the credibility of telecommunications reform in a small island developing states' context.

The third motivation which originated as a policy challenge in small island states governments is the fundamental issue whether smallness matters. Can successful telecommunications regulatory policies of developed and larger developing countries be successfully replicated in a small island developing states context? The focus of this study anticipates to contribute to the telecommunications policy literature by examining the effectiveness of commonly prescribed telecommunications reform policies (competition and establishment of an independent regulator) of larger developing countries, in a small island states context.

Overall, the selection of fixed-rules policy is important since, methodologically speaking; fixed-rules policy (WTO telecommunications commitments) can be objectively measured and is easily accessible since it is commonly used in recent empirical studies.[3] The inclusion of this international trade policy variable provides fresh insight into the much debated effects of sectoral trade liberalization in small island developing states.

Research question

Motivated by the renewed global policy debate on fixed-rules over discretionary rules and the recent telecommunications reforms in small island developing states, the research has two objectives. First, this study will examine policy initiatives that promote the development prospects of small island developing states. More importantly, it aims to examine policy prescriptions that overcome the natural challenges impeding their

[2] Existing literature on telecommunications policy in the last 30 years has focused on independent regulators as the most common policy option for instilling credibility. See further discussion in Chapter 2.

[3] See Keck and Djiofack-Zebaze (2009) for a recent empirical study using the WTO telecommunications commitment variable.

development potential (that is, telecommunications reform). Second, the research examines the impact of fixed-rules policy—WTO telecommunications commitments and discretionary rule policy—independent regulators—on the credibility of telecommunications reforms in small island developing states.

Based on these objectives, the main research question posits: Do multilateral policy restraints enhance the credibility of telecommunications regulatory reforms in small island developing states?

The research adopted a mixed-methods approach[4] to examine the effect of different levels of policy restraints on the credibility of telecommunications reform in small island developing states. The qualitative phase examined the hypotheses through comparative case study analyses of five Pacific island states (Fiji, Papua New Guinea, Tonga, Samoa and Vanuatu) drawing from primary fieldwork data collected through semi-structured expert interviews. The quantitative phase triangulated the case study findings by estimating the effectiveness of selected policy restraints on the credibility of telecommunications reform in small island developing states. The quantitative approach was based on estimates from multiple regression analyses of a panel data set of 160 developing countries (including 26 small island developing states) over the period 1995-2006.

Research contributions

This research aims to make four contributions to policy debate on telecommunications reform in small island developing states. First, Telecommunications liberalization is a complex and relatively new process in developing countries (Fink et al. 2003:444). However, this process has just begun in small island developing states. Therefore, the findings of the research provide fresh insights by identifying key regulatory successes and pitfalls that early reformers in the Pacific islands encountered, which provides a wealth of policy lessons for late-adopters

Second, the research linked three strands of literature: telecommunications reform in small island developing states, credibility problem, and multilateral trade agreements, something that contemporary policy debate on telecommunications policy grants lesser attention to. In

[4] Mixed method approach is discussed further in Chapter 3.

particular, this study would examine how technology through telecommunications connects isolated communities. Since remoteness and isolation incur costs on the socio-economic development prospects of island states, the role of technology in the telecommunications sector could contribute positively to small island developing states.

Third, the thesis aims to contribute to the current policy dialogue on trade liberalization in small island developing states. Few studies have comprehensively examined the impact of WTO telecommunications commitment on the credibility of reform policies in a small island developing states context. Using one service sector, the thesis attempts to provide preliminary evidence on the important role of commitments to the WTO on the credibility of telecommunications reform in small island developing states. The research further estimates empirically this relationship, across a panel data set for 160 developing countries, including 26 small island developing states.

Fourth, the early positive outcome of the telecommunications reforms in the Pacific islands provides anecdotal evidence to support sectoral reform over the single undertaking approach. Inserted as Paragraph 47 of the Doha Declaration, the Single Undertaking principle is defined as follows: "virtually every item of the negotiation is part of a whole and indivisible package and cannot be agreed separately" (World Trade Organization 2009). That is, nothing is agreed until everything is agreed upon. The study aims to contribute to the current policy dialogue on trade liberalization and small island developing states by suggesting that sectoral trade reform is easier (politically and economically) to adopt and perhaps sensitive enough to the domestic pressures of island states. On the other hand, a full-fledged and comprehensive trade reform across all sectors has been shown to overwhelm both small island states' government and general public support. Further, it is also anticipated that the findings of this study could contribute to the utilities sector reform literature in island states, by providing important policy lessons from the telecommunications sector that could be replicated in other utilities sectors such as electricity and water.

Research limitations

This research also has several limitations that are important to highlight. The timing of the examination of Pacific islands telecommunications reforms may be argued by some readers as premature.

While this may indeed be true, a comprehensive study of regulatory options undertaken by these Pacific islands at an early stage is equally important to stand as a record for the benefits of other small island developing states who are about to pursue a telecommunications reform program. Also, the study should provide a useful basis of information for future researchers who may attempt to analyze the long-term outcome of such a policy reform program. Without time and financial constraints dictating its boundaries, the study could have undertaken a more comprehensive business opinion survey, in addition to the stakeholder's semi-structured survey. This could have provided a more comprehensive picture of the credibility of domestic investment policies.

Structure of the book

Chapter 1 introduces the book. Chapter 2 sets the theoretical underpinnings while Chapter 3 outlines the methodological design of the research. Chapter 4 provides a first stage analysis of telecommunications reform in the Pacific case studies by conducting an up to date regulatory policy survey on telecommunications policy.

The main bulk of the analytical research conducted is covered in Chapters 5, 6 and 7. Chapter 5 analyzes the impact of a multilateral policy restraint (WTO telecommunications commitment) on the credibility of telecommunications reform in small island developing states, focusing on Tonga and Papua New Guinea. Chapter 6 analyses the impact of domestic policy restraint (independent regulator) on the credibility of domestic telecommunications reform in Fiji, Samoa and Vanuatu. In Chapter 7 the case study findings from Chapter 5 and 6 are triangulated by empirically estimating the effects of multilateral, bilateral and domestic policy restraints on the credibility of telecommunications reforms in small island developing states.

Chapter 8 concludes by linking the case study and empirical findings to the policy debates on the credibility of telecommunication reform in small island developing states and WTO. This chapter also attempts to outline the policy implications of the research findings and their usefulness to various users. Suggestions on issues for future research are also outlined.

Earlier versions of Chapter 4, 6 and 7 have been published in a refereed journal—Pacific Economic Bulletin. Also, an earlier version of

Chapter 5 was published as a book chapter in an Asian Development Bank publication edited by Ronald Duncan (Crawford School of Economics and Government, The Australian National University).

CHAPTER TWO

THE CREDIBILITY OF TELECOMMUNICATIONS REFORM IN SMALL ISLAND DEVELOPING STATES

1.0 Introduction

> "States entering into international agreements have at their disposal several tools to enhance the strength and credibility of their commitments, including the ability to make the agreements formal treaty rather than soft law". (Guzman 2005:579)

The idea that a non-credible investment environment characterized by non-transparent rules and property rights, political instability, high corruption, and frequent policy reversals translates into lower investment and growth is well established (Brunetti et al. 1998). Investors are reluctant to commit large sunk cost resources in an uncertain environment (Dixit and Pindyck 1994). This is particularly valid in the natural monopoly sectors including telecommunications. Levy and Spiller (1996:3) define telecommunications investment as containing three key characteristics. First, often there are only a handful of major telecommunications operators established in a country. A small number of telecommunications operators have implications for potential monopolistic collusion behaviors. Second, the investment's assets are usually non re-deployable with very little technological usability to any other utility sector or industry. Third, the telecommunications service has traditionally been state-owned. Therefore, policies affecting the sector will most often be highly politicized. A fundamental policy challenge therefore is how to develop a regulatory policy reform framework that instills credibility.

This chapter sets the contextual background for the research. I discuss three main strands of literature; telecommunications regulatory reform in small island developing states; the credibility problem; and the policy restraint literatures (multilateral trade agreements, bilateral investment treaties and independent regulators) which map out the theoretical arguments of the research. The structure of the chapter is as follows. Section 2 discusses literature on telecommunications reform in small island developing states. Section 3 discusses the credibility problem, while section 4 discusses policy restraints argued to instill credibility from the multilateral trading agreement, bilateral investment treaties and independent regulators literatures. Section 5 concludes the Chapter.

2.0 Telecommunications Reform in Small Island Developing States

2.1 Small Island Developing States

It is well documented that small island developing states have special characteristics that deter their growth prospects.[1] These characteristics—generally including small size of nations, geographical isolation, high susceptibility to natural disasters[2] and tropical diseases—are argued to limit development potential (Briguglio et al. 2006:13). Chand (2003:121) explained that "most of these disadvantages emanate from the lack of a sufficiently large population and domestic resource base to allow production of goods and services at the minimum efficient scale. Geographical isolation raises transportation costs, imposing a competitive disadvantage on high bulk-to-value exports such as primary commodities." Further, susceptibility of small island developing states to natural hazards such as cyclones, tsunamis and, in the long term, rising sea levels could adversely affect their narrow-based economies.

No defined boundary exists to what exactly the characteristics are of small island developing states. [3] International institutions such as the World Bank, United Nations Conference on Trade and Development (UNCTAD), the Commonwealth Secretariat and WTO have varying interpretations as to who is small and what are the characteristics of

---

[1] See Kuznets (1960); Robinson (1960); Streeten (1993); Briguglio (1995, 1998); Armstrong and Read (1998); Goetschel (1998); Limao and Venables (2001); Limao and Olarreaga (2006); Srinivasan (1986); Baldacchino (2006); Grynberg (2006); Horscroft (2006); Weatherhead (2006); Winters and Martins (2006) for detailed discussion on the economic characteristics and disadvantages of small states.

[2] The most recent tsunami that destroyed a large part of Samoa, and to a lesser extent American Samoa, and Tonga in September 2009, is a clear example of recent geographical vulnerability in the Pacific islands.

[3] A contentious issue to date in the small island states policy debate.

smallness they possess. Some of these interpretations are anchored in small island developing states' preferences and each institution's overall mandate. Academics alike posit a broad range of interpretations on small states.

Nevertheless, two fundamental criteria emerge out of these interpretations. First, specific to the purpose of this research is the recognition of the sovereignty of smaller island states to determine their own policy fate and consequences. Fully independent and sovereign island states (understood as small island developing states in this context) could differentiate themselves from small island states classified as trusted territories and colonies of developed countries. Such demarcation is crucial to ensure a valid inference is made when discussing policy issues determined by small island developing states themselves and not necessarily influenced by external colonial power. Sovereignty, however, is often used by Pacific island states as a political and economic instrument in regional and international forums for negotiating aid (Sutherland 2009). Second, the special characteristics of small island states are generally accepted as natural features.

A smallness concept could be adopted containing three broad categories. The broad categories are small population size (and land mass), insularity and geographical remoteness, and susceptibility to natural disasters.

Small size

The total number of people (population size) is a common and readily available measure for comparing country sizes. Empirical studies have used population as proxy for size of the market and domestic labor force (Armstrong and Read 1998:566). There have been other measures used such as gross domestic production and land area. A smaller economy puts severe constraints on a country's ability to sustain prolonged economic or political shocks. This line of argument originated from early writings of Kuznets (1960) and Vakil and Brahmananda (1960). Smaller economies suffer from limited capacity to exploit economies of scale, high dependence on a narrow range of export products and limited natural resources. Smaller size also results in higher reliance on imports, a smaller number of businesses leading to limited competition in key service sectors, and limited institutional capacity.

Small island developing states suffer from supply-side constraints, often depending on one commodity for export and a limited skilled labor force to exploit the commodity. Vakil and Brahmananda (1960:133-150) stated that ceteris paribus, "geographical size has significance because of the possibility that a large-sized country may possess a larger quantity of natural resources or a greater diversity in their supply". Knox (1967:35-44) echoed similar messages, using population size and land area as his distinguishing variables between small and larger nations. Knox emphasized two fundamental issues. First, smaller land area leads to fewer diversified resources than might be found in larger nations. Secondly, the small domestic market deters investors, as costs of doing business are higher. Knox's comparative findings point to small island states' heavy reliance on foreign trade, lower diversity of the exports base and a smaller market for investment.

It is often argued that the economic structure of small nations is typically less diversified than that of larger ones (Kuznets 1960:15-18). Kuznets suggested three reasons to explain this phenomenon. The first is the "size" of the area and its limiting effect on the supply of natural resources. Second, the limited size of the nation deters "optimum scale of plant for industries", which is essential for promotion of growth. Third, there is a danger of high specialization by a small workforce in a few economic activities for they may well concentrate on one valuable resource to the point where there is minimal incentive to pursue new initiatives. Hence, a limited pool of expertise in critical regulatory institutions including telecommunications could affect their overall effectiveness.

Insularity and geographical remoteness

All islands are by definition insular, but not all islands are situated in remote areas (Briguglio 1995:1617). The insularity of smaller states when coupled with their remote geographical locations imposes transportation and communication costs that impede their development prospects. Hausmann (2001) considered two major engines of growth—access to markets and technological progress—to understand why geography matters for economic growth.[4] If specialization increases productivity,

[4] Barro (1996) empirically investigated other major determinants of economic growth based on a panel of around 100 countries from 1960 to 1990 provided evidence that growth rate is enhanced by higher initial schooling and life

Hausmann (2001:47) argued, the gains can only be materialized when producers have access to markets where they can sell these specialized outputs. With multiple international sourcing of raw materials and parts for production, transportation costs play an important role in competitiveness. Unfortunately for remote Pacific island states, transportation costs are often determined by a country's geographical location in the globe.

The impact of geography through a country's location in the earth's latitude is argued to reflect development levels of countries. Gallup et al. (1999:180-181) claim that "nearly all countries in the geographic tropics are poor, and almost all countries in the mid-and high latitudes are rich". They found that among the tropical countries, the simple average GDP per capita in 1995 was US$3,326 [while] among the non tropical countries, it was US$9,027. Gallup et al. (1999) illustrate this point using graphical maps on the distribution of economic wellbeing and tropical disease (Figures 2-19 & 2-20, Appendix A)

The relationship between tropical diseases and development was popularized by Acemoglu, Johnson and Robinson (2001). In an attempt to estimate the impact of institutions on economic performance, Acemoglu et al. (2001) empirically tested mortality rate of early European settlers in the colonies. The authors hypothesized that the prevalence of tropical diseases (mostly malaria and yellow fever) during the colonization era deterred European settlers from fully establishing "neo-European" institutions and societies. "Extractive states" where instead established "to transfer as much resources of the colony to colonizer" (Acemoglu et al. 2001, p. 1370). Consequently, the long-term effect of extractive states institutions on economic performance were detrimental to some developing countries as these poor institutional arrangements remained even after independence. Acemoglu et al. (2001:1376) discussed that as colonies gained their independence, small elite ruling classes stepped in to run governments and preferred to exploit extractive institutions for their own benefits. So, it was a mere change of rent recipients from European Governments to local powerful elites. By contrast, the opposite could be said about Australia, New Zealand, Canada and the United States of America of which early European settlers encountered less mortality rate from diseases and where therefore able to established themselves with

expectancy, lower fertility, lower government consumption, better maintenance of rule of law, lower inflation, and improvements in the terms of trade.

better structured institutions which led to eventual higher economic performance.

The combined natural characteristics of small island developing states coupled with geographical isolation from major markets ultimately hamper their development prospects. Armstrong and Read (2006[a]:79 & 87) noted that "Pacific islands are extremely remote from global markets…with no fewer than 73 per cent of the small Pacific states being more than 5,000 kilometers from their nearest global market compared with only 37 per cent of the small states taken as a whole". Gibson (2007:83-86) echoed Armstrong and Read's line of argument on Pacific islands' remoteness by stating that "out of the 219 countries…the Melanesian and Polynesian countries have an average rank as the 207th most remote, while Micronesian countries have an average rank of 176th most remote." This figure illustrates how geographical isolation put small island developing states into a uniquely challenging circumstance hampering their development prospects.

Susceptibility to natural disasters

Natural disasters such as tsunamis, cyclones, drought, earthquakes, and floods tend to be more frequent in specific geographical areas, affecting both small and large states. However, larger states have higher resilience to natural shocks compared to small island developing states (Briguglio 1995:1617). Most Caribbean and Pacific island states are concentrated in regions with the highest frequency of natural disasters—within the tropics. The United Nations Disaster Relief Organization has estimated that the impact on the 25 most disaster-prone countries (including 13 small island developing states) has entailed costs between 28 per cent and 1,200 per cent of their annual GDP (Commonwealth Secretariat and World Bank 2000:11). The negative monetary costs of natural disasters experienced by a smaller island state will be larger in damage per unit of area than in a larger state (Briguglio 1995:1617). Also, small island developing states are generally dependent on one or two commodities, often agriculture, fisheries and tourism, which are highly vulnerable to natural disasters. The recent tsunami that devastated coastal communities in American Samoa, Samoa[5] and Tonga in September 2009 reflects the vulnerabilities of Pacific islands to natural disasters.

[5] Samoa which was the hardest hit lost 170 lives with an estimated damage cost of SA$130 million (Stuff.co.nz online source, 2009).

Weatherhead's (2006:33) flow diagram reproduced in Figure 2-1 best captures the complex dynamics of the smallness concept in recent times. Based on the literature of small island developing states, Weatherhead has consolidated the common factors often raised in the literature as common characteristics of small island developing states. This flow diagram demonstrates that the natural disadvantages of small island developing states natural disadvantages discourage investment in general. Poor foreign and domestic investment overall contribute to slower economic growth. Geographical isolation from major markets leads to higher production costs, reducing profit margins, which overall discourages investments. Thus, the impact of natural disasters such as seasonal hurricanes or occasional earthquakes which lead to potential destructive tsunamis and drought further worsens the investment potential of small island states.

Smallness in terms of population size limits the pool of innovative and proactive skilled people required for developing relevant and conducive socio-economic and public policies. Further, Duncan and Chand (2002:4) argued that the small size of the populations makes the establishment of the checks and balances necessary for good governance difficult to establish. In a situation where the educated élite who form the judiciary, the polity, the disciplinary forces (police and military), and the senior bureaucracy have been to the same schools and universities and may be related through marriage, a democratic process of checks and balances is difficult to achieve. Harberger (1988) cited in Duncan and Chand (2002:4) termed the "tyranny of demography".

The reality of this tyranny is reflected in many Pacific islands administrations, with skilled expatriates filling key positions in government—for instance, as part of the bilateral aid arrangement between Tonga and Australia, Also, the Tonga Police Force was led by a New Zealander as part of a similar bilateral cooperation arrangement. An Australian is the head of the Customs Department in Tonga. Overall, Weatherhead's flow diagram outlines the impact of the natural characteristics of small island states on their development potential.

There are, however, counterarguments on the extent to which the smallness concept has hindered growth and development prospects in small economies. Some small island states perform exceptionally well compared with other island states—Singapore is a classic example. One of the most influential empirical studies, undertaken by Easterly and Kraay

(2000), concluded that smallness is not a disadvantage to development. Easterly and Kraay (2000:2013 & 2015) found that small states have the same range of per capita incomes as the rest of the countries of the world and therefore concluded that small states are no different from large states and so should receive the same policy advice that large states do.

Figure 2-1: Characteristics of Small Island Developing States

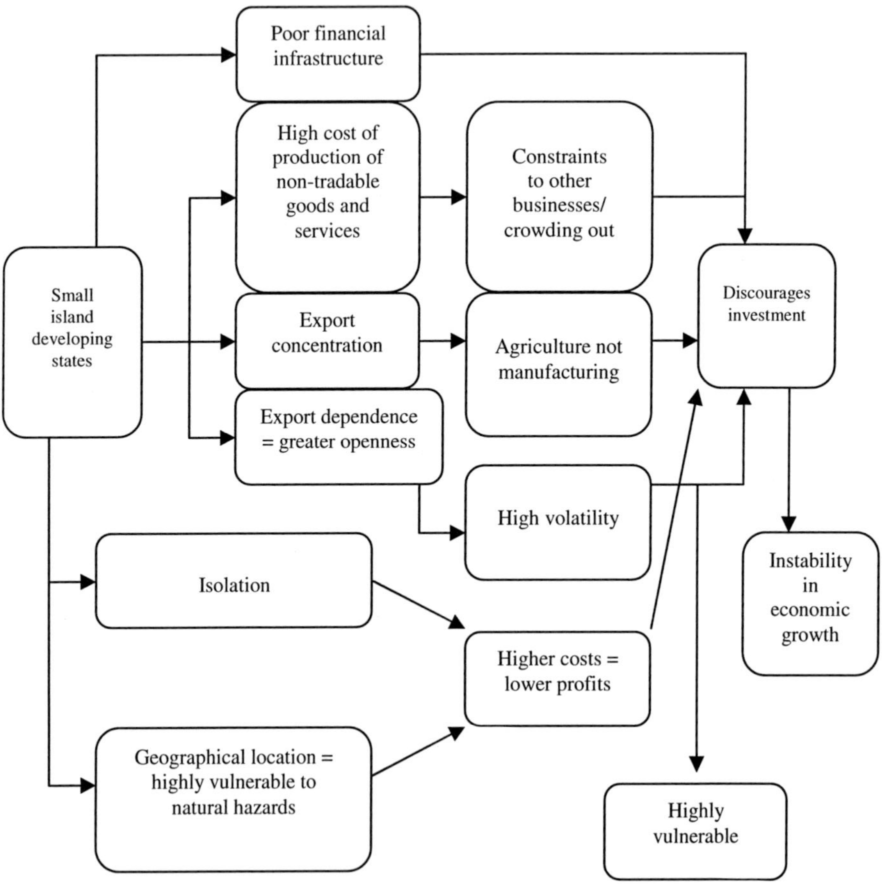

Source: Adapted from Weatherhead (2006:33).

The policy debate on the extent to which the smallness concept affects the development prospects of small island states remains open. While there has been widespread support from the small island states literature on Easterly and Kraay's (2000) line of argument, other scholars have undertaken a cautious approach to the case of small island states. Chand (2003:120) best captured this cautious approach by admitting that "while size does create particular problems, smallness does not constitute an insurmountable development hazard." According to Chand (2003), the policy challenge therefore is to draw successful lessons from other island states that have successfully developed and emulate those within less successful small island economies.

A major part of the recent studies on small island states follows this line of argument, that is, building socio-economic resilience and good governance of small island developing states through macro-economic stabilization policies[6] and institutional, social, political and environmental policy reforms, to overcome their natural disadvantages. The policy diagnostic is specific to small island states' characteristics, rather than general reform policies adopted from larger developing and developed economies being imposed on small island states. Major international institutions appear to have followed this line of argument as well, with the continued commitment to small states through special units within their organizations—for instance, the World Bank, Asian Development Bank, United Nations (several organizations within), WTO, IMF and the Commonwealth Secretariat have dedicated units and/or work programs for small island states.

One fundamental issue that has dominated the small island states policy debate (and been partially agreed upon from both sides of the debate) is that poor economic management and governance in small island developing states further worsens their development prospects. In a smaller economy, the consequence could be more detrimental compared to larger economies. This research adopted this line of reasoning but proposed that smallness should be an integral factor when considering the socio-economic and political reform of small island developing states. Any policy initiative that ignores this factor has a risk of imposing a complex

---

[6] See Jayaraman (2006); Chand (2006); Worrell, Codrington, Craigwell and Greenidge (2006); Jankee (2006); Downes (2006); Armstrong and Read (2006[b]); Briguglio, Cordina, Farrugia and Vella (2006); for discussion on building economic resilience of small states through various type of economic policy and social, political and environmental type policies.

policy diagnosis relevant to advanced larger economies on a simple and resource-constrained island state. In the case of telecommunications reform, the institutional and regulatory design success of larger developing countries since the 1980s may not necessarily be successful in small island developing states. The extent to which the telecommunications policy reform initiative is effective predominantly depends on how well the telecommunications design framework addresses the disadvantages of being small.

Overall, a small market with limited human and capital resources coupled with geographical isolation impedes small island developing states' growth. The literature on small states therefore renders two important issues relevant to this research. First, small island developing states have special characteristics that must be considered in drafting their respective reform programs. Second, telecommunications reform and particularly the role of technology in eliminating geographical isolation and remoteness are crucial in the small island developing states' telecommunications reform process.

The next section links the literature on small island states with the telecommunications literature. The discussion on the smallness concept provided a fuller appreciation and understanding of small island states' characteristics. It is therefore anticipated that the discussion in the next section, in particular the regulatory experiences in telecommunications reforms in developing countries should be understood in the context outlined by the smallness concept.

2.2 Telecommunications Reform

In the last decade, the question of the impact of telecommunications liberalization on the sector's performance has been well addressed. Scholars have undertaken national and cross-national studies on telecommunications reforms (Keck and Djiofack-Zebaze 2009; Shiu and Lam 2008; Armstrong and Sappington 2006; Lee and Findlay 2005; Fink et al. 2003; and Wallsten 2001). The consensus is that there has been a positive impact on telecommunications sector performance, with higher infrastructure and technological investment leading to reduction in prices and improvement in the quality of services. The majority of recent studies on telecommunications policy have focused on three regulatory policy instruments: privatization, competition and the establishment of independent regulators in developing countries (Flacher and Jennequin

2008; Fink et al. 2003, Wallsten 2003 and 2004; Li and Xu 2002; and Ros 1997).

Telecommunications liberalization is a complex and relatively new process for developing countries (Fink et al. 2003:444). It is however, a more recent policy initiative in small island developing states. Three Caribbean island states began reforms in the early 2000s (Jamaica, Barbados and Trinidad and Tobago)[7] while only five out of fourteen Pacific island states have liberalized their telecommunications sectors in the past five years.[8] While it is still early days to fully capture the outcomes of such regulatory reforms, it is crucially important to account for the selection and implementation of key policies during the early stages of the regulatory reform process in a small island developing states context.[9]

The credibility of domestic telecommunications reform policies to foreign investors is crucial when enormous financial and capital investments are at stake. This is particularly relevant in the case of telecommunications sector reform where investment involves large sunk costs in asset-specific infrastructure that cannot be re-deployed (Garcia-Murillo and Kuerbis 2005:785). A credible policy environment therefore in promoting a legal and transparent competitive environment is vital. The next section discusses the credibility literature.

3.0 The Credibility Problem

3.1 Credibility Problem

The idea that the outcome of government policies can be crucially affected by their perceived credibility is well established (Srivastava 1994:449). If governments were able to announce future policy reforms and comprehensively implement them, assuming that all other political and socio-economic factors remained constant, the credibility literature[10] suggests that credible policies would result in higher productivity and growth. Roller and Waverman (2001: 909-911) found that

[7] See Lodge and Stirton (2002).

[8] See Chapter 3 for further discussion on the Pacific islands.

[9] Chapter 3 discusses in detail the telecommunications reform policies in the Pacific islands.

[10] See Kydland and Prescott (1977); Blackburn and Christensen (1989); Cottarelli and Giannini (1997); on influential researches on the credible policy literature.

telecommunications development generates substantial positive externalities economy-wide, while Brunetti et al. (1998:353-356) found constant policy surprises and reversals, uncertain contract enforcements, and high levels of corruption most likely to translate into lower investment and growth.

Yet, governments frequently encounter domestic and international pressures that compel policymakers to renege on previously announced policies. This uncertainty about policies is often termed the "time inconsistency problem." In their seminal work, Kydland and Prescott (1977:487) highlighted the importance of credible commitment to announced policy. They argued that "policymakers should follow rules rather than have discretion. The reason is that they are not stupid or evil, but rather, that discretion implies selecting the decision which is best, given the current situation." Discretionary rules are therefore popular practices with policymakers due to their enablement of immediate responses to policy challenges and most importantly, for the predictability and certainty they can offer outside policymakers' political sphere.

While policymakers strive to draft and implement policies that serve their constituencies, they are in some cases subject to conflicting socio-economic and political pressures that require readjustment and changes to previously announced policies over time. Regulatory capture therefore could serve the interests of these groups instead of the general public they serve (Etzioni 2009:319). Regulatory capture exists when concerted pressure from certain interest groups influence public policy outcomes. These interest groups could include ministers and government bureaucrats, state-owned telecommunications operators, or politicians who write and control the regulations.

Originally developed by George J. Stigler (1971), the regulatory capture concept explained how lobbying interest groups pressure government to achieve their own interests. The capture theory was refined later by Peltzman (1976), Posner (1975) and Becker (1983). The later contributions advanced on Stigler's (1971) original work by recognizing that other pressure groups constantly compete for government's attention on a particular regulation. The later contributions are in line with Mancur Olson's (1965) collective bargaining argument on interest group theories. Majone (1997:145 cited in Gilardi 2002:875) stresses that it is difficult for elected politicians to be credible, notably because they have a very short time horizon, namely the next election. Policymakers dynamic political responses to their constituencies tend to undermine the long-term credibility of some announced policies. Buthe and Milner (2008:742) argued that unilateral domestic policy choices could often be easily changed due to pressure from vested interest groups.

Evidence from the Pacific case studies show that policymakers implementing telecommunications reform policies encountered conflicting pressures which resulted in revising or reneging of early announced telecommunications liberalization policies. Figure 2-2 illustrates the main stakeholders responsible for capture and the rationale behind capture. Before reform, historical pressures from rural and isolated communities combined with urban and business communities, based on the high costs and lack of basic telephony services, drove the pressure for the liberalization of the telecommunications sector. Once competition was introduced, the state-owned operator encountered challenges in how to be competitive (requiring management restructuring, funding for further development, and a transitional period for adapting to the competitive environment) and pressured government to revise its competition policy on telecommunications. The capture process is particularly strong when government continues to retain commercial interests within the sector retaining majority ownership shares of the incumbent telecommunications operator.

The pressure against a liberalized telecommunications sector from the state-owned incumbent operators in Pacific case studies does carry some legitimate foundations. Since the overall objective of liberalized telecommunications is long-term sustainable competition, most small markets in the Pacific have adopted a controlled duopoly market structure for competition. Often, this might include a foreign private investor together with the state-owned operator. Since state-owned operators have existing network infrastructure in place, and considering that it is publicly owned—hence, any policies affecting its long-term sustainability will likely be highly politicized—governments are therefore obligated to ensure the efficient and sustainable operation of such companies.

Often a government's main concern on sustainable competition in telecommunication is based on the need for two (or more) players to be efficient and compete with each other to ensure the benefits of competition are realized. Hence, disregarding the sustainability of state-owned operators during competition could risk a transition from a public to a private monopoly. This was a concern that many policymakers and regulators within the Pacific case studies shared and continue to monitor.

Figure 2-2: Credibility Problem on Telecommunications Reform in Pacific Case Studies

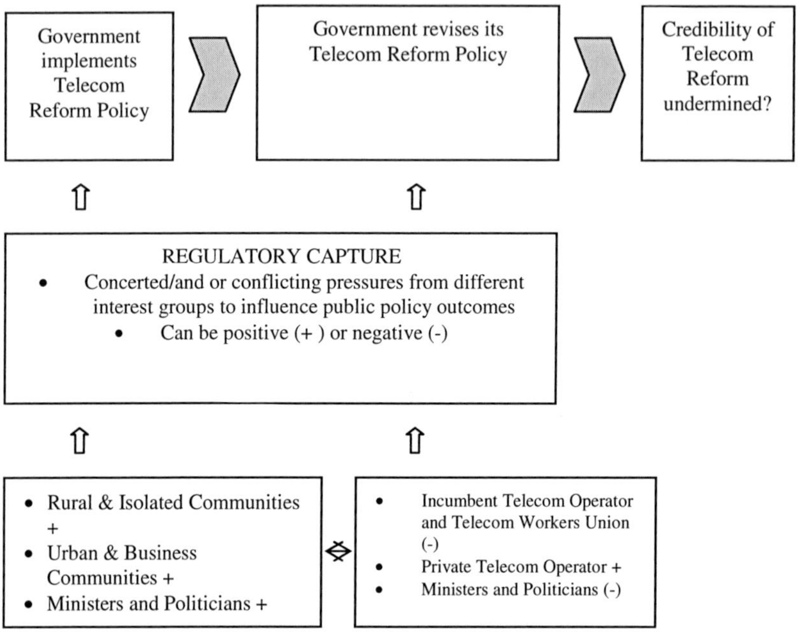

Note: (-) Pressures against telecommunications reform; + Pressures for telecommunications reform.

Source: Author's consolidation of conflicting interest group pressures on telecommunications reform in Pacific case studies.

Telecommunications liberalization however, continues to encounter conflicting pressures from pro-competition interest groups including private telecommunications operators. The governments of the Pacific case studies therefore constantly encounters a policy challenge on how to strike a balance between these two conflicting interests. This source of conflicting interest is the source of uncertainty and frequent policy reversals after the telecommunications reform was introduced.

The policy outcome resulting from interest group pressure may not necessarily be biased towards a minority group's interests at the cost of the general public (that is, the pressure of some interest groups yield positive outcome). A policy reform could be implemented with an outcome favoring the general public and certain narrow based interest groups. In the case of telecommunications reform in the Pacific islands, the introduction of competition in the mobile phone sector not only benefited the general public (connecting isolated and rural communities), but also aligned with the respective agendas of some government bureaucrats, politicians, regulators, and competitors' respective agendas. Similarly, other possibilities that the capture argument may not adequately explain include policy outcomes based on other factors such as political systems and political beliefs.

4.0 Policy Restraints: Independent Regulators, Multilateral Trade Agreement, and Bilateral Investment Treaties

To instill policy credibility, the regulatory design of policy frameworks is of fundamental importance. Policy restraint mechanisms can be put in place to lessen the credibility problem. The literature on fixed and discretionary rules sheds useful insights on this aspect. Discretionary policy over fixed rules is commonly debated in monetary policies (Mihov and Sibert 2006; Lohmann 1992; Fischer 1988; Barro and Gordon 1983). The discretionary policy[11] is often supported as it allows flexibility for regulators to react based on the policy issue at hand.

Three policy restraints are discussed in this section: first, the conventional independent regulator implemented as a domestic policy restraint to instill credibility in an industry sector; second, the discussion on the role of the multilateral trade agreement (WTO) implemented as an external policy restraint on the credibility of an industry sector; last, the role of bilateral investment treaties as another form of external policy restraint on the credibility of an industry's sector.

4.1 Independent Regulator

The most common discretionary rule from the banking sector literature is the delegation of discretionary power to independent central banks in

[11] Policy direction relies on the judgment and discretion of regulators or policymakers to allow for policy flexibility and quick response to the policy dilemma.

order to increase the credibility of their policy commitment (Gilardi 2002; Majone 1997; Dixit 1996; Shepsle 1991).

The role of independent regulators in providing certainty is well established (Lee and Levendis 2006; Stern and Trillas 2003; Wallsten 2003; Baudrier 2001; Noll 1999; Ros 1997; Levy and Spiller 1994; Tyler and Bednarczyk 1993). Bertelli & Whitford (2009:520) best capture the role of independent regulators:

> "Put simply, a government's commitment to a regulatory rule creates the expectations of a predictable investment environment; regulatory independence helps to supply that commitment. Firms can contract to deliver goods and services at lower risk if they believe regulators are unlikely to change the rules of the game during the period of the contract. This diminution of risk can be seen as reducing transactions costs".

The regulator should be independent from government control (Ros 1997:40), which enhances the efficient and fair allocation of resources in the telecommunications sector (Lee and Levendis 2006:407). However, even with the best intentioned reforms, with domestic restraint policies in place such as an independent regulator, the time-inconsistency problem could still create credibility problems. The independent regulator could be vulnerable to political influences through amendments of legislation which cater for interest group pressures. Melody (1997:195) argued that "the regulator either lost, or never had, the independence to make professional decisions on their merits because of undue influence either from politicians, politically driven Ministries, or the regulated monopolies." The outcome of such uncertainty for potential private investors is hesitation about investment. Rodrik (1991:230) suggested that rational behavior on the part of the private sector calls for withholding investment until much of the residual uncertainty regarding the success of the reforms is eliminated. The uncertainty drives up prices of services or leads to the withholding of a part or whole of the investment until the investor can be sure that a reform policy is irreversible (Aryeetey 1994:1212).[12]

---

[12] Hesitation to invest in infrastructure on the part of the Indonesian mobile phone company, Greencom, which was granted a mobile licence in PNG, lends support to this argument.

4.2 Multilateral Trade Agreements

The multilateral policy restraint provided by the WTO's commitments provides such fixed and binding rules. Bosworth and Duncan (2002:10) argued that:

> "The importance of [WTO] international commitment should not be underestimated. The political and bureaucratic systems of most countries are biased towards providing protection to influential inefficient industries, thereby adversely affecting the economy in general, and efficient exporters and consumers in particular".

Rodrik (1989:758, 770-1) argued that adopting a gradual pace on policy reform may give negative signals about government's real intentions. Therefore, genuine, reform-minded governments need to "overshoot"[13] policy to address the uncertainty posed by the time inconsistency of policies.[14] At the broadest level, overshooting policy could imply a case for credible fixed rules that bind governments. The main difference between this multilateral policy restraint and the domestic policy restraint provided by an independent regulator is the domestic and international costs of policy reversal by governments.[15] Commitments to telecommunications liberalization reforms in the WTO are legally binding and failure to adhere to the commitments can be challenged by other member countries through the WTO's Dispute Settlement Body. Bosworth and Duncan (2002:10) in this regard argue that:

> "The main economic benefit to be gained by a country from WTO membership is help in facilitating policy reforms that liberalize trade and, as a by-product, support a market economy...By 'locking in' such reforms internationally, WTO accession [commitments] provides governments with a defense mechanism against future policy backsliding or 'de-liberalization' in response to domestic protectionist pressures".

One of the core principles[16] of the WTO system is predictability of trade and investment rules through binding and transparency principles.

---

[13] Rodrik (1989) discussed the size of the reform as one signal.

[14] However, the costs of overshooting policy may act against government's real intentions.

[15] International reputation, borrowing capacity, aid programs, and political and socio-economic partnerships of countries are at stake when reneging on international rules.

[16] See WTO (2008), for a discussion of the WTO's principles.

The predictability of WTO agreements stemming from legally binding rules are crucial in minimizing trade costs and unnecessary barriers to trade. The WTO Secretariat's (2008:12) document on understanding the WTO best captures this predictability point as "to make countries' trade rules as clear and public ('transparent') as possible. Many WTO agreements require governments to disclose their policies publicly with the country or by notifying the WTO." The predictability and transparency of information therefore assist private investors to adopt informed trade and investment decisions.

The WTO's General Agreement on Trade in Services agreement formalizes the commitments made by WTO members under services including telecommunications. Services commitments are generally understood through the "schedule of specific commitments." The forthcoming discussion on GATS will provide a foundation to better understand and appreciate the WTO telecommunications commitment undertaken in the case of PNG and Tonga, as discussed in Chapter 5. [17]

General agreement on trade in services

GATS was launched in 1995 with the objective of establishing rules that ensure that WTO members' domestic regulations do not discriminate against other members'—most-favored nation (MFN) principle. [18] The main discriminatory measures prohibited by GATS are: limitations imposed upon number of services; limitations on number of foreign nationals[19]; limitations on the forms of legal entity (for example, the requirement of a partnership with a local business in a particular sector); and limitations on foreign equity participation (for example, the percentage participation requirement for a particular form of commercial presence).

---

[17] Efforts have been made to consolidate the key concepts ideal for understanding the case studies WTO commitments and as such, the discussion may not cover all the finer details of GATS.

[18] For understanding the WTO commitments of case study countries, each government is required to accord immediately and unconditionally to services and service suppliers of any other member no less favorable treatment than that it accords to like services and service suppliers of any other country (WTO 2002 :287).

[19] Professional and higher management levels only.

Trade in services is categorized according to four different modes of delivery[20]: (i) cross-border services supplied from the territory of one member to the territory of another member (for example, Digicel Tonga selling international connections to Telstra Australia); (ii) consumption of services supplied in the territory of one member to the consumers of another (for example, a Tongan national making a telephone call in Port Moresby through Telikom PNG's fixed-line network system); (iii) commercial presence—supply of services of one member in the market of another member (for example, establishment of Digicel branch in PNG); and (iv) temporary movement of natural persons—that is, service supplied by nationals of one member in the territory of another—(for example, a foreign national from Digicel's Jamaican branch posted as Country Manager to Digicel Tonga's branch).

Negotiations towards liberalizing limiting measures among members were operationalized through the use of a standard GATS Schedule of Commitments format (WTO 2006). The document requires that each member schedule (offer to commit) all limitation measures currently imposed upon services sectors. These initial offers have been the basis for further rounds of negotiations since 1995.

The services schedule consists of four main sections. First, the horizontal commitments are general limitations that apply to all sectors, including: business and foreign investment regulations requirements; any limitations on land tenure; and immigration requirements for movement of workers. Second, there are specific vertical limitations applying to each sector (as regulated by domestic regulations). These specific commitments produce the most valuable information in terms of which sectors are included and what types of limitations are imposed upon each mode of delivery.

Third, the telecommunications reference paper is one of the important outcomes of the telecommunications service negotiations completed in February 1997. The paper describes a set of pro-competitive regulatory principles on competition conditions, including safeguard measures and interconnection. The paper is legally binding once adopted by a WTO member. In practice, some members have adopted the reference paper

[20] See Altinger and Enders (1996); Egger and Lanz (2008) for detailed discussion of GATS.

partially or wholly as part of their commitments in the telecommunications sector.

Fourth, Article II "MFN exemptions" provides an exemption to a member not to follow the MFN principle under GATS. In principle, the GATS agreement provides for a ten-year timeframe. However, most WTO members have kept these limitations in place for more than ten years. Table 2-1 illustrates the four main sections on a typical schedule.

Table 2-1: Schedule of Specific Commitments Composition

(1) Cross-border supply	(2) Consumption abroad	(3) Commercial presence	(4) Movement of natural persons
	Limitations on Market Access (MA)	Limitations on National Treatment (NT)	Additional Commitments
HORIZONTAL COMMITMENTS			
Across All Sectors	(1) (2) (3) (4)	(1) (2) (3) (4)	
SPECIFIC COMMITMENTS			
Service Sub-sectors	(1) (2) (3) (4)	(1) (2) (3) (4)	
TELECOMMUNICATIONS REFERENCE PAPER			
ARTICLE II MFN EXEMPTIONS			

Source: Author's adaptation of GATS guidelines from WTO (2006)

The limitation measures are classified in the schedule under two categories. First, Market Access (MA) measures are limitations that discriminate between one foreign service supplier and another. Second, National Treatment (NT) limitations are measures that discriminate against foreign service suppliers in favor of local service suppliers.

Specific limitations for each mode of delivery under the two categories are commonly classified into three main measures. First, the limitation termed "None" indicates that the member concerned does not impose any limitations specified by GATS on that particular sector. Second, the limitation termed "Unbound" indicates that the member does not make any commitment to liberalization and is free to impose any of the GATS prohibited measures. Third, the limitation termed "Unbound except as indicated under horizontal commitments" indicates that the member has committed subject to limitations indicated under the horizontal commitments. It is common to find that Mode 4 commitments (see Table 2-1) are mostly unbound, as immigration laws are a sovereign issue for member countries. In addition, Mode 4 measures are only concerned with temporary movement of workers to other markets, rather than permanent migration.

Overall, the schedule of specific commitments has facilitated transparent communication of member countries' regulations on the services trade. The services schedules of most WTO members are publicly available from the WTO, which gives the business communities and governments an instant regulatory window into each member's rules and regulations on trade in services.

4.3 Bilateral Investment Treaties

Similar to multilateral trade agreements, bilateral investment treaties are another external fixed policy regime to provide protection for foreign investments. The proliferation of bilateral investment treaties since the 1980s has provided a general safeguard mechanism for investments between two countries. The United Nations Conference on Trade and Development calculates that fewer than 100 bilateral investment treaties were signed in 1980; in 1999, more than 2,000 of such Treaties (UNCTAD 2000 cited in Yackee 2008:805). Bilateral investment treaties usually involve the signatories between a developed and developing country providing guarantees of appropriate compensation for expropriation, provisions against discriminatory measures between foreign and domestic investors, fair treatment through the legislation and laws of foreign and domestic investors, measures for the provision of a mechanism to settle any investment related dispute, and a commitment that the signatory governments commit credibly to their obligations.

Several studies show evidence that signing bilateral investment treaties increases investment inflows (Kerner 2009; Buthe and Milner 2008; Kim 2007; Neumayer and Spess 2005; Salacuse and Sullivan 2005). However, the positive link between bilateral investment treaties and foreign direct investment is not universally accepted. Other studies show a limited positive or no effect for bilateral treaties on investment (Yackee 2008; Tobin and Rose-Ackerman 2005; Aisbett 2007; Guzman 1998). Investment agreements are controversial principally because they tend to place a variety of obligations on the host government—often the developing country—and no obligation on the foreign investors. A disproportionate cost falls on the smaller and poorer partner government (Aisbett 2008:1). The low numbers of bilateral investment treaties signed by the Pacific case study countries[21] provide anecdotal evidence of the reluctance of poorer smaller countries to participate may be due to the disproportionately high costs of obligations and implementation by host governments. In general, smaller and poorer countries have signed lower numbers of bilateral investment treaties compared to larger and wealthier countries as illustrated by Figure 2-3.

Figure 2-3 shows the total aggregate number of bilateral investment treaties signed by 160 developing countries from 1995 to 2006. Based on population—(Graph1); and GDP per capita constant (2000 US$)—(Graph 2), both scatterplots show positive relationships with bilateral investment treaty signings. Looking closer to Small island developing states signatories generally show that small island developing states sign up to lower total aggregate numbers of bilateral investment treaties compared to larger developing countries.

[21] See Chapter 3 for details on bilateral investment treaties in the Pacific case studies.

Figure 2-3: Aggregate Numbers of Bilateral Investment Treaties Signed—Developing Countries (1995-2006)

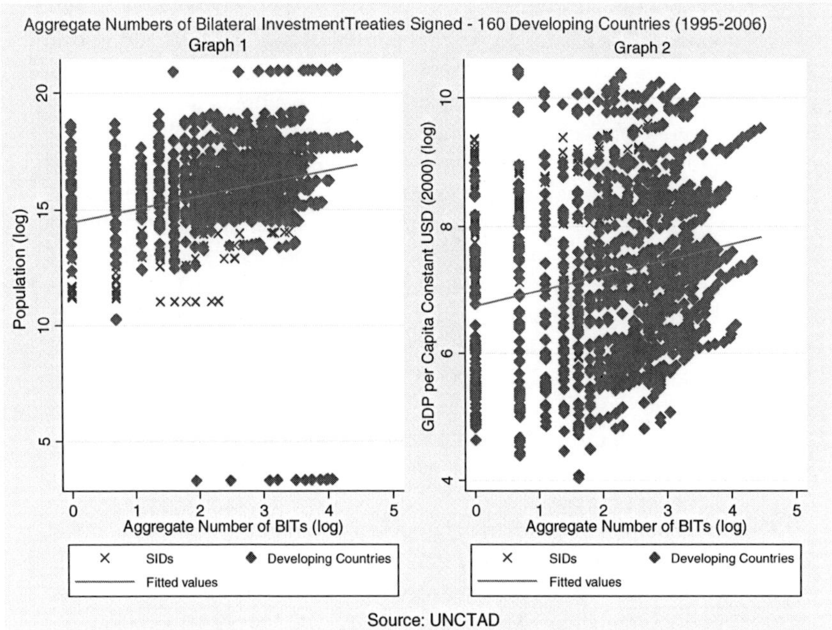

(2000)

5.0 Conclusion

This chapter has set the contextual background for the study. I discuss three main strands of literature on telecommunications regulatory reforms in small island developing states, the credibility problem, and the policy restraints mechanisms, which map out the theoretical arguments of the research.

The chapter presents a counterargument—the effectiveness of independent regulators to instill policy credibility in small island developing states is undermined by the existence of regulatory capture—against a well established credible role of independent regulators from the banking and telecommunications literatures in developed and larger developing countries. The vulnerability of the independent regulators could be partly caused by weak institutional and regulatory frameworks in small island developing states, but equally influential are the supply-side constraints—

lack of financial and technical capacity to effectively empower independent regulators—commonly found in small island developing states.

The research therefore proposes that the fixed rules of the World Trading Organization provide certainty and higher costs for policy reversal on telecommunications reform in small island developing states. While it is crucial that a clear regulatory demarcation exists between policymakers, regulators and operators, the supply-side constraints of small island developing states may render establishing a domestic independent regulator impracticable. Appropriate measures are suggested to remedy this natural disadvantage in Chapter 8. Furthermore, it is widely accepted from the literature and policy practitioners that bilateral investment treaties impose a protection mechanism for foreign investors in developing countries. This research however, suggests that the effectiveness of bilateral investment treaties in imposing credibility on investment in small island developing states could be less pronounced. The low number of signatories to bilateral investment treaties from small island developing states could have limited the effectiveness of this bilateral mechanism.

The next chapter outlines the research design and conceptual framework of this study. The research design section discusses the main hypotheses and methodological considerations. The conceptual framework section outlines the theoretical underpinnings of the system model, its effectiveness and the analytical adaptation for analyses of the case studies.

CHAPTER THREE

RESEARCH METHODOLOGY: FROM THEORY TO DESIGN

1.0 Introduction

To recapitulate, the main research question stipulates: Do multilateral policy restraints enhance the credibility of telecommunications regulatory reforms in small island developing states? The insights shed by the literature on multilateral trading agreements proved useful in considering the effectiveness of WTO telecommunications commitments in enhancing the credibility of telecommunications regulatory reform in small island developing states.

2.0 Research Hypotheses

The literature on telecommunications reform suggests that the establishment of independent regulators provides credibility to the reform process. However, as I demonstrate, the independent regulator provides limited credibility compared to multilateral policy restraints since the effectiveness of independent regulators is undermined by regulatory capture, and, when newly established independent regulators are resource constrained—financial and technical expertise. Hypothesis 1 posits as follows:

Hypothesis 1: Independent regulators are vulnerable to political influence, undermining the credibility of telecommunications reform in small island developing states.

Informed by the theoretical discussion on fixed rules and the multilateral trading system, I propose that the credibility of telecommunications reform can be enhanced through commitment to the WTO telecommunications agreement. The WTO agreements are legally binding, enforceable by a dispute settlement body. Also, the political and economic costs of policy reversal are higher for small island developing states. Other consequences of multilateral enforcement include risks of damaging a country's international reputation, or economic or trade sanctions; and jeopardizing aid programs, which are important to small island developing states development. Hypothesis 2 therefore proposes as follows:

Hypothesis 2: Commitment to the WTO telecommunications agreement increases the credibility of telecommunications reform in small island developing states.

Small island developing states' commitments to international trade agreements are nevertheless, controversial. The smallness literature emphasizes that the development prospects of small island developing states are hindered by their natural disadvantages. Hence, we would expect that public opposition in small island developing states to telecommunications liberalization policy relies on how telecommunications technology directly addresses the disadvantages of smallness for individuals. Hypothesis 3 therefore proposes as follows:

Hypothesis 3: Public support in small island developing states increases when improved telecommunications technology directly addresses the disadvantages of smallness for individuals.

The phenomenon studied is the impact of multilateral trade agreements (the WTO telecommunications commitment) on the credibility of telecommunications policy reform in small island developing states. Table 3-2 outlines the main independent and dependent variables.

I employ the WTO's telecommunications commitments as the multilateral policy restraint. The credibility of the telecommunications regulatory reform process—dependent variable—is operationalized through responses collected from expert interviews in the five case studies on policy amendments and reversals. It is also quantitatively measured using telecommunications sector performance variables discussed further in the empirical study in Chapter 7.

Table 3-2: Main Independent and Dependent Variables

Independent variables	Dependent variables
Multilateral policy restraint	Credibility of telecommunications sector reform
Qualitative measure: WTO telecommunications commitment made by a case study	*Qualitative measure:* Policy certainty (number of policy amendments/reversals)
Quantitative measure: WTO telecommunications commitment dummy variable	*Quantitative measure:* Telecommunications sector performance*

Source: Author's consolidation of research main independent and dependent variables.

Note: * Measured by total number of subscribers per employee and, total number of fixed and mobile subscribers per 100 people. As discussed in previous sections, credible policy results in higher investment and growth. Hence, a credible telecommunications reform program is expected to experience a higher sector performance and vice versa. Qualitative and Quantitative measures for main independent and dependent variables are used since the research adopts a mixed-method approach.

3.0 Methodologies

The general premise of the research falls into the epistemological perspective between the positivist[1] and interpretivist continuum. The positivist design phase of the research focused on empirical analyses of WTO's telecommunications commitments on telecommunications reform in 160 developing countries (including 26 small island developing states). On the other hand, the interpretive phase focused on comparative case study analyses with small-n expert interviews. The expert interviews extracted qualitative information that figures alone fail to explain. Accordingly, the mixed methods approach[2] adopted in this research reflects this balance.

[1] See Crotty (1998) and Yanow (2000) for discussion on research premises, methods and theoretical underpinnings.

[2] See Bryman (2006) for a literature survey on mixed-methods research.

The objective of a mixed method research design is to provide a methodological triangulation—quantitative and qualitative—on a study of a particular phenomenon. Tashakkori and Teddlie (1998:19) defined mixed model studies as "studies that are products of the pragmatist paradigm and that combine the qualitative and quantitative approaches within different phases of the research processes." Fundamentally, Tashakkori and Teddlie (1998) understood mixed methods studies as research designs with multilevel use of approaches at different levels of data aggregation. Data can be analyzed qualitatively at expert (individual) levels while undertaking quantitative analyses at national level.

The division between the two styles of research is a historical one, the supporters of each claiming that one is superior to the other. However as King et al. (1994:4) suggested, "the differences between the quantitative and qualitative traditions are only stylistic and are methodologically and substantively unimportant". Similar lines have been echoed by Van Evera (1997:4), "I regard large-n and case study methods as essential equals. Each has its strengths and weaknesses." Shively (2009:21) best captures the mixed methods approach by stating that, "it is probably best that studies with varying degree of quantification be carried on in any given field of political research, for different levels of quantification complement each other."

The study therefore pursues a complementarily mixed method research approach with qualitative case study analyses cross-checked by large-n quantitative analyses. The quantitative analysis's methodology is discussed in Chapter 7 while the qualitative comparative case study's design is discussed further below.

3.1 Case Studies from the Pacific Islands

The research was interested in examining the credibility of telecommunications reform in small island developing states. The Pacific islands are among the smallest isolated independent archipelagos in the world. Even when compared by geographical region, the Pacific islands (Oceania) are the smallest in aggregate terms among the world's regional populations (Table 3-18, Appendix B). The selection of cases based on the world's smallest and most isolated group is therefore important to the validity of the study in terms of effective sampling. Further, the selected cases are Pacific countries that had undertaken significant moves towards telecommunications reform. This method ensures that more useful information is collected by intelligently choosing the cases which amplify the relationship of interests, rather than randomly drawing cases (Shively 2005:103). The Pacific islands have traditionally consisted of 14 independent island states.[3] Apart from being characterized as small vulnerable economies, huge variation exists across the region's socio-economic structures (Table 3-19, Appendix C).

With the exceptions of Solomon Islands and Papua New Guinea whose gross national income[4] per capita is around the US$1,000 mark, the other twelve Pacific islands' economic standard ranges from low to middle economy ADB bench marks. The contribution of the services sector (telecommunications included) to the economy dominates any other sectors—50 per cent or more of GDP is due to services sector input—with the exception of Solomon Islands and Papua New Guinea. Urbanization is mixed within the Pacific, with smaller Micronesian and Polynesian countries slightly more urbanized than the Melanesian countries (Table 3-3).

Five Pacific islands countries—Fiji, Papua New Guinea, Samoa, Tonga and Vanuatu—were selected as case studies for this research. The selection of case studies is based on four fundamental issues. First, the criteria for case selection were based on the highest observed variation of the explanatory variable to lower the number of third factor influences (Van Evera 1997:52). The control for other potential variables effect is crucial in establishing the isolated causal relationship between the multilateral policy restraint and telecommunications sector performance.

---

[3] Also known as the 'Pacific Islands Forum States' consisting of Cook Islands, Federated States of Micronesia, Fiji, Kiribati, Republic of Marshall Islands, Nauru, Niue, Palau, Papua New Guinea, Samoa, Solomon Islands, Tonga, Tuvalu and Vanuatu.

[4] The use of per capita Gross National Income instead of the traditional GDP per capita is more appropriate since these island states receive significant resources from foreign aid and remittances (AusAID 2006:17). However, since GNI data is limited on Pacific Islands, the empirical estimates and discussion in Chapter 7 use GDP per capita (US$ constant 2000).

Table 3-3: Selected Socio-economic Indicators for Pacific Islands

Pacific Islands*	GNI per capita [a] (current US$) 2008	GDP per capita (constant 2000 US$) 2008	Services sector (% of total GDP) 2006	Urban population (% of total population) 2008
Cook Islands	..	..	77.7	70.2
Fiji Islands	3,930	2,195	64.3	50.7
Kiribati	2,000	560	78.3	43.6
Marshall Islands	3,270	2,240	70.7	70.7
Federated States of Micronesia	2,340	1,817	76.8	22.5
Nauru	..	..	78.3	100.0
Palau	8,650	6,571	79.8	77.0
Papua New Guinea	1,010	680	23.4	12.6
Samoa	2,780	1,714	59.9	22.8
Solomon Islands	1,180	1,165	45.4	17.6
Tonga	2,560	1,664	57.0	24.5
Tuvalu	..	..	69.7	48.1
Vanuatu	2,330	1,354	77.1	24.3
Low-income	524	387	50.4	..
Middle-income	3,260	1,997	35.1	..
High-income	39,345	28,696	65.1	..

Source: Asian Development Bank (ADB) (2008) and; United Nations Economic and Social Commission for Asia and the Pacific (UNESCAP) 2008.

Notes: [a] Based on World Bank Atlas method; * Niue not included for lack of statistical data; .. not available.

The cases were therefore allocated into case studies that had made commitments at the WTO on the telecommunications sector—Papua New Guinea and Tonga—and, the case studies that had not made any WTO telecommunications commitment—Fiji, Samoa and Vanuatu.

Table 3-4 outlines the Pacific case study selection criteria. The selections of case studies were determined on similar institutional, political, socio-economic, and geographical factors.[5] I use the presence of an independent regulator to reflect domestic policy restraint. Further, bilateral investment treaties are also controlled for bilateral policy restraint. The similarities in case conditions create a semi-controlled environment that limits third variable effects within case studies between values of the independent variable and the dependent variable (Van Evera 1997:52).

Table 3-4: Pacific Case Studies Selection

Case studies	Multilateral policy restraint (WTO telecom commitment)	Domestic policy restraint (independent regulator)	Telecom institutional framework	Key socio-economic and political factors
Papua New Guinea and Tonga	Yes	Controlled*	Controlled	Controlled*
Fiji Samoa Vanuatu	No			
Source: Author's consolidation of key variables of the research. Note: * Not fully controlled for all Pacific case studies and therefore some variation exists, for example, Tonga has no independent regulator. Economic standards and population sizes also vary.				

[5] To ensure that we observe only the effects of factor A on factor B, no other factors (C, D or E) should be changing at same time when A changes. This should ensure us that we observe only the relationship we are interested in (A on B) and not by chance or some other factors (C, D or E) influences. In practice, controlling for influences of third variables (C, D or E) is not always clear cut and therefore, any limitations in the research design on controlling for third-variable influences is clearly stated. Semi-controlled environment therefore indicate this reality that the relationship of interest is not fully controlled due to natural or socio-economic characteristics of each case study.

Singleton and Straits (2005:50-51) explained that,

> "whenever a variable [or group of variables] is held constant in research, that variable can not account for (or explain) any of the variation in the explanatory variables…holding variables constant thus simplifies complex social situations. It is a means of ruling out variables that are not of immediate interest but that might otherwise explain part of the phenomenon of interest".

It is, however, important to note that the Pacific islands are a group with great diversity in socio-political and economic backgrounds. Controlling for third variable influence is therefore a methodological challenge. The most notable differences important to acknowledge are population size, economic standard and traditional cultures. PNG has a population of more than six million, compared to a population of 100,000 in Tonga. Economic standards are quite varied within the Pacific case studies, with lower economic standards in larger Melanesian countries compared to relatively higher economic standards in smaller Polynesian countries. The traditional cultures in the Pacific Islands also are diverse, with different ethnic backgrounds, language and dialects, and way of life.

While there is no independent regulator in Tonga, the Department of Communications (now Ministry of Information and Communications) claims that it strives to act independently from policymakers. Variation also exists within the political structure of Pacific case studies, with Tonga and Fiji under more authoritarian governments—Tonga is a constitutional monarchy while Fiji is under a military government—while other Pacific case studies have implemented more democratic political structures.

Attempts however, were undertaken to identify the dynamic similarities in Pacific Islands' socio-economic and political endowments (Table 3-19, Appendix C). Table 3-19 shows some general characteristics in the Pacific case studies including telecommunications reform policies, WTO telecommunications commitment, and several socio-economic characteristics. The Pacific case studies are all small archipelagos with populations of less than 1.5 million.[6] The telecommunications institutional framework and signatories to free trade agreements show almost homogenous characteristics across the case studies. Socio-economic characteristics are also similar, with relatively low annual economic growth and similar social hardship levels. The World Bank (2009),

[6] With the exception of Papua New Guinea, for reasons discussed in Chapter 7.

"Worldwide Governance Indicators Project" shows visibly similar features on four indicators for all Pacific case studies: voice and accountability, government effectiveness, regulatory control and rule of law.

The selection of several Pacific case studies instead of one, together with the pre-selection requirement of extreme case studies, minimizes the potential for subjective bias[7] in the research. Structured research questions were employed in all five case studies, which not only ensured parallel comparative analyses between cases but also assisted the researcher in collecting fieldwork data objectively. The fieldwork visits were based in capital cities of the respective Pacific case studies. Empirical data collections were based on three sets of research techniques: semi-structured expert interviews; collection of secondary sources; and direct observations.

3.2 Semi-structured Expert Interviews

The nature of the research question dictated the style of the interview and selection of potential interviewees. Two factors drove this selection process. First, the research was interested in examining the detailed mechanics of key regulatory policy initiatives in which only a handful of public and private institutions were directly involved. Second, the telecommunications sector in most of the case studies contained two operators. Hence, only a limited pool of experts could be realistically identified for the study.

It was therefore necessary to select expert personnel from relevant institutions. The experts were not only perceived to be well acquainted with the historical evolution of telecommunications reform, but also, they have in-depth knowledge of the subject crucial for the study. [8] Hence, positional-sampling was developed with particular focus on Chief Executive Officers, Heads of Departments or regulatory policy specialists. The interview questions format was semi-structured, with a pre-determined set of questions developed in advance, but with flexibility to modify order and framing of each question based on the context of the interview conversations (Appendix F). The main objective is to motivate

---

[7] The large-n quantitative study in Chapter 6 provides a further triangulation towards minimizing bias on verification though.

[8] Information produced is based on well-informed opinions of expert people based on comprehensive inside information they have access to. This information usually not reproduced anywhere else or made public for commercial or political reasons.

the interviewee to talk openly while making sure in-depth information is extracted on the research topic.

Sixty-two semi-structured interviews were conducted (Table 3-21, Appendix E). Interviews were mostly conducted in hosts' offices with average duration between 30 to 60 minutes each. The fieldwork began in June 2008 and was completed by December 2008. Roughly 14 days spent conducting a series of pre-arranged and on-spot interviews each month on a case study. Contacts with potential interviewees were established based on the use of local contacts and via electronic emails. Interview data were recorded either on written accounts, in digital recordings format or both.

3.3 Secondary Sources

A broad range of secondary information were collected during fieldwork and afterwards. Table 3-20 (Appendix D) lists key secondary data collected with sources and type of information. Several other, online resources were also accessed including the web pages of the International Telecommunications Union; IMF; ADB; and the Commonwealth Secretariat.

3.4 Fieldwork Observations

During fieldwork, stakeholders interaction and responses were observed during interview and non-interview periods. In particular, direct observation was useful in observing customer responses to how well the telecommunications industry is performing in each case study. This was possible by simply observing customers' responses when serviced by telecommunications operator branches in capital cities. Also, I observed telecommunications sector performance based on instant media coverage in the newspapers and through television commercials during the period I spent in each case study country. This technique was critical in providing a broader understanding of the behaviors of key stakeholders in the research. Digital pictures were also taken of key stakeholder's offices and operations.

4.0 Conceptual Framework

Policy analysis can involve the examination of either the causes or consequences of government policies (Dye 1976:5). By looking at the causes of public policies, Dye suggested that public policies themselves are the “dependent variables” and researchers seek to explain the impact of those policies by reference to social, economic or political forces which are believed to be the causes of public policies. Dye (1976) labeled this type of research “policy determination research“. The studies of the consequences of public policy used public policy as the “independent variable” and the dependent variable is the economic, political and social factors in the society believed to be affected by the public policy. Dye (1976) called this research “policy impact research”.

To generate a meaningful and useful contribution to current policy dialogues in small island developing states, the research attempted to merge Dye’s (1976) policy “determination” and “impact” research to equally account for the causes and consequences of public policy. The analytical framework adopted in this research reflects this objective.

Most models in public policy have limitations, and the conceptual framework developed for this research is no exception. To begin with, efforts have been made to account for most of the key stakeholders, although other factors may not be fully accounted for. Nevertheless, the systematic methodological design for the comparative case studies provides some certainty. Second, the availability of appropriate indicators to accurately reflect variables of interest was a challenging exercise.

Analytical framework

Based on the theoretical underpinnings discussed in the previous section, I introduce an analytical framework adapted from the studies by Levy and Spiller (1996), and Fiani (1998, cited in Tigre 1999:6). The selection of these two conceptual frameworks is important as Fiani’s framework emphasizes the interactions between key stakeholders (causes and outcomes of interactions) while Levy and Spillers’ emphasizes political, institutional and regulatory frameworks (by whom and under what design framework).

Tigre (1999) studied the impact of international institutions and domestic regulation on the telecommunications sector in Latin America. One way of examining the impact institutional and domestic policies according to Tigre (1999:4) is the proper identification of factors affecting national telecommunications policies, including the examination of the relationship between national regulation agencies and key stakeholders. The key stakeholders include government ministers and bureaucrats, independent regulators, state-owned telecommunications operators, competitor, the public & private sectors and the WTO. Figure 3-4 demonstrates the analytical framework and relationships between key stakeholders.

Figure 3-4: An Analytical Framework

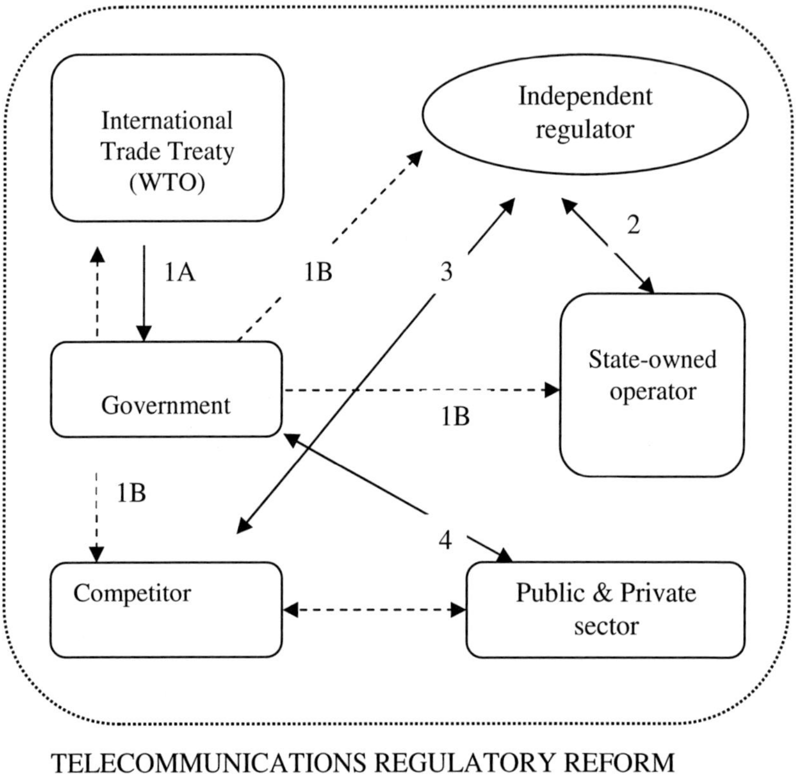

Source: Adapted from Fiani R (1998) cited in Tigre (1999, p.6) and Levy and Spiller (1996).

Relationships 1A & 1B discuss the relationships between the multilateral trading system, government and the independent regulator. This relationship portrays the multilateral policy restraint imposed by WTO agreements on government. Domestic regulatory telecom reform policies are consolidated by WTO commitments. Tigre (1999) suggested that agreements between the actors involved are influenced not only by technical or local issues but also foreign policy issues.

Also, the interaction between government and independent regulators is reflected. This relationship deals with the hypothesized political interference by government on independent regulator. The conditions for government's incentive to renege reform policies are based on government's commercial interest in the sector and overall weaker institutional and governance structure.

Relationship 2 involves the independent regulator and state-owned telecommunications operator. This relationship according to Tigre (1999) is influenced by three main factors; first is the political environment—ideology assumed by the national government, second is the conflicting interest between the regulator and the monopoly player. Third, is political ownership of public telecom operators and how it can be politicized in national telecom policies.

Relationship 3 involves between independent regulator and competitors. The competitor's objective is driven by commercial interests—for example, pursuing its network expansion only on commercially viable areas (usually urban areas only). The independent regulator on the other hand—acting on behalf of the general public's interest—favors universal coverage which includes non-profitable areas (remote islands and rural areas).

Relationship 4 looks at the interaction between government and interest groups. Becker (1983) emphasized on pressure groups competition for political influence. Political equilibrium depends on certain criteria which include group efficiency in producing pressure, the effect of additional pressure (economy of scale however up to a certain point), the number of persons in different groups and the impact of inefficient distortionary use of taxes and subsidies on actors, what Becker termed as "deadweight costs". The emphasis on the incentive for pressure and its impact on how it is operationalized pressure vary. Thurber (1991) cited in Furlong (1997:236-327) suggested that, "the source of interest group's power depend on their resources (such as money, total membership, and the dispersion of members) and their ability to transform those resources (such as leadership and communication) into action."

The comparative case study analyses in Chapters 4, 5 and 6 therefore focuses discussion around the policy interactions identified in this analytical framework.

5.0 Conclusion

This Chapter set out the methodological tool for the research based on the theoretical discussion in Chapter 2. The Chapter outlined the design of the research with specific references to the research question, hypotheses, independent and dependent variables and the range of data collection techniques employed.

The next Chapter proceeds to the actual case study analyses by examining an updated account on the key regulatory framework on telecommunications in the Pacific case studies.

CHAPTER FOUR

TELECOMMUNICATIONS POLICY REFORM IN PACIFIC ISLAND CASE STUDIES[1]

1.0 Introduction

Moving towards case study analyses, this chapter introduces telecommunications reform policies in the Pacific island case studies. The Chapter discusses the key regulatory policy variables and outlines the early expansion of the Irish-owned mobile operator Digicel Pacific Limited, instrumental in the recent investments in the mobile service in all the Pacific case studies. The discussion on recent changes to the telecommunications policies provides useful platforms for forthcoming chapters on what type of policy frameworks have been implemented and how telecommunications policy has evolved in recent years. In addition, this chapter provides much needed updated regulatory information on the telecommunications sector in the Pacific case studies deemed useful for future empirical studies.

In the past decade, five Pacific island states have undergone some form of deregulation in their telecommunications sectors, with major reforms intensified in the past fours years. The motives behind the push by Pacific island states for reform vary case by case; however, two factors which emerge as common to all reforming Pacific case studies are their smallness and isolation. Island states push for telecommunications regulator reform to promote infrastructural development, as a means of promoting economic development and connecting isolated islands. The use of ICT as a mode of service delivery for education by the University of the South Pacific is a good example of telecommunications impacting on distance and isolation (Duncan and McMaster 2008:193-211).

---

[1] An earlier version of this Chapter was published in the *Pacific Economic Bulletin*, Volume 23, Number 3, pp. 69-100, 2008[b], visit <http://peb.anu.edu.au/pdf/PEB23_3-OFA_WEB.pdf>.

The early outcome of telecommunications reforms in the Pacific case studies reaffirm some of the fundamental aspects of telecommunications liberalization established by the literature in developing countries.[2] Although there has been a cross-country survey on developing countries' telecommunications regulatory policies[3], little attention has been granted to the Pacific islands. This Chapter attempts to fill that gap by conducting a regulatory policy stock-take on the evolution of telecommunications policies in Tonga, Fiji, Samoa, Papua New Guinea and Vanuatu.

Section 2 discusses the Pacific case studies' regulatory policies on telecommunications, while Section 3 discusses distinct cross-country similarities of regulatory policies in Pacific case studies. Section 4 concludes this chapter.

2.0 Regulatory Policies in Pacific Case Studies

2.1 Tonga

Tonga was the first Pacific island state to introduce competition into its telecommunications sector. The entry of a second mobile operator (TONFON) in 2003 led to a sharp reduction in mobile charges and an increase in total teledensity. TONFON had the lowest costs for peak mobile calls[4] in the Pacific region (World Bank 2006:83 and AusAID 2008[a]:46). Mobile phone ownership increased from 3.4 per cent in 2002 to 30 per cent in mid 2007 (AusAID 2008[a]:43).

The Pacific Economic Survey 2008 reported that the price of mobile calls (US$ per minute) in Tonga was the lowest in the Pacific since the introduction of competition (AusAID 2008[a]:43)—Figure 4-5.

[2] See Chapter 2 for discussion on the literature on telecommunications policy.

[3] See Ros (1999); Gasmi et al. (2000); Wallsten (2001); Madden et al.(2003); Fink et al. (2003); Varoudakis and Rossotto (2004); and Painter and Wong (2007).

[4] US$ per minute, about 50 cents per minute in the case of TONFON.

Figure 4-5: Cost of Peak Mobile Calls (US$ per minute) in the Pacific Region

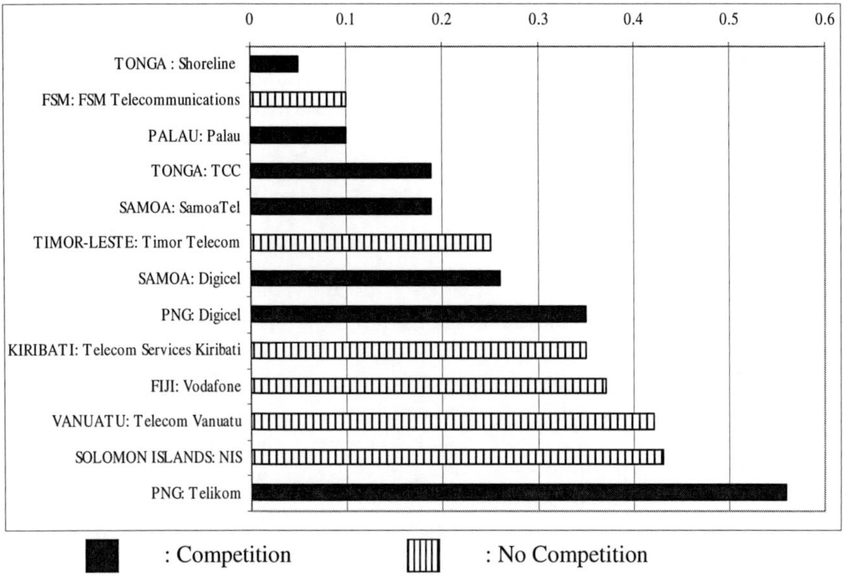

Source: Adapted from AusAID (2008)

Note: Prices and exchange rates effective September 2007. In some cases operators offer per minute, per two minute or per 30-second rates. Some have introduced per second billing. Where more than one rate is provided by a company (for example, mobile-to-mobile and mobile-to-landline) a simple average was taken.

Figure 4-5 also shows that Pacific countries which have introduced competition, have in general, lower costs of peak mobile calls per minute compared to Pacific countries that have not introduced competition. PNG Telikom was the most expensive mobile phone provider in 2008.

Regulatory policy

In an arrangement common to most Commonwealth countries in the Pacific and Caribbean, Cable & Wireless from the United Kingdom established the main telecommunications infrastructure for the island kingdom in 1978. A joint venture agreement with the Tongan Government lasted 22 years and provided all telecommunications services for inter-island[5] and international communications.

By 2000, the Tongan Parliament had passed two pieces of legislation for the regulation of the sector. First, the Communications Act 2000 established the Department of Communications as the central regulatory body to regulate and maintain telecommunications. The minister responsible for communications, the Prime Minister, led the Department. The Communications Act was the first piece of legislation to set out rules and procedures on consumer protection, tariffs for services, universal-service commitments, economic regulation, general competition practice, and arbitration. It was the first attempt by the Tongan Government to comprehensively address the regulatory environment for telecommunications.

As of 2009, no regulations have been passed on the key specific provisions (such as tariff management) of the legislation. The key principles of the Communications Act 2000 are outlined briefly in Table 4-5. The Communications Act 2000 covers several important features for effective regulation such as consumer protection, tariff management, fixed licensing terms with opportunities for renewal, universal-service policy, anti-competitive policies and arbitration. Provisions were not made, however, for an independent regulator and for the funding of universal-service obligations.

Second, the Tonga Communication Corporation Act 2000 was passed to absorb the incumbent monopoly, Cable and Wireless (UK). After the joint venture with Cable and Wireless (UK) expired in 2000, the government established a company under the Companies Act 1995, which was initially known as Tonga Telecommunications International Ltd (TTIL). This company was used to carry on the telecommunications service after the expiry of the service franchise. From February 2001, TTIL was renamed the Tonga Communications Corporations (TCC) with all rights and obligations legally transferred, based on the Tonga Communications Corporations Act 2000 (Tonga Department of Communications 2000:5).

[5] Between the main island Tongatapu and, ‘Eua island; Vava’u Group, Ha’apai Group and, the two Niua islands.

Table 4-5: Tonga's Communications Act 2000

	Key Sections		Key Principals
1	Objectives	o	To establish a communications licensing and regulation framework in support of the national development policy objectives.
		o	To establish powers and functions of a Department of Communications where regulation and policy control of the communications sector will be administered.
		o	To promote fair and sustainable competition in the supply and provision of network facilities, network services and applications services.
		o	To promote and protect the interests of customers.
2	Licensing	o	The minister grants licences subject to approval of the chair of the Privy Council. The terms of licences should not exceed 10 years.
3	Consumer protection	o	To establish consumer standards for licences issued on provision of information to consumers regarding services, tariffs and performance, handling of consumer complaints, protection of individual consumer information, advertising or representation of services, and consumer charging, billing, collection, and credit practices.
4	Tariffs	o	Licensees must provide the Department of Communications with a list of charges for their existing services or new services to be offered.
5	Universal-service system	o	The minister may direct the department to determine a universal system to promote the widespread availability of services in Tonga.
		o	The universal system may include: the needs of under-served areas in Tonga or under-served groups within a particular community; measures to encourage the installation of network facilities and the provision of network services in those

			designated areas; and consideration for the affordability and costs of providing services to such areas.
6	Social regulation	o	The minister may direct the department to set standards for content applications services, which should address unsuitable content, advertising content, and representation of Tongan culture and national identity.
		o	A licensee shall not supply any content that is indecent or obscene, displays excessive violence, is blasphemous, treasonous or seditious, or defamatory, or contravenes with the laws of Tonga.
		o	The minister may declare in writing a licensee to supply without charge divine worship content or other content of religious nature.
		o	The minister may determine the extent and manner in which a licensee may provide political or controversial content.
7	Economic regulation	o	Prohibition on anti-competitive behaviors, collusive agreements, and discrimination in services provided to consumers.
8	Arbitration	o	The department conducts arbitration on interconnection disputes between operators. The department has final decision.
9	Inquiries and investigations	o	The minister may direct the department to hold an inquiry on any aspects of the Act.
		o	The minister may direct the department to hold investigation into any civil or criminal offence committed under the act.

Source: Government of Tonga (2000[a])

In addition, a communications policy was drafted in 2000 (Tonga Department of Communications 2006:1). The policy set forth four key policy principles: nurturing a sustainable and financially viable communications sector; maximizing infrastructure availability; supporting industry investment; and attracting and maximizing strategic and economic benefits from communications assets (Soakai 2004:5). The new policy ensured that introduced competition would encourage growth in a universal manner. The competition would raise the infrastructure standard of telecommunications necessary in supporting economic development.

Ownership

In 2000, Tonga essentially shifted from partial private ownership to near full nationalization of the incumbent monopoly. The shift of rights and obligations to TCC granted the public corporation the authority to control its expenditure and to undertake "business-like decisions" on investment and daily development without the need for formal approval from government. TCC's daily operations were therefore left to its executive officer and management team. This was considered important for maintaining a business-like management team to run the daily operations of the corporation rather than telecommunications operators being run by political leaders (Noll 2000:203). On the other hand, the policies that regulated the industries were the sole responsibility of politicians, ensuring that the activities of the sector does protect the Tongan culture and traditional (for example, social regulation set the standards for the proper use of telecommunications to uphold Tongan cultures and traditions).

Political sensitivities led the government to adopt a less drastic approach, yet it still undertook what was considered to be neoliberal reform[6] of its telecommunications sector. The ownership shares have remained unchanged since 2000. Ten per cent of the shares were advertised to Tongan nationals under the Tongan Participation Scheme stipulated by Section 13 and 14 of the Tonga Communications Act 2000. The government's rationale, as reflected in its communications policy, indicated a belief in widespread ownership of national carriers as set by global precedents. It was therefore important for Tongan nationals to be given the opportunity to participate in the ownership of TCC. This was a political rather than economic move—something that is seen as necessary to increase popular support for reform in developing countries (Noll 2000:203). Noll (2000) explained, 'that selling shares in "atomized quantities" is uneconomical as the realized price of these shares is less than the price of shares sold to [a] controlling consortium because

[6] See Noll (2000) for discussion of neoliberal reform of telecommunications in developing countries.

atomized sales have greater transactions costs and because the domestic capital market is underdeveloped'.

The Tongan Government, however, maintains a close affiliation through the board of directors to which the management of TCC is accountable. As stipulated by Part VI of the Tonga Communications Corporation Act 2000, "there shall be no more than seven directors and not less than four at any one time". The Minister of Finance appoints directors, with the consent of the cabinet. Cabinet ministers usually form a majority of the seven directors, although the Minister of Public Enterprise announced in February 2008 that "all Cabinet Ministers including Prime Ministers will relinquish their directorate positions by January 2009 to be filled by the private sector as part of [the] Government's public reform' (Matangi Tonga 2008[b]:1). As of April 2010, little progress has materialized on this front.

Market structure

In 2000, a licence for telephone and mobile service provision was granted to TONFON—the domestic mobile service arm of parent company Shoreline Communications Incorporated—to operate local services, domestic fixed and international fixed long-distance lines, mobile services and internet services (ITU 2000:2). Other segments, such as data, digital subscriber line (DSL), leased lines and paging, were reserved for the incumbent state-owned operator. Operations on the mobile service segment began in 2003. King Siaosi Tupou V was the owner of Shoreline Communications Incorporated and held a close business affiliation with TONFON when it was first established. In 2007, the King's involvement in telecommunications ceased when Digicel acquired TONFON (see further discussion in Chapter 5).

TONFON competed aggressively with TCC for mobile services in the first few years of operation. Competition in mobile services was intense as both providers attempted to improve service quality at a lower price. In less than two years, Shoreline Communications Incorporated established a Global System for Mobile Communications (GSM) network in collaboration with Globecomm, a United States based communications company,[7] while TCC offered its GSM-900 network earlier in 2001. In

---

[7] Visit <http://www.globecommsystems.com/rs/home.aspx> for more information on Globecomm and the Tongan Case.

2006, TCC, through collaboration with Alvarion[8], an Israeli communications company, further upgraded its GSM network with "wimax technology' to offer broadband data services (Alvarion 2006:1). The fixed line segment continued to be solely served solely by TCC, although competition in the internet services between the two companies was as active as for the mobile services.

Although competition between the two telecommunications operators led to positive outcomes for consumers, the Government planned a gradual introduction of "sustainable" competition. The communications policy outlined the Government's position for the adoption of a limited market entry model, which was deemed appropriate to address the unique set of challenges it believed faced by the industry. It was also noted in the policy statement that these restrictions were necessary to avoid the dramatic erosion of revenue per subscriber and to avoid competition between operators being based on the cannibalization and fragmentation of the existing customer base (Tonga Department of Communications 2000:4).

Irish-based company Digicel acquired TONFON from Shoreline Communications Incorporated in November 2007 (Reuters 2007:1). Digicel was granted a licence to operate in the fixed line, mobile and internet segments, as well as television cable services (Tonga Department of Communications 2008). Within six months, Digicel invested more than TOP$20 million (about US$10 million) to build and upgrade its network in Tonga (Matangi Tonga 2008[a]:2). On 8 May 2008, the company opened its first office in Nuku'alofa, recruiting Tongans in professional positions, with a comprehensive plan to establish more than 12 branches throughout Tongatapu, the Vava'u Group, the Ha'apai Group and 'Eua Island (Matangi Tonga 2008[a])

A third privately-owned telecommunications company—Tongasat (Friendly Islands Satellite Communications Limited)—was established earlier in 1988, although its core service was satellite communications. Tongasat leased out satellite orbital slots in outer space to multinational telecommunications providers (Tongasat 2008). It currently has nine geostationary satellite orbital positions leased to international clients. It operates a satellite called ESIAFI-1, with a footprint covering southeastern Europe, North Africa and the Middle East (Tongasat 2008).

[8] Visit <http://www.alvarion.com/> for further company detail and technology produced.

No other telecommunications provider within the Pacific region provides this type of service.

Universal service

The Communications Act 2000 contains general provisions for the universal-service system. The objective is to promote the widespread availability of services to under-served areas of the country. The universal-service system also promotes the establishment of appropriate infrastructure networks for under-served areas and consideration for the affordability of the services (Government of Tonga 2000[a]:25). There are no specific financial requirements (such as a universal fund) for the providers within the Act, although the Tongan Participation Scheme indirectly stipulates that revenue from sales of the 10 per cent of shares be committed by TCC for the development and improvement of communications network infrastructure. The Tongan Participation Scheme is regulated under the Tonga Communications Corporation Act 2000. The Minister of Finance on behalf of the Tongan Government is responsible for the scheme, which encourages private local ownership of TCC. The universal service commitment is the responsibility of TCC but not other licensed operators.

Although Shoreline Communications Incorporated's mobile arm TONFON was granted a licence to operate within the fixed-line segment, it has never done so—probably because of the market power of the incumbent and the high initial sunk costs required for investment. In comparison, the fixed costs of building a wireless network are relatively low.

The entrance of TONFON has expanded the mobile services market. Its Chief Executive Officer, Mr. Soane Ramanlal, stated in 2007 that "the mobile market has about 30,000 mobile subscribers in aggregate and TONFON claims about two thirds of that" (Matangi Tonga 2007:2). The costs of establishing wireless towers for mobile telephony compared to installing copper wire networks were far smaller. New providers therefore, were able to build wireless networks and attract large number of customers relatively quickly (Wallsten 2004:306). The overall impact on the telecommunications market was that the total teledensity for mobile and fixed lines increased from 10.8 phones per 100 people in 2001 to 44 phones per 100 people in 2005 (Soakai 2006:1). The mobile segment covered areas that the incumbent's fixed-line network had not covered and therefore made a contribution to universal-service commitments.

Bilateral investment treaties

In London on 22 October 1997, the then Minister of Labour, Commerce and Industries for Tonga, Dr Giulio M. Paunga, signed a bilateral investment treaty on behalf of the Tongan Government between Tonga and the United Kingdom. The objective of the treaty was to promote and protect investments of the two nationals in the two countries. Treatment of investments by nationals was adopted in similar approach to WTO's "national treatment" and "most-favored-nation" provisions. Three other important provisions of the treaty deemed relevant include provisions dealing with; expropriation risks; repatriation of investment and returns; and a mechanism for the settlement of disputes between investors and the host state, and between contracting parties. Dispute settlement between investor and host state, though, could be submitted to independent international arbitration bodies including: the International Centre for the Settlement of Investment Disputes; the court of arbitration of the International Chamber of Commerce; or an international arbitrator under the arbitration rules of the United Nations Commission on International Trade Law.

Multilateral trade commitments

Tonga negotiated offers on trade in services in its negotiations for accession to the WTO. Tonga committed to non-discriminatory treatment in basic telecommunications, with sub-sectors covering voice telephone services (fixed-line and mobile services) and value-added telecommunications services, including sub-sectors covering electronic mail, voice email and online information and database retrieval (internet segment).[9] These service offers were approved by the WTO's General Council in 2005, although, a transitional period was granted for the incumbent to adjust and, as of January 2008, foreign direct investment (Mode 3 - Commercial Presence) for fixed and mobile services was committed for non-discrimination in terms of market access and national treatment.

[9] See WTO document WT/ACC/TON/17/Add.2 dated 2 December 2005 and subsequent updates for full service commitments.

In addition, Tonga adopted the Telecommunications Reference Paper as part of its commitments on telecommunications. The reference paper is a result of the negotiations on basic telecommunications made by WTO members in 1996-97. The paper's main objective was to allow derogation from the basic rules of GATS allowing domestic regulation to limit the delivery of basic telecommunications services for social or cultural reasons. The reference paper was also drafted to tackle anti-competitive use of market power by incumbent or powerful service providers entering the market, to promote competitive market practices and to ensure an independent regulator made policy decisions that were non-discriminatory, transparent and objective. The reference paper also promotes universal-service obligations, although each member has the right to develop and define the scope of its universal coverage. Most of these commitments are reflected in the Communications Act 2000.

2.2 Papua New Guinea

Regulatory reform in the telecommunications sector in PNG was marked by the introduction of competition into the mobile service sector in September 2006. The beginning of operations for Digicel PNG Limited in March 2007 ended the exclusive rights for Telikom PNG Limited. The early results indicate a sharp increase in coverage and doubling of mobile phone subscribers (AusAID 2008[a]:43). The PNG government has estimated that the expansion in mobile services contributed around 0.7 percentage points to gross domestic product (GDP) growth in 2007 (AusAID 2008[a]:43).

Regulatory policy

The PNG government via the direction of the National Executive Council (NEC), endorsed a National Policy on Information and Communication (NPIC) in 1994. This was the first policy paper on regulatory reform for telecommunications in PNG. The policy paper briefly outlined seven objectives covering telecommunications services, including: the need for access of all users to telecommunications, including in rural and remote areas; the development of telecommunications through business efficiency, cost reductions and appropriate tariffs; appropriate policies to attract private investment; telecommunications regulations to be consistent with national objectives; and the privatization of state-owned Telikom (Papua New Guinea Ministry of Information and Communications

Services 1993:13-15). To varying degrees, these objectives are reflected in the telecommunications legislation that currently governs the sector.

Three pieces of legislation constitute the principal regulatory framework for the telecommunications industry in PNG: the Telecommunications Act 1996 (and amendments), the Telecommunications Industry Act 2002 and amendments (Government of PNG 2002), and the Independent Consumer and Competition Act 2002 (Government of PNG 2002). The ICCC's involvement as the economic regulator for telecommunications sector was gradually phased out when the new regulatory body on telecommunications, the National Information and Communication Technology Authority—NICTA—was established in March 2010. The Telecommunications Act 1996 (and amendments) was the first major legislation implemented for the regulation of the telecommunications sector in PNG. The key principles of the Telecommunications Act 1996 are outlined briefly in Table 4-6.

The Telecommunications Act ensures that the sector is supplied as efficiently and economically as practicable by creating a regulatory environment that promotes fair and efficient market conduct.[10] The 1996 Act also established the Papua New Guinea Radio Communications Telecommunications Technical Authority (PANGTEL), which is responsible for providing technical inspections and setting technical standards and technical regulation for the telecommunications industry. PANGTEL is required by law to consult with the government—and vice versa—on policy issues relating to telecommunications.

[10] See Section 2 – General Objectives of the Act, Telecommunications Act 1996, No. 57.

Table 4-6: Papua New Guinea's Telecommunications Act 1996 (and amendments)

	Key Principals	Key Sections
1	Objectives	o The Telecommunications Act to be consistent with PNG's Constitution. o The Act ensures that standard telephone services are supplied as efficiently and economically as practicable, carriers will achieve high levels of accountability, infrastructure development, fair and efficient market conduct, and will promote PNG's telecommunications capabilities, industries and skills.
2	Independent regulator	o The commission (established under the Independent Consumer and Competition Commission Act 2002) is the economic regulator for telecommunications. o PANGTEL (Papua New Guinea Radio Communications and Telecommunications Technical Authority) is responsible for provision of technical standards. o In the event of these two entities being unable to reach agreement in filling their respective duties, the commission's view shall prevail. o The commission shall provide economic monitoring, control, inspection and regulation of the sector, grant licences and consult with industry and consumers on matters relating to the supply of telecommunications.
3	Licences	o The commission shall grant licences. o The licensee is required to comply with regulations and conditions set out by the commission.
4	Consumer protection	o The dominant carrier[1] will not discriminate between consumers of telecommunications services in relation to charges for services rendered or terms and conditions under which the services are supplied.
5	Tariffs	o Carriers to supply the commission, in writing, tariffs or charges for each telecommunications service supplied. The commission may disallow any tariff that does not comply with the Act.

6	Network Access	o The carrier has the right to interconnect its facilities with the network of any other carrier. o The commission may participate in negotiations over network access between carriers if one carrier proposes its inclusion. o The commission shall act as arbitrator if two carriers cannot agree on the terms and conditions of an access agreement. The commission makes the final decision.
7	Rural development obligations and fund	o All carriers to fulfill rural development obligations in PNG to ensure that the standard telephone service becomes reasonably accessible to all people in the country. o The minister may consult with PANGTEL on policy directions relating to designated areas to be covered, set rules on how carriers may recover costs from such obligations, and specify the method of disbursing the Rural Development Fund. o PANGTEL may declare universal-service carrier and rural development service carriers.
8	Inquiries and investigations	o The commission may conduct an inquiry into any matter relating to the performance of any of the commission's function and powers. o The commission may investigate the conduct of any carrier deemed to contravene the act. o A person may complain to the commission about matters relating to the act. o The commission may direct a carrier to remedy a breach of licence conditions.

Source: PANGTEL, Telecommunications Act 1996 (amendments). Available from <http://www.pangtel.gov.pg/Legislation/legislation.htm> (viewed 24 March 2008).

Note:[1] A dominant carrier is defined by the act as by virtue of the terms of its licence, or by government policy, or by reason of its share of the market, or because of its access to technology, infrastructure or capital, which gives it a substantial degree of power in the market for the supply of a telecommunications service.

The granting of telecommunications licences is the responsibility of the Independent Consumer and Competition Commission (ICCC). The ICCC Act 2002 established its legal authority to promote economic efficiency in the industry. The ICCC is tasked with price access pricing, licensing and regulation in all sectors. It is also responsible for investigating complaints concerning market conduct and for reviewing operation of regulated entities. PANGTEL and the ICCC are required to cooperate in terms of policy issues relating to telecommunications. An appeal panel was established under the act to deal with any dispute.

Ownership

Telikom PNG Limited, which has served PNG for more than 55 years, is 100 per cent state-owned. Telikom PNG Limited and other state-owned enterprises are managed by the Independent Public Business Corporation of Papua New Guinea (IPBC). The IPBC is a 100 per cent state-owned statutory corporation with its own Act tasked to independently hold the majority of state-owned commercial assets in trust and to manage those assets to improve commercial performance and economic development.[11] Telikom provides services in voice and data, including fixed-line services and the internet.[12] In November 2008, Telikom PNG Limited sold 50 per cent of its ownership shares in B-Mobile (its mobile service branch) to foreign private investor Capital Way Consortium for an amount of US$45 million (Paine n.d.).

Market structure

Mobile service licences were granted to Digicel PNG from September 2006 and to Greencom[13] from September 2007, effectively ending Telikom's monopoly in the mobile sector. Presently, the mobile sector is being served by B-Mobile (which used to be owned by Telikom's wholly owned mobile subsidiary, Pacific Mobile Communications Limited) and Digicel PNG. Greencom (Dawamiba PNG) has not yet begun operations.

---

[11] Visit IPBC's website at <http://www.ipbc.com.pg/index.html>

[12] Visit <http://www.Telikompng.com.pg> for more information on Telikom PNG Limited.

[13] Greencom is a telecommunications, engineering and construction company from Indonesia that joined a local family business to form Dawamiba PNG. Visit Radio New Zealand International report for further information, <http://www.rnzi.com/pages/news.php?op=readandid=26574> (viewed 12 January 2008).

Universal service

One of the key major objectives of the NPIC (and subsequent revisions) was the need for access of all users to telecommunications, with particular emphasis on the rural population. Strategy guidelines were set, including the provision of funding for rural telecommunications and encouraging local and provincial governments to improve access to telecommunications for all PNG citizens (PNG Ministry of Information and Communication Services 1993:13).

The rural development obligations and funds in the Telecommunications Act 1996 focused on basic telephony becoming reasonably accessible to all. The consultation between minister and PANGTEL declares specific areas for rural development obligations. The operators declared by PANGTEL to be universal-service carriers may access the Rural Development Fund to pursue infrastructural developments which was drafted with a view to gradually introducing competition and privatization.

Bilateral investment treaties

PNG has signed bilateral investment treaties with Germany (in 1980), United Kingdom (1981), Australia (1990), China (1991), and Malaysia (1992), although the treaty with Malaysia has not been ratified (UNCTAD 2000). The treaties have similar characteristics in terms of promotion and protection of investments—in particular, the equal treatment of investment returns for domestic and foreign investors. Expropriation measures were also restricted, although in the treaty between PNG and Australia, an exception was included to allow expropriation rights by the PNG Government of private investment on national interest grounds. Independent arbitration is to be established in the case of investor-to-state or investor-to-investor disputes. Dispute cases are allowed to be referred to the International Centre for Settlement of Investment Disputes or other relevant international bodies.

Multilateral trade commitments

PNG made multilateral commitments during the WTO telecommunications sectoral negotiation in 1997. Offers were committed on basic and added-value services, including basic telephony, the mobile phone sector and the internet. PNG scheduled under service delivery Mode 1 (Cross-border supply) for basic telephony that all international service must go through Telikom's gateway network. Additional derogation on commercial presence was for the protection of the monopoly rights of Telikom for all services subject to five-year exclusivity (1997-2002) which has lapsed.

2.3 Samoa

Samoa is one of the success stories of the Pacific in terms of comprehensive regulatory reform of its telecommunications sector. With collaboration from the World Bank, Samoa has successfully transformed its telecommunications sector with the introduction of competition to the mobile services sector in 2006. Mobile teledensity increased from 1.5 per cent of the total population in 2002, to 46 per cent in mid-2007 (AusAID 2008[a]:43).

Regulatory policy

The Telecommunications Act 2005 provided the key regulatory framework for the liberalization of telecommunications sector in Samoa. The key principles of the Act are outlined briefly in Table 4-7.

Table 4-7: Samoa's Telecommunications Act 2005

	Key Sections		Key Principles
1	Objectives	o	Facilitate the development of the telecommunications sector to promote social and economic development.
		o	Promote universal access, provide reliable and efficient services through competition and private-sector investment.
		o	Encourage sustainable foreign and domestic investment.
		o	Establish a framework for the control of anti-competitive behavior.
		o	Protect the interests of subscribers.
2	Independent regulator	o	Establish an independent regulator with functions relating to advising the minister on telecommunications policy, implementing the Act, issuing licences, resolving disputes between customers and operators or between operators and providing appropriate regulations to avoid anti-competitive behavior on the part of

		the dominant operator. o The regulator is independent in its operation and policy decisions from any influences, including the government. o An appeal against the decision of the regulator can be made to the Supreme Court.
3	Licences	o The regulator will grant all licences. o All people providing telecommunications services must hold a licence to do so.
4	Universal-access policy and universal-access fund	o The regulator may propose to the minister a policy relating to the obligations of providing universal services. o The universal-service policy shall consider the inclusion of basic telephone services, the designated areas and the costs of such obligations. o The minister may establish a fund to subsidize the net costs of providing universal services.
5	Competition policy	o The regulator shall establish policies that will promote efficient and sustainable competition for the benefit of customers, provide an open and transparent regulatory framework that minimizes regulatory barriers to entry of new operators, make orders designating dominant service providers*, prevent anti-competitive behavior from dominant service providers, dispose of complaints and resolve disputes.
6	Interconnection	o The regulator shall establish an open, non-discriminatory and commercially viable network for interconnection. o The regulator shall intervene to settle any interconnection disputes between providers.
7	Tariffs	o The dominant service provider shall file with and obtain approval from the regulator for all tariffs for services rendered. o The dominant service provider is required to publish its tariff schedules on its web sites for public information.

8	Consumer protection	o A service provider shall charge a customer only for the specific telecommunications service or equipment ordered. o A service provider shall not disclose any customer's information without the customer's written consent. o Service providers shall take all reasonable steps to ensure the confidentiality of customer communications. o A service provider shall identify a specific person to receive customer's complaints o A dominant service provider shall offer all customers the same terms and quality of services including tariffs charged.
9	Dispute settlement	o In disputes between providers or between customers and providers, the regulator may assign a staff member or consultant to mediate, or refer such disputes to the Supreme Court or issue an order to settle a dispute. o Parties to a dispute may agree to refer the dispute to private mediation or arbitration.**

Source: Parliament of Samoa, Telecommunications Act 2005, Ministry of Communications and Information Technology. Available from, <http://www.parliament.gov.ws/documents/acts/TELECOMMUNICATIONSMUNICATIONS_ACT_2005_-_Eng.pdf> (viewed 24 March 2008)

Note: * Every service whose gross revenue in a specific telecommunications market constitutes 40% or more of the total gross revenues of all services providers in that market; ** This provision was later revised by the Samoan Government and it is now required that the regulator settle all disputes and any appeals can be made directly to a Telecommunications Tribunal instead of the Supreme Court.

The main task for the regulator is the provision of policy advice to the minister responsible for telecommunications.[14] The regulator has the power to grant licences to telecommunications service operators, set licence fees, resolve disputes between service providers and the Government or between service operators, monitor and act on anti-competitive behavior and investigate complaints against service operators. The Act also covers other essential aspects, such as consumer protection, tariffs management, competition policies, consumer protection and

[14] Minister of Communications and Information Technology.

arbitration mechanisms. There is, however, no fixed time limit for granting licences; this is subject to the discretion of the Samoan Government and the independent regulator.

Ownership

The incumbent operator, Samoatel, is under joint private and public ownership: the government owns 40 per cent, Samoa's National Bank Provident Fund owns 27.5 per cent and the Bank of Samoa owns 22.5 per cent (both are government-owned entities), Samoa Life Insurance owns 10 per cent (World Bank 2006: 86).

Market structure

The Telecommunications Act 2005 introduced competition to the mobile sector. Previously, Telecommunications Samoa Cellular (TSC) had exclusive rights to the mobile segment.[15] In 2006, the Samoan Government issued two licences for mobile services—one to Digicel Samoa Limited (which acquired 90 per cent ownership of TSC from Telecom New Zealand) and one to Samoatel (AusAID 2008[a]:45).

Universal service

The Telecommunications Act 2005 set guidelines for the development of a universal service policy. The regulator is responsible for advising the minister on universal-service policies. The prices of basic telecommunications services and network coverage are the two guiding universal policy principles outlined in the 2005 Act. In addition, the 2005 Act details the establishment of a universal-service fund, to which the minister may require all licensees to contribute.

Bilateral investment treaties

Samoa had not signed any bilateral investment treaty as of April 2010.

---

[15] TSC is 10 per cent government-owned and 90 percent owned by Telecom New Zealand.

Multilateral trade commitments

Samoa is currently acceding to the WTO. As of April 2010, it had not finalized any trade in services offers under the general agreement on GATS.

2.4 Fiji

The Radisson Accord signed in November 2007 between Amalgamated Telecommunications Holdings Limited (ATH)—on behalf of the three telecommunications companies holding exclusive rights for local, international and mobile services—and the Fijian government ended the monopoly in the telecommunications sector in Fiji. The accord set October 2008 as the date for open competition and granting of licences to any telecommunications service provider (Baselala 2007:1). Fiji's regulatory environment for telecommunications has evolved gradually in the past two decades. The following discussion attempts to capture the gradual but significant milestones in regulatory policy development.

Regulatory policy

The Department of Communications, under the Ministry of Industry, Tourism, Trade and Communications, is responsible for the regulatory environment relating to telecommunications sector. The Posts and Telecommunications Decree 1989 (PTD) continues to regulate the sector. Because the PTD was a cabinet decision[16], it was instrumental in setting comprehensive rules for the telecommunications sector.[17] It covered rules on licensing, the telecommunications code and the role of the Communications Department. The PTD also granted 25-year exclusive rights for national telecommunications to Fiji Posts and Telecommunications Limited (FPTL) as the domestic operator, and for the international telecommunications to Fiji International Telecommunications known as FINTEL (ITU 2004:24).

After the 1989 decree, a comprehensive bill was drafted for the deregulation of the telecommunications sector: the Telecommunications Bill 2006. Key sections of the Telecommunications Bill 2006 are outlined

---

[16] There were no parliamentary sessions during the period 1987-1992.

[17] Posts and Telecommunications Decree No. 37 1989 contained 9 parts and 4 schedules, with 168 sections containing 136 pages.

in Table 4-8. Three characteristics of the bill are worth discussing. First, the bill envisaged a more predictable and transparent regulatory authority with the establishment of the Telecommunications Authority of Fiji (TAF). The statutory body is comprised of five board members, a chief executive officer and staff. Its duties under the bill include the right to grant licences, implementation of policy, regulation of technical aspects of access and interconnection, management of the radio spectrum and frequencies, and consumer protection (Parliament of Fiji 2006[a]:25). TAF's funding is in the form of annual appropriations to be approved by the Parliament.

Second, the bill would dismantle the monopoly rights granted by the 1989 decree by offering non-exclusive licences to any entity wishing to provide telecommunications services within Fiji. A licence would have a lifetime of 15 years subject to renewals. Third, universal service was included, with an advisory committee to develop "economically feasible schemes" for implementation.

Table 4-8: Fiji's Telecommunications Bill 2006*

	Key Sections		Key Principals
1	Management of telecommunications	o	The minister will formulate, monitor and review telecommunications policy.
		o	Establishment of the Telecommunications Authority of Fiji (TAF) with functions to implement telecommunications policy, mediate disputes, manage state assets, promote investor confidence and protect consumer interests. TAF will also be responsible for granting, suspending or revoking licences.
2	Regulation of telecommunications	o	Term of a licence may not exceed 15 years.
3	Universal service	o	Establishment of a universal-service advisory committee to advise TAF on matters relating to a universal scheme, its goals and implementation strategies.
		o	Universal-service scheme to be economically reasonable and technically feasible to enable the people of Fiji access to telecommunications services.

		o The minister may declare universal-service areas. o A service operator may become subject to universal service subject to market power and application to the universal-service fund. o TAF must levy charges for universal services up to a maximum prescribed percentage of licensee's gross revenue. Funds collected from this levy plus funds from other sources collected shall be deposited into a universal-service fund. The universal fund must only be used for the purpose of universal services.
4	Consumer protection and technical matters	o All service providers to provide consumers with all terms and conditions of services, charge consumers only for services and products ordered or used, keep information about consumers confidential and adopt a simple and transparent complaints-handling procedure for dealing with consumer complaints and disputes. o TAF may set technical rules and standards applicable to the importation, use, supply, installation or maintenance of telecommunications equipment.
5	Telecommunications Appeal Tribunal	o Establishment of a telecommunications Appeal Tribunal to hear and determine any appeals against TAF determinations, including granting or revoking licences.

Source: Parliament of Fiji (2006[b])

Note: * Bill introduced to Parliament on 11 September 2006. Parliament has been suspended since the 5 December 2006 coup.

In addition, consumer protection and a Telecommunications Appeal Tribunal were to be set up to ensure that the rights of consumers and providers were protected.

Ownership

The 1989 decree set guidelines for the acquisition and transfer of all public assets and liabilities on telecommunications and posts to the Fiji Posts and Telecommunications Limited (FPTL). In 1996, FPTL was renamed as Telecom Fiji Limited (TFL) as a result of the separation of the telecommunications and posts sectors from the old FPTL.

Before 1998, the government owned 100 per cent of TFL. With the creation of ATH in 1998 and its subsequent partial sale to private interests, TFL transformed from 100 per cent to 34.6 per cent public ownership (ITU 2004:24). The partial sale privatization of ATH enabled Fiji's National Provident Fund (FNPF) to buy a 49 per cent share for US$130 million. Later, an additional 2 per cent was purchased for F$23 million to give ATH majority private ownership. Other private investors had minority ownership shares of about 7.2 per cent (ITU 2004:24). The mobile service was provided through exclusive rights by Vodafone Fiji. Vodafone Fiji is 51 per cent owned by ATH and 49 per cent by Cable and Wireless (UK). FINTEL provides the international service, with 51 per cent ownership by the government and 49 per cent by Cable and Wireless (UK).

Market structure

Under the 1989 decree, the market was dissected artificially through exclusive licences into three major segments namely, international services, domestic services and mobile services. This artificial segmentation posed challenges for the main operators when deregulation talks intensified in 2007. Deregulation would open traditional segments to competition from the other domestic players, effectively reducing each provider's market share. Discussions by FINTEL and TFL to arrange a merger in order to share costs while protecting each other's market segment began in 2007, but a merger did not materialize (Island Business 2008).

FINTEL has exclusive rights to provide international voice, data, internet and video services. All telephone calls, including mobile services, are routed through FINTEL's network under a service interconnection arrangement with the domestic network operator, TFL. Internet services are leased directly from FINTEL.

Vodafone Fiji operated in the mobile service segment although it did not hold a mobile licence but claimed exclusivity for mobile services until 2014 through its association with ATH (ITU 2004:26). The very nature of market segmentation proved challenging for Vodafone Fiji due to land ownership issues and because all long-distance transmissions went through TFL, effectively adding costs to a limited network capacity (ITU 2004:26).

Discussions between the Fijian Government and incumbent telecommunications companies intensified only in the last three years and, on 20 November 2007, the government endorsed the "Radisson Accord" (Fiji Government Online 2007[a]). The main terms of the accord reflect the key characteristics of the proposed Telecommunications Bill 2006, including the liberalization of the telecommunications sector and granting of 15-year non-exclusive licences to all providers. Compensation for loss of exclusive rights came in the form of extended transitional periods. An 18-month transitional period from the date of the signing of the accord was granted to FINTEL, with Telecom Fiji not to provide direct international service before that date (Island Business 2008:1). FINTEL was granted licences to provide services in all three segments although its participation in the mobile sector was limited to the status of mobile virtual network operator only.

In February 2008, Digicel Fiji Limited won a bid to operate as the second mobile operator in Fiji with an investment of US$10.25million. Digicel Pacific chief executive officer, Vanessa Slowey, stated that Fiji was a very important market and the company had big investment plans for Fiji (Reuters 2008). Digicel's financial strength allowed it to eliminate three other bidders by meeting four tender requirements: 1) bid submissions were to be by individual entities; 2) a F$2 million non-refundable deposit was needed for bid validation; 3) bid must be higher than US$5 million; and 4) there was a deadline for all submissions. A government press release stated that, "there was only one successful and compliant bid and that was the bid from Digicel" (Fiji Government Online 2008[a]). The setting of such strict financial requirements could be seen as an anti-competitive measure to weed out smaller bidders; it could also, however, be seen as an appropriate policy to eliminate high-risk investors and ensure that potential investors had the financial and technological means to meet universal commitments and other economic policy requirements aligned with Fiji's developmental objectives.

Universal service

The Telecommunications Bill 2006 set criteria and responsibilities for the Government to establish a universal service advisory committee to advise TAF on universal funding schemes and implementation strategies. Most importantly, the Bill set guidelines for universal-service levies, with a set percentage of the licensee's gross revenue to be collected for the purpose of universal schemes. A universal-service fund was to be established to collect the Government's subsidies, as well as loans on behalf of the sector, and the levies charged. The fund may only be spent only on the installation of eligible networks and services, as outlined by the schemes developed.

Bilateral investment treaties and Multilateral trade commitments

As of April 2010, Fiji had not signed any bilateral investment treaty—as reported by UNCTAD. Fiji had also not made any offers to the WTO on telecommunications services.

2.5 Vanuatu

Until very recently, the telecommunications sector in Vanuatu was a monopoly with even lower teledensity and quality service provision than most of its Pacific neighbors—Figure 4-6.

Attempts had been made in the past—either indirectly through government[18] or via the Judicial Court in 2007—to introduce competition to certain segments of the industry. Vanuatu has, however, pursued a telecommunications reform package in the past three years in collaboration with the World Bank. In 2007, the Government granted a mobile service licence to Digicel.

[18] In 2001, one of the hotly debated issues between the Government of Vanuatu and WTO Members during its WTO accession package was the request from WTO members to liberalize the telecommunications sector as 'of date of accession' rather than expiry period of the exclusive monopoly rights in 2012.

Figure 4-6: Total Telephone Subscribers (Fixed and Mobile per 100 people)

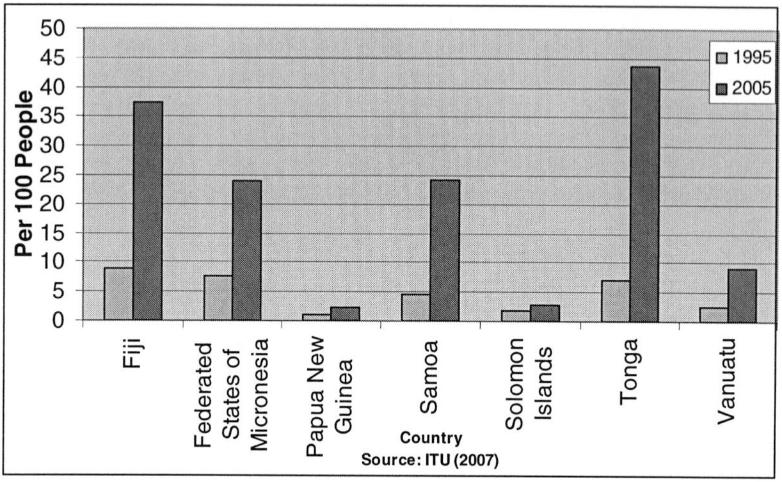

Regulatory policy

The Telecommunications Act 1982 (Government of Vanuatu 1982, 1986, 1988) was the first piece of legislation to establish the legal provisions for the regulation of the telecommunications sector in Vanuatu. The Department of Telecommunications was created with power to establish, maintain and operate telecommunications services. The Act granted rights for the Department to enter into contracts with international telecommunications operators for the establishment of an international telephone service, the establishment of basic telecommunications infrastructure on private property and compensation (Government of Vanuatu 1988:4).

Telecommunications regulations[19] passed between the period 1983 to 1988 focused on regulating fees and charges for services. The fees collected by the Government of Vanuatu included: service connection fees; annual fixed-lines rentals, telephone instruments costs and domestic and international call charges.

---

[19] Order 19 of 1983, Order 65 of 1983, Order 11 of 1985 and Order 14 of 1988. See Telecommunications Act 1988.

In 1989, a new Telecommunications Act[20] provided new regulations for the sector. The 1989 act established a Telecommunications Authority. This corporate body comprised five members, with the Prime Minister appointing all members, including a representative from the Ministries of Finance and Telecommunications. The Telecommunications Authority was tasked with monitoring the provision of domestic and international telecommunications services. These tasks involved close monitoring of standards and the performance of service operators and advising the minister responsible for telecommunications on granting licences. The funding of the operations was the responsibility of the Minister of Finance. An amendment, however, to the 1989 Telecommunications Act made in 1993 dissolved the power and rights of the authority granted under the Telecommunications Act 1989, and there was a complete re-centralization of powers back to the Minister.

A significant provision introduced in the 1989 Act was the power of ministers to grant licences to telecommunications operators—something that was missing in the 1982 Act. Before 1983, the minister had the right to grant licences with the advice of the Telecommunications Authority and, afterwards, the minister alone had that right, with prior approval of the Council of Ministers. The Act also defined a monopoly market structure for the sector.

In 2006, in collaboration with the World Bank, the Vanuatu Government undertook a major reform in its infrastructure sector with telecommunications as a priority. The work-in-progress reform program involved development of new regulations for the sector, including establishment of an independent Utility Regulatory Authority, introducing competition to the mobile service market, non-discriminatory measures against foreign investors, and optimal use of scarce resources (Government of Vanuatu 2007[b]:5).

The Utilities Regulatory Authority Act was passed in 2007 with commencement date of 11 February 2008. The Act established an independent corporate body, comprising three commissioners, to be appointed by the Minister of Finance. The main function of the Authority is to act as an independent advisory body to the Government in matters relating to regulate utility sectors. The Authority does, however, have authority to set safety, inspection and reliability standards as well as

[20] And subsequent amendments; No. 24 1989, No. 18 1993 and No. 15 of 2007.

setting maximum prices for the provision of utilities. Regulated services described by the Act include only electricity and water (Government of Vanuatu 2007[c]:4), with no mention of telecommunications services. The Telecommunications Bill 2009, however, refers to the Utility Regulatory Authority as the regulatory authority for telecommunications.

When the liberalization of the mobile service sector was announced by Government on 14 March 2008, the Government appointed an independent telecommunications regulator (Vanuatu Ministry of Infrastructure and Public Utilities 2008:1). With no linkage to the Utilities Regulatory Authority Act 2007, the independent regulator operates its legal capacity based on an amendment made in 2007 to the 1989 Telecommunications Act. This amendment gave additional powers to the Minister in granting of licences and the delegation of his powers to an authorized officer. This remained the regulatory arrangement until December 2009 when the Telecommunications Bill was passed. The key sections of the draft Telecommunications bill are outlined in Table 4-9.

The Telecommunications Bill was passed in December 2009 and renamed the Telecommunications and Radiocommunications Regulations Act 2009 (Government of Vanuatu 2009[a]). Two additional parts incorporated in the final act that were not included in the Bill involved the conditions allowed for challenging the decisions of the regulator through the judicial system, and specific provisions for the immunity of the regulator from judicial reviews. It is also worthy to note that the 2009 Act outlined the responsibilities and powers of an independent regulator for telecommunications with no reference to the Utility Regulatory Authority.

Table 4-9: Vanuatu's Telecommunications Bill 2007*

	Key Sections		Key Principals
1	Preliminary	o	The purpose of the Bill is to regulate the supply of telecommunications services for the long-term benefit of end users.
		o	The objectives of the Bill are to establish an open, non-discriminatory, transparent licensing regime for service providers; to define the institutional framework for policy development and regulation of the telecommunications sector; to promote universal service, to encourage foreign and domestic investment; to establish anti-competitive framework; and protect consumer interests.

2	Management of telecommunications	o The Minister's responsibility is to formulate, monitor and review policy for telecommunications following consultation with the Utility Regulatory Authority. o The responsibility of the Utility Regulatory Authority is to regulate the sector through implementation of the act, to grant licences, monitor and enforce compliance by licensees, resolve disputes between customers and service providers, and maintain appropriate measures for the purpose of preventing dominant service providers from engaging in anti-competitive practices.
3	Licences	o The Utility Regulatory Authority to grant licences. o Licensing procedures to be transparent. o The Utility Regulatory Authority to establish conditions of licences. o Terms of licences are not stated and open to respective licence application circumstances.
4	Universal service	o The Utility Regulatory Authority is to propose and the minister may approve a policy setting out objectives and related principles for universal access. o The universal service policy shall consider development of the costs of universal service, basic telecommunications services, geographical areas coverage and any barriers to the use of available resources. o The Minister may approve a regulation to establish a Telecommunications Development Fund to be used to subsidize the net costs of implementing the universal-service policy. o The fund will be administered by the Utility Regulatory Authority.
5	Competition policy	o The Utility Regulatory Authority to promote efficient and sustainable competition, establish an open and transparent regulatory framework, dispose of complaints and resolve disputes related to anti-competitive practices, designate dominant service providers* and appropriate measures to avoid taking advantage of dominance.

6	Interconnection	o	The Utility Regulatory Authority to promote adequate, efficient and cost-oriented interconnection of telecommunications networks.
7	Tariffs	o	All service providers to file all tariffs with the Utility Regulatory Authority.
8	Relations between service providers and customers	o	The Bill is to regulate fair dealing practices for service providers, and assure confidentiality of customer information, confidentiality of customer communications, protection of personal information and appropriate measure by service providers to address customer complaints.
9	Disputes, offences and enforcement	o	The Utility Regulatory Authority may assist in resolving any dispute between service providers or customers. The Utility Regulatory Authority may refer such disputes to the Supreme Court or issue an order to resolve the dispute. Parties may agree to refer the dispute to private mediation or arbitration.

Source: Government of Vanuatu (2007[a]).

Note: * Every service provider whose gross revenues in a specific telecommunications market constitute 40% or more of the total gross revenues of all service providers in that market shall be designated a dominant service provider.

Ownership

Until recently, Telecom Vanuatu Limited (TVL) was the sole provider of telecommunications in Vanuatu. The ownership structure was partially private, being a joint venture between the Government of Vanuatu, Cable and Wireless (UK) and France Cable and Radio. Each had equal ownership shares in TVL. In March 2008, however, the Vanuatu Government's shares were "released" to Cable and Wireless (UK) and France Cable and Radio, as compensation for prematurely breaking the exclusive rights agreement with TVL (Willie 2008:1).

Market structure

Although much of the reform program is still work-in-progress, certain milestones have been reached. These include the drafting of a national ICT policy, passing of the Telecommunications and Radiocommunications Regulations Act 2009 establishing the independent regulators powers, and most importantly, the introduction of competition to the mobile service sector in March 2008, with granting of a GSM mobile licence to Digicel (Digicel Vanuatu 2008:1).

Universal service

There was no mention of any universal-service provisions in either the Telecommunications Act 1982 or the 1989 Act. However, under the new draft Telecommunications Bill 2007, a Universal Service Policy and a Telecommunications Development Fund is to be developed to increase rural access to telecommunications services and to the internet (Government of Vanuatu 2007[a]:26-27). Providers of telecommunications services will be obligated to make a contribution of a percentage of their adjusted gross revenue to the fund (Government of Vanuatu 2007[b]:13). These provisions were included in the final Telecommunications and Radiocommunications Regulations Act 2009.

As part of the requirement for Digicel under its GSM mobile licence, Digicel was to launch its new network within 6 months with 75 per cent population coverage, to be increased to 85 per cent coverage within 18 months (Vanuatu Ministry of Infrastructure and Public Utilities 2008:1). Digicel reached 85 per cent of Vanuatu in December 2009 (Government of Vanuatu 2009[b]).

Bilateral investment treaties

Vanuatu signed one bilateral investment treaty with the United Kingdom in December 2003, as notified by UNCTAD. The treaty for the promotion and protection of investments is not, however, in force yet. However, the provisions within the treaty give priority to protection and promotion of investment, with most-favored-nation and national treatment provisions, protection against expropriation, free repatriation and an investor-to-host state dispute mechanism.

Multilateral trade commitments

Vanuatu is currently acceding to the WTO[21] and has not finalized any commitment on telecommunications sector. In its accession package, Vanuatu has offered to undertake commitments on trade in services, and, in particular, the telecommunications sector. Based on the draft services commitments offered in 2001, it has offered non-discriminatory treatment to foreign telecommunications providers (especially under Mode 3—Commercial Presence), conditional to the expiration of the monopoly rights held by TVL until 2012 (WTO 2001). This derogation measure however is irrelevant since the telecommunications market was liberalized in 2008.

3.0 Telecommunications Policy: Regulatory Convergence?

While variations in the regulatory policies of the reformed Pacific states can be found, the convergence of certain policies is worth mentioning. With the exception of Tonga, which introduced competition in 2003, and Samoa, which introduced competition in 2006, other Pacific islands began to introduce competition only in the past three years.[22] All reforming Pacific case studies drafted and implemented comprehensive telecommunications legislation for the regulation of the sector, with the view to gradually introducing competition and privatization. Table 4-10 summarizes key regulatory policies across the Pacific case studies.

---

[21] For more information on Vanuatu's WTO accession, visit <http://www.wto.org/English/thewto_e/acc_e/a1_vanuatu_e.htm> (viewed 11 July 2008).

[22] Papua New Guinea liberalized its mobile service sector in March 2007; Vanuatu liberalized its mobile service sector on 14 March 2008; and Fiji liberalized in October 2008.

Table 4-10: Telecommunications Regulatory Framework in Pacific Case Studies (April 2010)

	Tonga	Fiji	Samoa	Papua New Guinea	Vanuatu
Principal Telecom Legislation	1. Communications Act 2000 2. Tonga Corporation Act 2000	1. Posts and Telecommunications Decree 1989 2. Telecommunication Promulgations 2008	1. Telecommunications Act 1982. 2. Telecommunications Act 1989. 3. Telecommunications Act 2005.	1. Telecommunications Act 1996 (and subsidiary amendments). 2. Independent Consumer and Competition Commission Act 2002. 3. Telikom PNG Ltd Act 1996.	1. Telecommunications Act 1982. 2. Telecommunications Act 1989. 3. Telecommunications and Radiocommunications Regulation Act 2009.
Telecom Policy Statement/ICT Policy	Communications Policy 2000			National Policy on Information and Communications of Papua New Guinea 1994 and Revisions (2007, 2008 and 2009)	Telecommunications Policy Statement 2007.
Telecom Appeal Tribunal	None	Yes, via the Telecommunications Promulgations Act 2008.	Yes, via the amended Telecommunications 2005.	Yes, via the Independent Consumer and Competition Commission Act 2002.	Yes, via Telecommunications and Radiocommunications Regulation Act 2009.

	Tonga	Fiji	Samoa	Papua New Guinea	Vanuatu
Consumer Protection	Yes, under the Communications Act 2000.	Yes, under the new Telecommunications Promulgations Act 2008	Yes, under the Telecommunications Act 2005.	Yes, under the Independent Consumer and Competition Commission Act 2002.	Yes, under the Utility Regulatory Authority Act 2007[f] and the Telecommunications and Radiocommunications Regulation Act 2009.
Independent Regulator	No, The Department of Communications is part of the Prime Minister's Office; accountable to Prime Minister; annual budget approved by Parliament.	Yes, the new Telecommunications Authority of Fiji (TAF) will be a statutory board independent of government.	Yes, under the Telecommunications Act 2005. Budget is to be approved by parliament.	Yes, Papua New Guinea Radiocommunications and Telecommunications Technical Authority (PANGTEL) is responsible for technical standards for the telecommunications sector, as prescribed by relevant sections of the Telecommunications Act 1996 and subsequent amendments.	Yes, an amendment to the 1989 Telecommunications Act in 2007 provided the legal capacity for the minister to delegate power to an independent regulator. In December 2009, the Telecommunications and Radiocommunications Regulation Act 2009 provided the specific legal responsibilities for the telecommunications regulator.

	Tonga	Fiji	Samoa	Papua New Guinea	Vanuatu
				The Independent Consumer and Competition Commission (ICCC) is the second independent body that has authority over telecommunications including licences, dispute settlement, and consumer protection.	
Privatization/ Corporatization Program	Corporatized.	Corporatized.	Privatized.	Corporatized.	Privatized.
Market Structure	As of April 2010: 1. Domestic Fixed long distance: Competition [a] 2. International gateway: Competition [a] 3. Mobile Services: Competition [a] 4. Internet Services: Competition [a]	As of April 2010: 1. Domestic Fixed long distance: Monopoly 2. International Gateway: Monopoly 3. Mobile Services: Competition 4. Internet Services:	As of April 2010: 1. Domestic Fixed long distance: Monopoly 2. International Gateway: Competition 3. Mobile Services: Competition 4. Internet Services: Competition	As of April 2010: 1. Domestic Fixed long distance: Monopoly 2. International Gateway: Monopoly 3. Mobile Services: Competition 4. Internet Services: Competition	As of April 2010: 1. Domestic Fixed long distance: Monopoly 2. International Gateway: Competition 3. Mobile Services: Competition 4. Internet Services: Competition

	Tonga	Fiji	Samoa	Papua New Guinea	Vanuatu
		Competition			
Ownership of main domestic fixed line operators	As of February 2010: Tonga Communications Corporation (90% government ownership, 10% Tongan Nationals)[d]	As of February 2010: Telecom Fiji Limited (34.6% government ownership, 58.2% National Provident Fund of Fiji, 7.2% Others).[b]	As of February 2010: Samoatel (40% government ownership, 27.5% National Provident Fund, 22.5% Bank of Samoa, 10% Samoa Life Insurance).[c]	As of February 2010: Telikom PNG Limited (100% government ownership)	As of February 2010: Telecom Vanuatu Limited (TVL) (50% Cable and Wireless and 50% France Cable and Radio)
Anti-competitive provision	Yes, under the Communications Act 2000.	None.	Yes, under the Telecommunications Act 2005.	None.	Yes, under the Telecommunications and Radiocommunications Regulation Act 2009.
Universal service	Yes, under the Communications Act 2000.	Yes, under the Telecommunications Promulgations Act 2008.	Yes, under the Telecommunications Act 2005.	Yes, under the Telecommunications Act 1996 and subsequent amendments.	Yes, under the Telecommunications and Radiocommunications Regulation Act 2009
Universal service fund	None	Yes, under the new Telecommunications Promulgations Act 2008.	Yes, under the Telecommunications Act 2005.	Yes, under the Telecommunications Act 1996 and subsequent amendments	Yes, under the Telecommunications and Radiocommunications Regulation Act 2009

	Tonga	Fiji	Samoa	Papua New Guinea	Vanuatu
WTO telecommunications commitment	Yes.	None.	None.[e]	Yes.	None.[e]
Bilateral Investment Treaty Signatory.	Yes.	None.	None.	Yes.	Yes.
Telecom framework for dialogue with stakeholders	Yes, a public-private consultative committee is currently developing specific for telecommunications services.	Yes	Yes, facilitated by the independent regulator	Yes, facilitated by the independent regulator	Yes, facilitated by the independent regulator
Digicel Pacific	Yes, granted full licence in November 2007, began operation on 8 of May 2008.	Yes, operation began in October 2008.	Yes, granted licence to operate in November 2006.	Yes, granted licence for mobile service in September 2006, began operation in March 2007.	Yes, granted a GSM mobile licence in 2007 and began operation on 14 March 2008.
	Acquired 100% ownership of domestic mobile operator (TONFON)		Acquired Telecommunications New Zealand's 90% ownership share of domestic mobile operator.		

Tonga	Fiji	Samoa	Papua New Guinea	Vanuatu
		Telecommunications Samoa Cellular (TSC).		

Sources: Consolidation by author of information from telecommunications operators, government telecommunications reports, telecommunications legislation, media reports from the Pacific case study countries; World Bank (2006); AusAID (2008[a,b]); and International Telecommunications Union (ITU) (2004).

Notes: [a] duopoly; [b] 2004 ownership status reported by ITU; [c] World Bank 2006, 'The Pacific infrastructure challenge: a review of obstacles and opportunities for improving performance in the Pacific islands, Pacific Island Country Management Unit, East Asia and Pacific Region, World Bank, Washington, DC; [d] Tonga Department of Communications 2008, Department of Communications web site, Government of Tonga. Available from <http://www.pmo.gov.to/artman/publish/printer_105.shtml> (viewed 14 March 2008); [e] acceding WTO Members. Vanuatu made an offer on telecommunications in 2001 although it has not been finalized yet. Samoa is currently negotiating its services offer; [f] The Utilities Regulatory Authority Act 2007 does not cover telecommunications sector under its jurisdiction. The definition of "regulated service" covered under the Utilities Regulatory Act only mentions electricity and water.

4.0 Conclusion

Across the five Pacific case studies, the important role of telecommunications policy statements in anchoring all subsequent telecommunications legislation is apparent in those island states that had such statements: Tonga, PNG and Vanuatu. Governments often refer back to their own communications policy in setting key criteria for regulatory reform. PNG's Information and Communications Minister, Patrick Tammur, said that his department "took the first step to install a National ICT Policy endorsed by [the] Government which sets the direction for the department to develop and benefit from the advances in ICT technology, trends and practices" (Joku 2008:2). The revision to the telecommunications policy in April 2008 granted Telikom the exclusive rights to operate the international gateway (Digicel 2008[a]). In a response to the outcry from competitors and the business community, the PNG government argued that granting a monopoly over the international gateway was necessary for PNG's social and economic development (Joku 2008:2).

Similarly, Tonga's Communications Policy 2000 was the pivotal policy guideline for regulatory reform in its telecommunications sector. In 2006, the Department of Communication's Annual Report outlined the progress achieved, including the limited[1] competition allowed in the mobile and internet sectors and plans for liberalizing customer telecommunications equipment services. Other issues included the establishment of a communications committee to consult with relevant stakeholders on certain policy issues—consumer and pricing policy protection through a mandatory requirement for operators to "seek the approval of the department to change the tariffs or condition of existing services" (Tonga Department of Communications 2006:14).

Fiji, PNG, Samoa and Vanuatu have an appeal tribunal specific to telecommunications issues embedded in their telecommunications legislation. Tonga, PNG and Vanuatu have signed bilateral investment treaties with major developed trading partners. Tonga and PNG have made multilateral commitments on telecommunications at the WTO for non-discriminatory treatment of foreign investments, while Vanuatu and Samoa might undertake telecommunications commitments as part of their WTO accession packages.

---

[1] Duopoly market structure with potential new entrants subject to 'national interests'.

Universal-service commitments are common in the legislation of all the Pacific case studies, while dedicated universal service funds can be found in four (with Tonga the exception). Protection of consumer rights is also covered by the communications legislation in all five of the Pacific case studies.

Competition regulation can be found on telecommunications legislation in Tonga, Samoa and Vanuatu. Privatization and/or corporatization programs have progressed at various levels in all Pacific case studies. Independent regulators are legislated for in Fiji, Samoa, PNG and Vanuatu.

The early outcomes of regulatory reforms in the five Pacific case studies can be measured through the depth and coverage of the private investments of Digicel. Digicel has been granted a licence to operate GSM mobile services in all five of the Pacific countries under investigation. Digicel's foreign direct investment strategy has been in the form of the acquisition of domestic mobile operators (in Tonga and Samoa), and foreign direct investment (in PNG). Digicel is discussed further in Chapters 5 and 6.

Informed by the discussion on the regulatory policies and institutional framework on telecommunications in the Pacific case studies, the next chapter examines the multilateral policy restraint hypothesis based on fieldwork evidence from PNG and Tonga.

CHAPTER FIVE

WTO AND THE CREDIBILITY OF TELECOMMUNICATIONS REFORM[1]

1.0 Introduction

This chapter examines two propositions. First, WTO telecommunications commitments (multilateral policy restraints) have enhanced the credibility of telecommunications regulatory reforms in Papua New Guinea (PNG) and Tonga. Second, successful domestic political adoption of multilateral policy restraints is easier when telecommunications technology overcomes some of the inherent challenges of isolated small island states. The case study evidence from Papua New Guinea and Tonga is found to support these propositions.

By drawing from fieldwork evidence on the early regulatory policy reform in PNG and Tonga, this chapter examines the impact of WTO telecommunications commitment on the credibility of telecommunications reform. I find evidence that WTO commitments have provided policy restraint in an uncertain regulatory environment. Evidence was also found that new technology for wireless telephony networks directly addresses the challenges of being small and isolated. Directly addressing the challenges of small and isolated island states reduces opposition from vested interest groups and the general public towards telecommunications liberalization.

This chapter is structured as follows. Section 2 discusses the context of WTO telecommunications commitments in PNG and Tonga. Section 3 analyzes regulatory behavior argued to induce policy uncertainty. Section 4 examines the policy implications of WTO telecommunications

[1] An earlier version of this chapter was published as, 'Telecommunications regulatory reforms and the credibility problem: case studies from Papua New Guinea and Tonga', in R Duncan (ed.), '*The Political Economy of Economic Reform in the Pacific*', Asian Development Bank, Manila, 2011.

commitments and the credibility of the telecommunications reforms. Section 5 concludes the chapter.

2.0 WTO Telecommunications Commitments: Papua New Guinea and Tonga

Introducing the WTO telecommunications commitments of the Pacific case studies, the chapter discusses the specific telecommunications commitments adopted by PNG and Tonga.

2.1 Papua New Guinea

PNG is one of three Pacific islands that became founding members of WTO in 1995. PNG submitted an offer on telecommunications services during the WTO's 1996-97 telecommunications negotiations (WTO 1997). The PNG Government made commitments not to implement any domestic policy measures that might impose limitations on foreign participants in mobile and fixed telephony. Table 5-11 shows the relevant commitments.

Table 5-11: PNG Schedule of Commitments: Fixed and Mobile Services

Modes of Supply (1) Cross-border supply	(2) Consumption abroad	(3) Commercial presence	(4) Presence of natural persons
Sector or Sub-sector	Market Access Limitations (Restrictive Measures by one foreign service against another foreign service)	National Treatment Limitations (Restrictive Measures between foreign services against domestic like services)	Additional Commitments

<table>
<tr><td colspan="4">I. HORIZONTAL COMMITMENTS</td></tr>
<tr><td>ALL SECTORS INCLUDED IN THIS SCHEDULE</td><td>(3)
(a) Normal government approval and registration is required for all foreign investors based on several criteria.

(b) Companies incorporated outside PNG must register the company's name with the Investment Promotion Authority in PNG.

(c) Foreign nationals and foreign-owned companies may not purchase land but only through leasing.</td><td>(3) Foreign employees are required to provide on-the-job training to local employees</td><td></td></tr>
<tr><td colspan="4">II. SPECIFIC COMMITMENTS</td></tr>
<tr><td>2.COMMUNI-CATIONS SERVICES

c. <u>Telecommuni-cations Services</u>

(a) Voice Telephone Services (7521)</td><td>(1). Only through the network of Telikom.

(2) Alternative calling or calls back are not allowed.

(3) All Telecommunications Services are subjected to a five year exclusivity (1997-2002) to Telikom, as the monopoly service provider. The issuance of additional operating licences and their terms and conditions will be considered and announced at least two years prior to the end of the exclusivity period.

Telikom is designated as signatory to the INTELSAT Operating Agreement.</td><td>(1) None

(2) None

(3) None</td><td>Papua New Guinea subscribes to the regulatory principles annexed to this schedule.</td></tr>
</table>

(o) Others Digital Cellular Services (75213*) Mobile Data Services (7523**)	Under the Articles of Association and Memorandum of Articles of Telikom, Telikom reserves the right to set up subsidiary companies in business ventures on particular services of telecommunications (4) Unbound except as indicated in the horizontal section.	 (4) Unbound except as indicated in the horizontal section.	

Source: WTO (1995 & 1997).

Note: The bracketed set of numbers following each sector or subsector are a Central Product Classification (CPC) number system used by relevant international institutions including the WTO to systematically harmonized classification of services sectors. For a complete listing of the WTO's CPC listing, please refer to WTO 1991, "WTO's services sectoral classification list", MTN.GNS/W/120, visit <http://www.wto.org/english/tratop_e/serv_e/mtn_gns_w_120_e.doc>, viewed 19 December 2009.

* Indicates that the service specified is a component of a more aggregated CPC item specified elsewhere in the WTO classification list; ** Indicates that the service specified constitutes only a part of the total range of activities covered by the CPC concordance (e.g. voice mail is only a component of CPC item 7523) (WTO 1991).

The commitments however, contained four important conditions. First, the normal trade-related rules and regulations of the country relevant to any business entity would be imposed on any foreign operator. Second, in the commercial presence of foreign investors, all telecommunications services were subjected to a five-year (1997-2002) monopoly for the national operator, Telikom[2]. Also, PNG committed not to put in place prohibited restrictions[3] discriminating between foreign and local service providers

[2] The WTO multilateral negotiations on Telecommunications Services began in 1997. As first offers, several members submitted offers which reflected the *status quo* (monopoly). It was seen as a positive move towards liberalization.

[3] Article XVI of GATS lists six prohibited market access restrictions including limitations on: numbers of suppliers, total value of transaction of assets, total

(Mode 3, National Treatment). Third, foreign operators must deliver telecommunications service across the border into PNG through Telikom PNG's network. Fourth, the PNG government subscribed to the telecommunications reference paper outlining international best practice telecommunications regulatory principles.[4]

2.2 Tonga

Tonga is one of three Pacific Islands which applied for membership after 1995. Tonga undertook bilateral services negotiations with members of the WTO Working Party prior to accession. The process was lengthy, costly and complex. Tonga's accession took place at the WTO Ministerial Meeting held in Hong Kong, China, in December 2005. Tonga's WTO accession package was submitted to the WTO's General Council and accepted by both parties (WTO and Tonga) in the Hong Kong China Ministerial Meeting in December 2005, subject to ratification before July 31 2006. However, the ratification was delayed due to domestic political and economic challenges in Tonga and was eventually submitted and accepted by the WTO on 27 June 2007. Table 5-12 outlines the telephone fixed lines (voice telephone service) and mobile services (digital cellular service) commitments made by Tonga.

Tonga made commitments on fixed-line telephone and mobile services. Three issues are worthy of note. First, the inclusion of taxation measures committed for non-discriminatory treatment across all services sectors is rare in WTO members' services schedules. In addition, the normal requirements of the investment regulations apply to foreign and domestic providers alike. Tonga also notified members through its schedule of the prohibition on the acquisition of land except through leasing arrangements. Also, Tonga committed not to apply discriminatory measures to non-resident workers from different member countries.[5] Second, Tonga adopted the Telecommunications Reference Paper. Third, Tonga notified via its schedule that some services subsidies could be made available only to Tongan citizens. Since Tonga's accession, and as of January 2010, no agreement on services subsidies had been tabled in the WTO. This is partially due to the suspension of the Doha Round (since

---

number of service operations, total number of people, legal restrictions on type of joint venture, and limitations on the participation of foreign capital.

[4] Refer to discussion on GATS for further information.

[5] See Table 12, Horizontal Commitments section.

2006) but also WTO members are currently negotiating to improve the quality of existing schedules commitments.

Table 5-12: Tonga Schedule of Commitments: Fixed and Mobile Services

Modes of Supply (1) Cross-border supply	(2) Consumption abroad	(3) Commercial presence	(4) Presence of natural persons
Sector or Sub-sector	Market Access Limitations (Restrictive Measures by one foreign service against another foreign service)	National Treatment Limitations (Restrictive Measures between foreign services against domestic like services)	Additional Commitments
I. HORIZONTAL COMMITMENTS			
ALL SECTORS INCLUDED IN THIS SCHEDULE Taxation Measures	(1) None (2) None (3) None (4) Unbound	(1) None (2) None (3) None (4) Unbound	
ALL SECTORS INCLUDED IN THIS SCHEDULE	(4) Unbound except for measures affecting the entry and temporary stay of nationals of another member who fall into the categories listed below: 1. Salespersons 2.Intra-corporate transferee 3. Managers 4. Executives 5. Specialists 6. Personnel engaged in establishment	2) and (3) Unbound with regard to subsidies Government approval under the Foreign Investment Act is required for foreign investors to invest into the Kingdom The Tongan Constitution prohibits the sales of land to all foreigners. Foreigners can only attain land through leasing, with the right to lease land for up to 99 years as well as sub-lease property	

		(4) Unbound except for measures listed under Market Access Subsidies available to natural persons may be limited to Tongan citizens	
II. SPECIFIC COMMITMENTS			
2.COMMUNICA-TIONS SERVICES *Telecommunications Services* (a) Voice telephone services (7521)	(1) As of 1 January 2008: None (2) As of 1 January 2008: None (3) As of 1 January 2008: None (4) Unbound except as indicated under horizontal commitments	(1) None (2) None (3) None (4) Unbound except as indicated under horizontal commitments	Tonga subscribes to the principles set forth in the reference paper attached
(o) Others	(1) As of 1 January 2008: None (2) As of 1 January 2008: None (3) As of 1 January 2008: None (4) Unbound except as indicated under horizontal commitments	None (2) None (3) None (4) Unbound except as indicated under horizontal commitment	Tonga subscribes to the principles set forth in the reference paper attached
Source: WTO (2005[a] & 2005[c])			

Overall, PNG and Tonga committed to liberalize fixed-line telephones and mobile services. [6] Both countries committed to liberalize, without limitations to Mode 3, Commercial Presence (foreign direct investment). Furthermore, both cases adopted the telecommunications reference paper emphasizing commitments to pro-competitive practices.

3.0 The Credibility of Telecommunications Reform

This section draws upon evidence of regulatory changes during the telecommunications reform process in PNG and Tonga. As I will

[6] Although, as the schedules show, both adopted transitional periods for the monopolies' exclusivity to end.

demonstrate, the early regulatory changes undermined the credibility of the reform process in PNG. Most importantly, I argue that the WTO telecommunications commitments provided certainty to the reform processes, whereas domestic (and bilateral) restraint provided limited or no certainty in PNG and Tonga. [7]

3.1 Papua New Guinea

The discussion on the credibility of telecommunications reform in PNG is divided into two sections. I first discuss the early policies and political lobbying against ICCC's effectiveness before competition began. The second section discusses the lobbying pressures on the telecommunications reform during and after competition was introduced.

Pre-reform policies (December 2005 to March 2007)

Since the December 2005 National Executive Council (NEC) decision[8] to introduce mobile competition, the regulatory reforms have seen several policies and pieces of legislation drafted, amended or repealed. Prior to introduction of mobile service, only two pieces of Information Communication Technology (ICT) legislation had been implemented. These were a Communication Policy drafted as a result of a Communication Policy seminar in 1978; and in 1992 the Department of Information and Communication was instructed to begin the process of formulating a coherent national ICT policy (PNG Department of Communication and Information 1994). The result was the National Policy on Information and Communication of Papua New Guinea passed in 1994. The latter policy was more comprehensive, setting out general policy guidelines on defining ownership, access, and content. The 1994 ICT policy emphasized the role of the state-owned telecommunications operator in providing access to rural communities and extending the network to complement economic development. Privatization plans for the state-owned incumbent operator were clearly stated whereas introduction of competition was not mentioned. A 1999 WTO Secretariat report (WTO 1999:121) confirmed this position by stating that the government's policy

---

[7] WTO commitments and obligations of a country are usually triggered only when another member raised concerns in the WTO.

[8] No public information made available for the details of the NEC decision except through information collected from some interviewees in PNG.

intention "is to gradually privatize Telikom PNG ...by divesting up to 49% of ownership."

A gradual policy shift toward liberalization of telecommunications services began when three key pieces of legislation[9] were passed in 1996. The three bills created three legal entities, namely: Telikom PNG Ltd, as the exclusive monopoly provider of all telecommunications services; the ICCC as the economic and social regulator; and PANGTEL, to act as the technical authority for telecommunications services. Internet services were introduced in 1997, with five internet service providers (Kelegai and Middleton n.d.: 3), using the Telikom network and international gateways.

Telikom continued to be the sole provider of all telecommunications services. Through a regulatory contract with ICCC, the state-owned incumbent telecommunications operator was granted another five-year monopoly from 2002 until 17 October 2007.[10] The capacity of Telikom to serve rural and isolated communities was severely constrained, however. The Acting Secretary for PNG's Department of State Enterprise and Information at the time, Mr. Iduhu Henao (2004:2-3), outlined the challenges to the development of telecommunications services, and basically pointed to the difficult geographic terrain, the largely rural population, and diversity of language and culture as the fundamental deterrents to network deployment. One telecommunications policy expert interviewed in Port Moresby stated that Telikom's operation "as a monopoly for the last 52 years was inefficient with poor infrastructure. It is a company run by engineers. It is not a company that is run by people with business mentality in terms of marketing, accounting, quality of services, innovations and so on" (Respondent 9, fieldwork interviews, 13 September 2008).

But geography and the largely rural population were not the main reasons for Telikom's underperformance. When Grand Chief Sir Michael Somare was elected Prime Minister in 2002, his administration set out to rehabilitate Telikom. Poor management was seen as one of the major contributors to inefficiencies. Somare reported to Parliament in 2005 that Telikom at one time had six Managing Directors over an eleventh-month period (Papua New Guinea Office of the Prime Minister 2005). The government stabilized the management structure and hired experts to assist

[9] Refer to Chapter 3 for detailed discussion on each of the pieces of legislation.

[10] On fixed line service, mobile service and international gateway.

in providing strategic direction to the Chairman and Board. The results were a series of positive business initiatives, including appointment of international firms to formulate strategic policies and further expand the network of fixed-line service.

The first major competition policy development was in December 2005 when an NEC decision was passed on the introduction of competition in mobile services. The main objective of the national ICT approved in 2005 was for the use of telecommunications for economic development in PNG. The Government stated in the 2005 NEC decision a preference to establish electronic connectivity for dissemination of information to the general public and as a means of reaching out to the outside world (e-government, e-commerce and e-education). Telikom's infrastructure, through which these services were to be provided, was limited and in need of major modernization. Therefore, rehabilitation of Telikom was stated to be one of the Government's priorities. However, according to the same NEC decision, competition was to be introduced in the mobile sector. A telecommunications policy expert in Port Moresby argued that:

> "To be able to rehabilitate Telikom PNG, they need a good stream of revenue and also need to attract finance for its developmental programs. Hence, the argument therefore was that, we can't do that if we have an inefficient Telikom company competing with an efficient multinational foreign telecommunications operator. Telikom argued that while it is trying to establish its network to the whole of the country, they can not afford for a mobile company to come in and "cherry pick" on the most profitable areas (Port Moresby, Lae, Mt. Hagen and Kakapu). This meant that Telikom would have to subsidize[11] the rates in profitable areas to cover the non-profitable areas, meaning that its tariff rates will be more expensive than any other operator which operates in the profitable areas only" (Respondent 9, fieldwork interviews, 13 September 2008).

Two aspects relating to Telikom's operations arise from this discussion. First, Telikom has had exclusive monopoly rights for more than 50 years. There have been no incentives for the incumbent operator to develop and invest in infrastructure services during this time. Second, when the incentive presented itself—competition—Telikom was inadequately prepared. The lack of ability of Telikom to operate effectively in a competitive market may have been the major issue that

[11] As of April 2010, Universal-service coverage and fund policies had not been implemented in PNG.

drove much of the political interference with the reform program, which led to regulatory uncertainties in 2007-08.

Telikom showed signs of a typical monopoly namely, inefficient and limited infrastructural development.[12] Looking more closely at one common telecommunications indicator—total telephone subscribers (fixed line and mobile) per 100 persons, often used to proxy network deployment—shows that PNG had the lowest total number of subscribers of all five Pacific island cases studied in the period 1995 to 2006. Papua New Guinea's network deployment per 100 people ratio remains fairly constant, from 0.99 in 1995 to 2.35 in 2005 (International Telecommunications Union 2007).[13] Further, there were six different Managing Directors leading Telikom within an eleven-month period as reported by Papua New Guinea's Prime Minister Sir Michael Somare to national Parliament in 2005.

A telecommunications policy expert in Port Moresby described Telikom's pre-competition era as follows:

> "As is the case with many state-owned entities, the infrastructure had deteriorated over the years as a result of ineffective management, constant political interference, tariffs not being cost-reflective, massive underinvestment and lack of incentives to improve services or roll out network. The infrastructure was outdated, unreliable, and network coverage was low" (Respondent 9, fieldwork interviews, 13 September 2008).

The low level of network expansion (indicated by total fixed-line and mobile phone subscribers per 100 people) is captured in Figure 5-7.

---

[12] A substantial body of research literature has found that removal of monopoly with the introduction of competition in the telecommunications sector results in lower prices, better delivery of service, wider access and faster expansion of capacity (Haggarty et al. 2002:3). See also Fink et al. (2003).

[13] Refer to Figure 4-6 for comparative telecommunications statistics on total subscribers per 100 people of Pacific case studies.

Figure 5-7: Total Fixed Lines and Mobile Subscribers per 100 People - PNG and Tonga

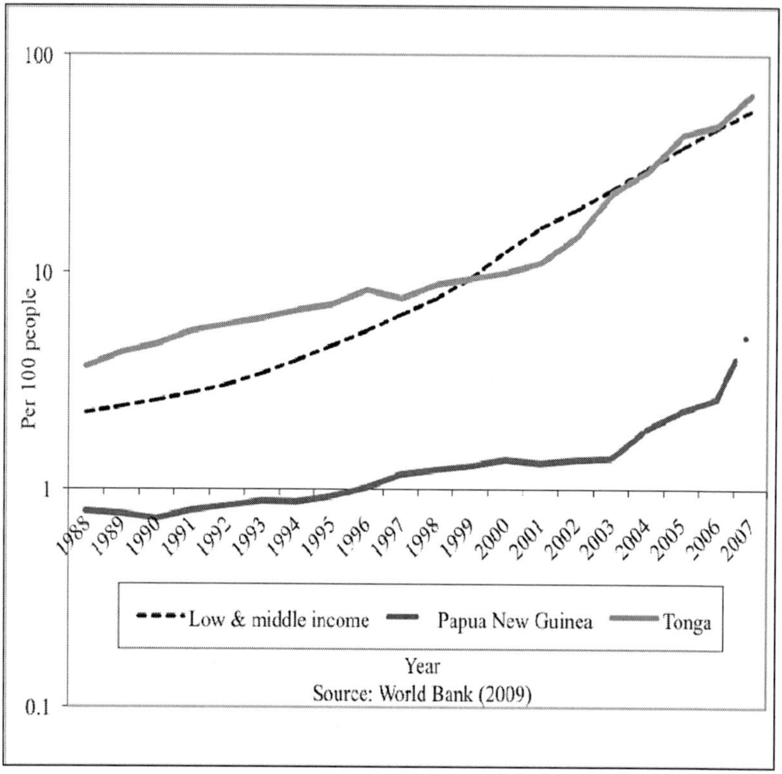

Source: World Bank (2009)

Despite PNG's long-term trend of low network deployment, the coverage improved significantly in 2006/07 when Digicel entered the mobile phone market. Figure 5-8 illustrates the linkage between key policy instruments and mobile service network deployment for PNG and Tonga. Figure 5-8 shows that mobile subscription before competition policy was relatively low in both countries, although both indicate significant improvements shortly after competition policy (or actual competition) was announced.

Figure 5-8: Mobile Network Deployment* - PNG and Tonga

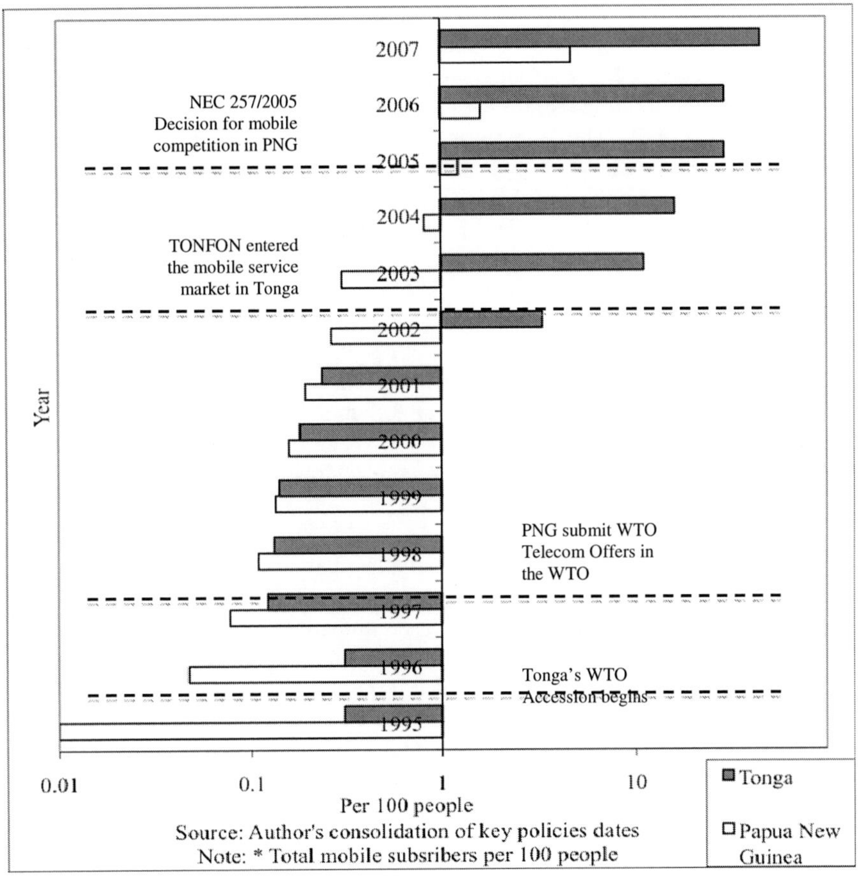

Three key statements in the December 2005 NEC decision are worth mentioning. First, through its regulatory contract with ICCC, Telikom was to agree to terminate its mobile phone monopoly by 31 March 2006. Second, ICCC was mandated to select, via public tender, two new licensees to compete with Telikom's B-Mobile. Third, March 2007 was the date set for open competition in mobile service. Following the Government's decision to introduce competition, the ICCC released a press statement in January 2006 (ICCC 2006:1-2) outlining the processes it would follow to undertake to fulfill its obligations. Figure 5-9 outlines the process.

The media release from the Office of the Commissioner, ICCC, on 18 January 2006 outlined four main steps. First, the public tender process would begin on 7 March and submissions would close in May 2006. Second, the assessment of the applications would be undertaken by ICCC, with the two new mobile providers to be announced by mid-October 2006. Contrary to the set timeline, the two new licensees were announced earlier, in September 2006. Third, construction of network infrastructure for the two new mobile entrants was tentatively scheduled for December 2006. Fourth, licences would be issued (these were issued to Digicel PNG and Greencom on 27 March 2007). Digicel PNG began operation on the 17 July 2007 while Greencom has not begun operation.

The ICCC was also required to consult with Telikom on procedures to terminate its monopoly rights over mobile service by the end of March 2006. The ICCC sought Telikom's approval in early January and received consent from Telikom via a letter dated 20 February 2006. In surrendering its exclusivity rights, Telikom requested ICCC to fulfill several conditions. ICCC claimed that these conditions were addressed, and amended the contract between Telikom and ICCC.

However, in September 2006, Telikom claimed that the conditions were not fulfilled and it did not consent to the release of its monopoly rights (ICCC 2007:1). Telikom may have studied its potential competitor further and realized the magnitude of the competition. Importantly, the PNG Government released a national ICT Policy on the same month that generally reneged on the December 2005 NEC decision for liberalization of mobile service. Against Telikom and government opposition, ICCC kept to its timeline and announced the two new licensees. The ICCC's position on the Government's September 2006 ICT policy is best captured by its Commissioner and Chief Executive Officer, Mr. Thomas Abe saying that "it is the prerogative of the government to make and change policies but this is a situation where government wanted the game to be re-played when the full time whistle had already gone" (ICCC 2007:2).

The Government maintained that "refinements" to the policy were due to the need for Telikom to rehabilitate in order to cope with a competitive environment. The interpretation of ICCC, on the other hand, was that the effects of any new policy must only come after March 2007, when the old policy ended. In addition, legal advice to ICCC suggested that the licences issued in March 2007 could not be legally challenged just because of a sudden government policy change (ICCC 2007:2). Substantial financial costs through infrastructure network deployment by the new entrant had already been incurred in the country and any significant policy change could impose legal action for compensation by the new entrant against the PNG Government. Figure 5-9 illustrates key stakeholders' policy input to the pre-reform process.

There were three public entities that pressured[14] ICCC to stall the mobile liberalization policy. First, Telikom commenced three separate judicial proceedings to challenge ICCC actions: one through an Appeal Panel[15] and the other two through the court system. The Appeal Panel however, ruled in favor of ICCC. The first court decision also dismissed Telikom's claim for abuse of process (Supreme Court of Papua New Guinea 2008:1). Soon afterwards, Telikom voluntarily discontinued the second Court proceeding.

Second, the ICCC Commissioner, Mr. Thomas Abe in a public speech in October 2007 stated that:

> "Unfortunately, not every government agency apparently felt the same way [to grant licences for Digicel and Greencom in March 2007]. The Independent Public Business Commission (IPBC), as the sole shareholder in Telikom, continued to advocate a position that would have prevented the introduction of mobile competition from March 2007 or [not] at all" (Abe 2007[a]:4).

The pressure from IPBC could have been the result of Telikom's utilizing this particular channel to protect its interest from apparent competition.

---

[14] See ICCC Commissioner Thomas Abe's press statement of 30 July 2007 and speech 5 of October 2007.

[15] Authorized by the Telecommunications Act.

Figure 5-9: Key Stakeholders Pre-Reform Milestones (December 2005 - March 2007)[1]

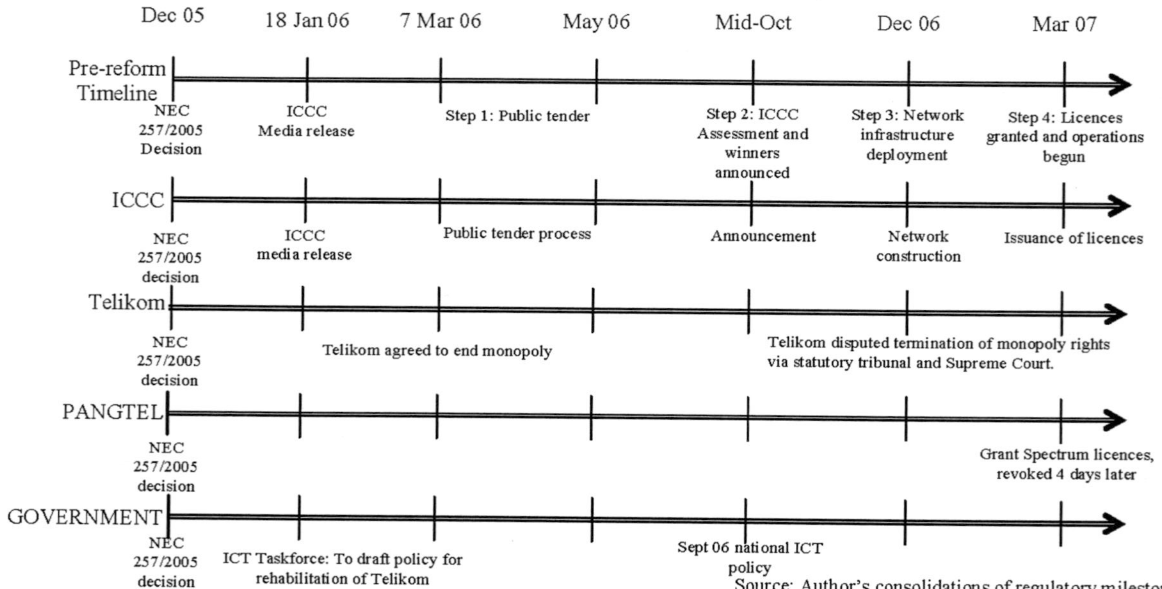

Source: Author's consolidations of regulatory milestones (2005-2007).

[1] Monthly periods are not drawn to scale.

Third, the Minister responsible for the Department of Public Enterprises, Information and Development Cooperation (DPEIDC), Mr. Arthur Somare, pushed for policy reversal to rehabilitate Telekom's capacity to compete effectively. A reporter from The National (a PNG online news media outlet), Mr. Alfredo Henandez, reported that "the order to cancel the telco's [Digicel] licence to operate in PNG came from the Prime Minister's son, Arthur Somare, Minister of Public Enterprise, Information and Development" (Hernandez n.d.). The ICCC's Commissioner, Mr. Thomas Abe, stated in his press release on 30 July 2007 that, "Minister Arthur Somare has also been trying for over a year to stop ICCC and PANGTEL from giving effect to this [December 2005 NEC decision] government policy" (ICCC 2007:2). A telecommunications policy expert in Port Moresby recalled the ICT Taskforce's frequent tense negotiations over ICT Policy. While ten members of the Taskforce accepted that competition should continue, two members consistently argued to stop competition. One was Minister Arthur Somare's DPEIDC and the other was IPBC; also within Minister Arthur Somare's portfolio' (Respondent 9, fieldwork interview, 13 September 2008). The ICT taskforce was established based on an NEC decision in 2006 to develop new ICT policies for the main purpose of stalling full competition in the mobile sector, for the rehabilitation of Telikom.

Minister Somare's objection to ICCC granting licences for competition in the mobile sector was reported in Parliament, claiming "that ICCC has failed to perform its functions under Section 19 of the Telecommunications Act, by not implementing ICT policy" (2007[b]: 5). [1] This statement is referring to the September 2007 ICT policy, which stated that Digicel should not be granted a licence for immediate competition but rather there should be a staged competition. However, the licence that ICCC granted in March 2007 was based on the December 2005 NEC decision, which the Government should have amended well before Digicel began to establish its infrastructural network from September 2006. Although there was an ICT Policy that was passed (but not implemented) in September 2006, coinciding with the announcement of the result of the tender process, it was rather late, as ICCC had followed the public tender process mapped out from January 2006.

The PNG Department of Public Enterprises, Information and Development Cooperation had drafted an ICT policy in September 2006 to

[1] Section 19 – Functions and Powers of the Commission

reflect its position on competition and the rehabilitation of Telikom. The September 2006 ICT policy contained two fundamental regulatory departures from the December 2005 NEC policy. First, the PNG Government recognized the need to rehabilitate and upgrade Telikom's network capabilities, including its inability to compete. It was stated that K$500 million to K$1.4 billion would be required over five years to rehabilitate the network (PNG Department of Public Enterprises, Information and Development Cooperation 2006:23). In particular, the rehabilitation program involved internal restructuring of Telikom to maintain its exclusive rights on network infrastructure services[2] (NETCO) while at the same time "addressing" the competition elements of the 2005 NEC decision through SERVCO. It was anticipated that any new mobile entrants might apply for a SERVCO licence to operate in the mobile service but must use the infrastructure NETCO provides. This September 2006 ICT policy recommended that the Government "postpone or cancel [the licences for Digicel and Greencom] for 18 to 24 months" (PNG Department of Public Enterprises, Information and Development Cooperation 2006:25).

This recommendation was contrary to the December 2005 NEC decision. Two reasons for the policy reversal were put forward in the September 2006 ICT policy. First, that Telikom's network is technically not capable of interconnecting to another carrier's network and therefore customers of one carrier would not be able to call customers of another carrier. Digicel requested interconnection with Telikom three months before its official launch in May 2007 (Joku 2008). [3] Digicel only began testing interconnection with Telikom on 31 January 2008 and it was another six months before nationwide connection in July 2008. Much of the delay had been focused on the technical capacity of Telikom for interconnection (Digicel 2008[b]). Also, there was a numbering plan limitation inside Telikom's network capacity to 400,000 customer subscribers.

Second, the September 2006 ICT Policy claimed that "ICCC has both a regulatory function under the ICCC Act 2002 and the regulatory authority to issue and revoke licences under the Telecommunications Act 1996. [This] is a conflict of interest and ought not be allowed to subsist" (PNG

[2] Network services include international gateway, fixed-line and mobile service infrastructures

[3] ICCC issued the Telecommunications Interconnection Code of Practice to facilitate interconnection negotiations earlier on the 17 November 2006.

Department of Public Enterprises, Information and Development Cooperation 2006:32). To highlight the point, the September ICT policy stated that "ICC[C] move to issue mobile licences ahead of schedule in the knowledge that the NEC is reviewing government policy as defined by the Telecommunications Act (1996) and therefore, may put it beyond the power of the Commission to issue the mobile licences in accordance with Section 57 (2) of that Act" (PNG Department of Public Enterprises, Information and Development Cooperation 2006:32). The ICT policy recommended that ICCC's power to issue and revoke licences return to a committee comprised of representatives from PANGTEL and ICCC with a former chief justice as chair. This recommendation would effectively return licensing power to government control rather than to an independent entity.[4]

The claim of "bringing forward" the end of Telikom's monopoly over mobile service deserves further discussion. Under the regulatory contract that ICCC agreed with Telikom in 2002, Telikom was given an exclusive licence until October 2007. However, the December 2005 NEC decision ruled that introduction of mobile service competition would be in March 2007. This effectively "brought forward" the end of exclusive rights over mobile service for Telikom by about eight months. Both of these decisions were formulated and approved by Government. A telecommunications policy expert in Port Moresby recalled that "the Chief Executive Officer of IPBC – Mr. Glen Blake, and Commissioner of ICCC, Mr. Thomas Abe, were called by Government and were told to implement this decision [December 2005 NEC Decision]" (Respondent 9 fieldwork interview, 13 September 2008).

The September 2006 national ICT policy was never implemented. No publicly accessible document is available to shed light on why it was never implemented, although its timing does provide hints about the purpose of the policy. The ICT policy was finalized at the same time as ICCC announced the winners of the public tender process for the introduction of two new mobile service providers. Since ICCC pressed on with the announcement and the timeline set for March 2007 was based on the December 2005 NEC decision, the usefulness of the September 2006 ICT policy diminished, as it clearly contradicted earlier policy. There is also

---

[4] The latest ICT Policy (March 2009) indicates that the power for issuing and revoking licences is granted to a new authority—National Information and Communication Technology Authority (NICTA)—primarily made up of PANGTEL officials and assets.

evidence that this policy document was not made publicly accessible, (as shown by the lack of discussion), either through the Government's later policy documents or the regulator's press releases.[5]

In March 2007, Digicel launched several mobile stations. In accordance with its legislative mandate, PANGTEL issued Digicel with a Spectrum licence. However, several days later it withdrew the licence stating "amended ICT policy" as the reason for withdrawal. The National online (The National 2007[a]) reported that "[Arthur] Somare notified PANGTEL of the "amended" Government Information Communications." PANGTEL Acting Director General, Mr. Charles Punaha, was also reported as saying that under the amended ICT policy, access to Spectrum would be restricted to NETCO, the proposed new operator of all telecommunications infrastructure. Nevertheless, Digicel obtained a court order shortly after, which cancelled PANGTEL's action and allowed Digicel to operate.

This section has shown how pressures from Telikom, IPBC, and the Communications Minister reversed telecommunications liberalization policy between December 2005 and 2007, severely interfering with the ICCC's independence. The next section examines the pressures on the reform during and after competition was introduced.

Post-reform policies (March 2007 – August 2009)

Since September 2006, the Government has reviewed the ICT policy yet again, in early 2007. A telecommunications blueprint was developed in May 2007, which was the basis for the May 2007 ICT Policy. The May 2007 ICT Policy generally reflected the recommendations of the September 2006 ICT policy in three crucial regulatory areas. First, there was a recommendation for the adoption of the "NETCO/SERVCO model" in which Telikom retains indefinite monopoly over NETCO infrastructure, whereas SERVCO would be opened for new licences. Second, competition (SERVCO operators) would only commence after 1 June 2008. Third, the PNG Government through DPEIDC, would establish new committees to

---

[5] The September 2006 ICT Policy may be confused with the NEC 188/2007 that resulted in a comprehensive ICT Policy which was never implemented. The characteristics of the NEC 188/2007 are identical to the mysterious September 2006 ICT Policy. Interestingly, it was another National ICT Policy (February 2008) that made this statement. It is also useful to note that in 2007, there were two new ICT policies passed by government that were implemented.

oversee licensing issues and the overall ICT policy. The authority of the ICCC to issue and revoke licences was to be "removed and will rest with the Minister for DPEIDC" (PNG Department of Public Enterprises, Information and Development Cooperation 2007:12).

The May 2007 ICT Policy was also never implemented, as tremendous pressure intensified against the government's 2007-08 ICT policy frequent amendments. Figure 5-10 illustrates a timeline of the policy interactions between key stakeholders during this period.

Digicel PNG was methodical but diplomatic in how it dealt with the policy uncertainties. It pressured government through two main channels. First, Digicel negotiated directly with the Government to ensure security for its investment. The Pacific Islands Broadcasting Associations (2007) reported that Digicel Group Board Director, Mr. Seamus Lynch, had met with the Prime Minister in early March (2007) and was given an assurance that Digicel's investment and licence to operate in PNG were protected. Digicel continued to engage in regular dialogue with Telikom, ICCC, PANGTEL and the Government to ensure that its initial licence, based on the December 2005 NEC decision, was protected. When PANGTEL withdrew Digicel's Spectrum licence in March 2007, Mr. Lynch was quoted saying that "Digicel obtained a National Court injunction to prevent PANGTEL from doing so and that PANGTEL acted illegally…the actions of PANGTEL yesterday appear to be very politically motivated" (Digicel 2007).

Second, as an Irish investment, Digicel protected its investment through government-to-government dialogue channels between the Irish and PNG governments. The Irish Ambassador to Australia and PNG, HE Mairtin O'Fainin, reportedly flew to Port Moresby to talk with PNG Government officials following the Government's moves to revoke Digicel's Spectrum licence (Island Business 2007). The Irish Ambassador was reported as saying that he was assured by the PNG officials of their government's continued commitment to competition in the telecommunications sector.

Figure 5-10: Key Stakeholders Post -Reform Milestones (March 07 - August 09)

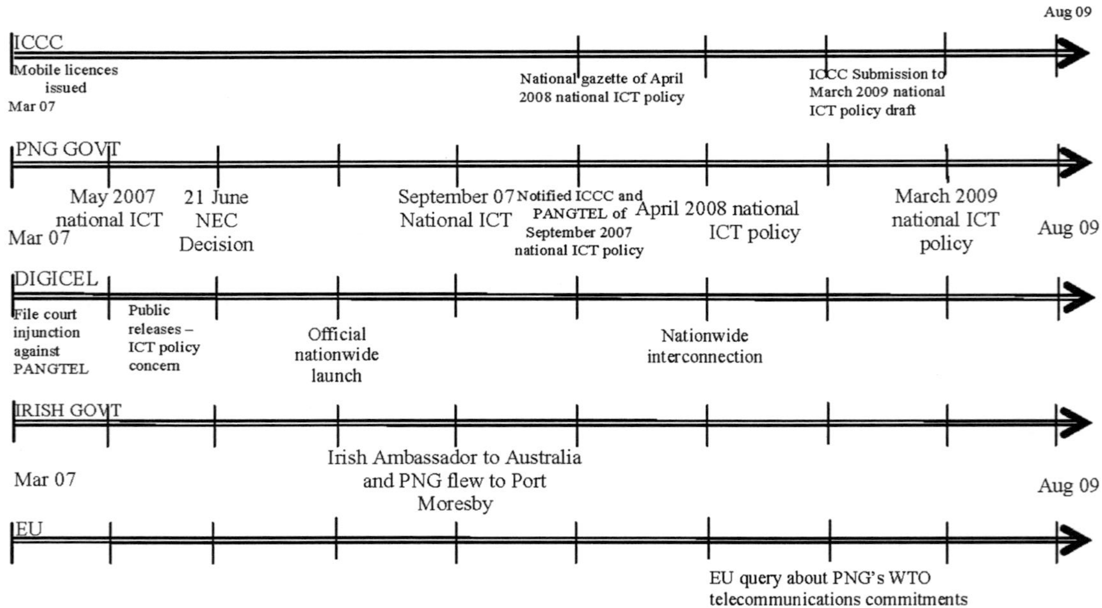

Source: Author's consolidation of key regulatory milestone.
Note: Monthly periods are not drawn to scale.

Digicel's main investment concerns up to the May 2007 ICT Policy were basically twofold. The first concern was the withdrawn of Digicel's Spectrum licence by PANGTEL in March 2007. The second concern was the NETCO "model", in which Telikom continued to control the international gateway. The chief executive officer of Digicel PNG, Mr. Kevin O'Sullivan, was reported as saying that:

> "With only one gateway operating, people will experience higher calling rates, lower quality of calls due to network congestion as well as limited international roaming services. He also added that, 'to remove Digicel's international gateway would be a step backward from the current open market approach. The people have tasted the benefits of competition and have the right to continue to enjoy those benefits – lower prices, better quality, increased coverage and introduction of new services" (Digicel 2008[c]).

There is also evidence that Digicel may have exploited other international legal avenues for the protection of its investments in PNG, including invoking PNG's WTO commitments on telecommunications. A member of the Manufactures Council of PNG[1] in Port Moresby said that:

> "There was a monopoly for telecommunications when we negotiated the WTO telecommunications commitment. It had a lapse time of five years (2002). The sensible thing was to make an application for extension and they [PNG government] would have got it. They did not do it. What has happened now, we got a letter from the EU notifying us of their interest in our WTO commitments in September 2008. The commitment has lapsed and it was triggered by a 'private sector' of course" (Respondent 2, fieldwork interviews, 09 September 2008).

Thus, a multilateral commitment pressured government to refrain from policy reversals on telecommunications reform.

Two crucial aspects of the telecommunications reform strengthen the case for this point. First, the latest ICT Policy released in March 2009 stated that the model proposed was consistent with PNG's WTO obligations (PNG Department of Communications and Information 2009:22). It is worth mentioning that the national ICT policies released earlier in February and April 2008 reaffirmed the Government's commitment to competition in the telecommunications sector and that the

[1] This person has been heavily involved with the PNG Government's WTO and Regional Trade Agreements negotiations in the past 20 years.

WTO will put PNG under pressure to open its telecommunications sector to competition. The March 2009 ICT policy statement indicates that the government ensured that its ICT policy is compatible with PNG's WTO commitments. The statement referring to PNG's WTO obligations since the February 2008 ICT policy may have not occurred by accident. Prior to the February 2008 ICT policy, the September 2007 ICT policy announced that competition would continue but all mobile operators must use Telikom's international gateway. It was during this time that the Irish Ambassador to Australia and PNG flew to Port Moresby, and also the PNG Government received the EU letter referring to PNG's WTO commitments.

Second, the September 2007 ICT policy directed a phased liberalization in which in Phase 1 Telikom retained its monopoly over the international gateway service. The two ICT policies in 2008 adopted similar frameworks. There was no timeframe indicated in the 2008 ICT policies as to when Phase 2 would begin. However, the March 2009 ICT policy came up with a clear timeframe and set milestones to be achieved. More interestingly, the international gateway was tentatively scheduled to be liberalized by October 2009, or as soon as practical. As of January 2010, the international gateway had not been liberalized. Digicel PNG is currently pursuing this issue through the local court system. There was discussion though of the possibility of NICTA granting an international gateway licence to Digicel when it commenced operation in April 2010, although this has not materialized either. Nevertheless, throughout the 2007-09 ICT policies, the PNG Government stated its long-term commitment to sustainable competition.

In consideration of how the WTO commitments could be fully triggered and thus take effect in the context of the PNG case study, it is useful to consider likely scenarios that could be pursued.[2] The international gateway dispute is a case in point. It is not clear whether the telecommunications licence granted by ICCC to Digicel on March 2007 included the right to operate its own international gateway. Based on the press releases, media dialogue and series of expert interviews I conducted, the ICCC and the PNG Government interpreted the right to the international gateway differently. Digicel understood that its licence to operate in PNG included the right to operate its own international gateway.

---

[2] Based on the September 2007 ICT Policy and subsequent ICT policies.

A telecommunications policy expert in Port Moresby shared a similar interpretation of ICCC's position on the issue by stating:

> "Clause 2.4 of the Digicel Licence requires that Digicel use an international gateway operated by a general carrier, unless the ICCC consents to Digicel using its own or another gateway. The ICCC gave its temporary consent to Digicel under the Licence to carry international communications using its own international gateway, until connection to the Telikom PNG [international] gateway was achieved" (Respondent 6, fieldwork interviews, 10 September 2008).

On the other hand, the government approach is that it did not grant international gateway rights to Digicel. A government official in Port Moresby stated:

> "It was never intended under the [December] 2005 mobile competition policy that these rights [international gateway] or other general carrier reserved rights would be granted to the new mobile carriers. Those rights were to remain with Telkom PNG at least until October 2007 and any subsequent change was to be a matter of government policy" (Respondent 4, fieldwork interviews, 10 September 2008).

The Government's interpretation is backed by Sections 45 (rights to reserve line links and ancillary facilities) and 46 (supply of telecommunications services by satellite based facilities or microwave facilities) of the Telecommunications Act 1996. These two provisions state that no operator other than the general carrier holds the right to operate a "reserve link within Papua New Guinea and a place outside Papua New Guinea". Section 46 states international linkage rights of a general carrier through satellites or microwave facilities.[3]

The latest ICT policy (March 2009) states that the operation of international gateways (since September 2007) is the exclusive right of Telikom. The most likely scenario for Digicel to pursue was to request the Irish Government (or the European Union, of which Ireland is a member), to challenge PNG's actions in the WTO on three potential derogation

---

[3] Reserve links are in-country telecommunications facilities that linked telecommunications services via cable lines (telephony system with a central controlling telecom hub). On the other hand, microwave facility is basically communications through wireless means (mobile services connected based on geographical wireless towers).

scenarios.[4] First, as a matter of principle, any foreign supplier that deems itself adversely affected by the measures of a host government could request its home country authorities to raise the issue with that government through the WTO.[5] Hence, depending on the nature of the measure in question, governments concerned discuss alternative solutions or if deadlock is reached, raise their concern at the WTO's dispute settlement body. This appears to be the most likely scenario that Digicel would have pursued in the international gateway dialogue during this period. Second, under PNG's WTO telecommunications commitments, Telikom's exclusive monopoly was scheduled for five years, to 2002. One potential interpretation is that there is a case for market liberalization after that end date. Hence, under this scenario, PNG's telecommunications sector should have been liberalized in 2002.

One important issue to keep in mind on this scenario is that PNG did not request an extension in 2002 and this option could have been exploited. In PNG's case—as shown by frequent attempts to reverse the liberalization policy—five years was not sufficient to allow for the PNG government to fund the rehabilitation of Telikom. An ambitious reform program with a short, fixed timeline increases the risks of future policy interference. State-owned monopolies with no competitive experience and limited financial resources to counter introduced competition could encounter extreme challenges. Hence, the Government was forced to consider revising its telecommunications policies to allow for the rehabilitation of the incumbent operator to competitive standards.

A similar problem occurred in Albania in 2003/04. It applied for a waiver in the WTO and was granted one when the privatization of its state-owned monopoly—Albtelecom—ran into difficulties. The waiver postponed the commitment's implementation date by one year (Adlung 2007:254-255). Similarly, Tonga through its accession process, requested a waiver on the ratification deadline of its WTO commitments (including telecommunications commitments) due to economic and political difficulties in July 2006. It was granted a one-year waiver, which was ratified in July 2007.

Third, in its WTO telecommunications commitment, PNG scheduled no limitations discriminating between foreign and local service suppliers.

---

[4] The Government of PNG scheduled to liberalize the international gateway by October 2009, but by the end of January 2010, had not done so.

[5] Many thanks to Rudolf Adlung for clarifying this point.

The granting of exclusive rights over an international gateway to Telikom after the 2002 deadline may be deemed a violation of its 1997 WTO telecommunications commitments. Any legal dispute formally established in the WTO on any of these scenarios could impose tremendous economic and political costs on PNG.

The local business communities in PNG also put pressure on the Government. Island Business reporter, Ms. Dionisia Tabureguci, reported that "public pressure resulted in the Government scrapping the very controversial NETCO/SERVCO competition model" (Tabureguci 2008). The Port Moresby Chamber of Commerce General Manager, Mr. David Conn, was quoted as saying, "they are not happy because government did not consult with them on the policy. He also criticized Government and Telikom for failing to attend a public workshop held in January 2008, attended by a wide spectrum of people and stakeholders" (Tabureguci 2008).

There was also limited political pressure from within government as there was much political lobbying going between those who supported competition and those who opposed it (Respondent 9, fieldwork interviews, 13 September 2008). A telecommunications policy expert in Port Moresby stated that,

> "eventually, an ICT policy [May 2007 ICT Policy] was adopted by the PNG Government, which was not agreed to by the majority of the Taskforce, but held the views of the minority, who thought that competition would be detrimental for Telikom PNG" (Respondent 9, fieldwork interviews, 13 September 2008).

The ICCC similarly had difficulties with the Government's May 2007 ICT policy. The ICCC's Commissioner Abe, in a press statement on 30 July 2007, stated that "ICCC was informed by Minister Somare at the end of June 2007 that, in a decision taken on 21 June during the election period, the Government had reversed its previous policy of introducing mobile competition, and wanted the ICCC to revoke the licences issued to Digicel…ICCC sought legal advice…and has been advised that the licences already issued to Digicel are proper and valid, and cannot now be legally cancelled because of a change in government policy" (Abe 2007[b]).

Since ICCC's involvement with the reform program in December 2005, its position has been to act as the independent regulator for telecommunications services (without any political interference) and provide competition in the mobile service sector through granting of a licence to Digicel. This position was reflected in several public statements by Commissioner Abe in 2007/08. [6] The provision of ICCC's functions in accordance with its legislation was effective during the reform program on one key regulatory aspect—independence. Maintaining independence amidst commercial and political interference was achieved by ICCC, although it may have contributed to the loss of its power to grant and revoke telecommunications licences.[7]

Looking at the effects of bilateral investment treaties on the credibility of telecommunications reform in Papua New Guinea reveals that while several bilateral investment treaties signed with other countries, Ireland (of where Digicel is based) was not one of them. [8] Since the legal effect of bilateral treaties on investment goes as far as two countries, the two countries involved predominantly determine its protection's effectiveness. This is probably why there was lack of coverage (if at all) by media, reports and series of interviews on the usefulness of bilateral investment treaties in telecommunications reform in PNG.

Overall, this section has discussed how pressures from key stakeholders including Telikom, IPBC, and government ministers undermined the independence and therefore effectiveness of ICCC to instill credibility. Furthermore, this section has argued that the WTO telecommunications commitments have limited the chances for policy reversal and thereby have stabilized telecommunications reform in PNG's telecommunications reform.

3.2 Tonga

Tonga's successful introduction of mobile competition in late 2002 was swiftly backed by a comprehensive telecommunications reform program. Competition in the telecommunications sector began when TONFON entered the mobile phone market as the second provider in July 2003. During that time, Tonga was negotiating its services commitments

---

[6] 18 January 2006; 30 July 2007 and 5 October 2007.

[7] The latest ICT policy in March 2009 stated that a new regulator—NICTA—be established and that all powers to grant and revoke licences shall be taken from ICCC to this new regulator. Although not clear at this stage, the new regulator will be heavily influenced by government in terms of Members of the Board and source of funding.

[8] See Chapter 3 for details of bilateral investment treaties signed by PNG.

as part of its accession to the WTO. As a result, Tonga's domestic and multilateral position on telecommunications policy was relatively aligned and consolidated in the multilateral trading system.

Tonga finalized its WTO accession package in December 2005 and in November 2007, Digicel entered the Tongan market via acquisition of TONFON. The motive behind the selling of TONFON, according to the Shoreline Group, was "part of the program for King Siaosi Tupou V to withdraw from commercial interests in Tonga" (Tonga-Now 2007). The Shoreline Group of Companies owned TONFON, in which the Crown Prince (now King) was a major shareholder. Ever since the November 2006 Riot, which resulted in the closure of Shoreline's main office in Nuku'alofa, the company now has a very limited presence in Tonga. Digicel Tonga commenced operation in May 2008. Since that time, the telecommunications sector has realized a reduction in mobile service prices with better quality of mobile service delivery through competition.

Since the expiry in 1999 of the franchise agreement between the Tongan Government and British's Cable and Wireless, the provider of international services in Tonga,[9] the Tongan Government's intention of reforming the sector was made clear in the swift move to draft and pass the Communications Act 2000. The motive behind the reform is not clear, although two pieces of anecdotal evidence shed some light. First, according to a telecommunications policy expert in Nuku'alofa explained:

> "The expiry of the franchise agreement with Cable and Wireless provided an ideal commercial opportunity for government to exploit…during those days the costs of an international call was US$ 3.30 per minute but now [December 2008] its down to about US$ 0.30 per minute…also the need for introduction of new services to Tonga via mobile services and internet connection" (Respondent 20, fieldwork interviews, 24 November 2008).

Second, the close business affiliation of then Crown Prince Tupouto'a[10] with Shoreline Groups (of which TONFON operates the mobile services) and the fact that he assented to the Bill, generated unquestionable political support from within government's executive branch for the successful implementation of the reform program. The Communications Act 2000

[9] International service was the most profitable segment during the Cable and Wireless time compared to domestic services and fixed line.
[10] Now King Siaosi Tupou V.

from the outset, therefore, was drafted to reflect the strong political support for a competitive telecommunications sector.[11]

Two regulatory aspects of the Communications Act 2000 deserve further discussion. First, the telecommunications reform in Tonga had clear objectives from the beginning as reflected by the Communications Policy Statement 2000. The communications policy mandated three regulatory priorities for the reform program. First, the development of the telecommunications infrastructure was deemed essential for economic development. The second priority was the introduction of competition to encourage growth across the sector, and lower prices. The introduction of competition for a second provider was considered as the "first stage in a wider liberalization process". The policy statement made clear that government reserved the right to permit any further new entrant, ensuring a sustainable duopoly competition allowing maximum benefits for consumers. Third, in an attempt to consolidate provision of all telecommunications services, a new public telecommunications operator—Tonga Communications Corporations (TCC)—was established, replacing the services previously provided by Cable and Wireless (international) and the Tonga Telecommunications Commission (domestic).

Second, the creation of a Department of Communication "as an independent regulator", stipulated by the Communications Policy Statement 2000 and the Communications Act 2000, indicated government's policy intention of creating a predictable environment for investment. As indicated in the Communications Policy Statement (2000), "the Minister's role has a particular emphasis on policy making, [while] the Department is primarily concerned with policy implementation." The Department however, is accountable to the Minister, responsible for Communications and funded by government. The regulator has continued to pursue regulatory neutrality and opted for market forces to regulate the sector. It has so far been effective.

The comprehensive reform program nevertheless did impose policy challenges to several key stakeholders including TCC. A telecommunications policy expert in Nuku'alofa recalled:

> "When the government deregulated the market, going from a monopoly situation to a competitive environment was quite a challenge, one of the

[11] See Chapter 2, Tonga's Telecommunications Policy for detailed discussion on the Communications Act 2000.

> major policy challenges for TCC was the short transitional period—seven months—it was granted by government to prepare for competition. At the same time, TCC was also going through internal restructuring on merging of the two companies (Cable and Wireless; and Tonga Communications International Limited—TCIL). In addition, there was tense competition in a small market; TCC had to balance out reducing tariffs on services (negative impact on revenue), while attempting to expand network (increasing demand on capital investment) at the same time[12]. Further, Digicel Tonga as part of a global company has more power (economies of scale) in terms of purchasing, trainings etcetera, than TCC, a small local company with limited funding sources. For example, if you buy 100,000 headsets you can receive 50 per cent discount whereas if you buy 1,000 similar headsets you get only 5 per cent discount. However, it's not doom and gloom for TCC since the good thing for us is that we know our market very well. It will take some time for Digicel to gain in-depth knowledge and public brand trust, a time which TCC can use to its advantage" (Respondent 19, fieldwork interviews, 24 November 2008).

Similar to the PNG case, there was an interconnection dispute between Digicel and TCC which originated in 2003. A telecommunications policy expert in Nuku'alofa recalled that:

> "Interconnection disputes between the two providers began in 2003 to 2004. The Department has not put in place an Arbitration policy and therefore had to call in experts to draft guidelines for the Department to use. The guidelines for Arbitration were completed in April 2005. An Arbitrator was appointed...and we started the process of submissions for interconnections fees and reports. The Department also brought in an economic advisor to advice the Arbitrator. But at the end of 2005, we received communications from the two operators that they have solved their interconnection disputes bilaterally outside the Arbitration system" (Respondent 20, fieldwork interviews, 24 November 2008).

As of April 2010, there had been no recorded disputes or legal proceedings against any key stakeholder in the sector. Also, remarkably similar to the PNG case, Tonga had not signed a bilateral investment treaty with Ireland. Hence, there was less chance that legal protection under a bilateral investment treaty context could be exploited by Digicel in the

---

[12] Universal-service coverage commitments and funds are included in the Communications Act 2000, however as of July 2009, the Tongan Government is currently drafting regulations and detail policies on implementing those commitments. A similar situation occurred in PNG.

case of future disputes. There had been no recorded disputes to April 2010 between Digicel and TCC.

Overall, the case of Tonga shows a regulatory reform program with clearly set objectives at the outset, dictating a predictable policy path for investors. The monarchial system of government provided a stabilizing and strong political commitment, coupled with the support from the Crown Prince's business interests. Further evidence of Tonga's observing its multilateral commitments in the WTO provided a lock-in mechanism for government to implement its telecommunications reform.

4.0 The Impact of WTO Telecommunications Commitments

4.1 Policymakers and Regulators

The PNG and Tonga case studies have shed useful insights on the impact of one WTO agreement—GATS—on the credibility of a domestic reform program in a small island developing states context.

The PNG Government's ICT policies[13], several ICCC communications[14], media reports[15], telecommunications policies and the expert interviews[16] conducted provide strong evidence of the importance of WTO telecommunications commitment in consolidating unilateral telecommunications liberalization. The PNG Government was reminded of its commitment by the Irish Ambassador's visit and the reported communication by the European Union to the PNG Government enquiring about its WTO commitments.

The latest ICT policy recognizes that open competition provides the best means of delivering benefits to consumers over the long term. For the first time, it recognizes that alternatives (closed or limited competition) "are unlikely to be acceptable to the PNG consumers or to the wider international community, where multilateral liberalization through forums

[13] PNG Government national ICT policy of May 2007, September 2007, April 2008, March 2009 and NEC Decision 2005.

[14] ICCC Commissioner's Press Statement of 18 January 2006, 30 July 2007, 5 October 2007, and 20 February 2009.

[15] Islands Business (2008) and Digicel (2007, 2008).

[16] Several requests for an interview appointment with Digicel PNG's country manager were unsuccessful.

such as APEC and the WTO will put PNG under increasing pressure to open its telecommunications sector to competition" (Papua New Guinea Government 2007:1).

The structural separation of Telikom into NETCO/SERVCO model was rescinded. This amendment imposed an important forward-looking regulatory step, that is, the recognition that Telikom is in need of serious rehabilitation and therefore there is need for a phased introduction to full competition.

In March 2009, the Department of Communications and Information released the final report of its latest national ICT policy – "National ICT Policy Phase 2 Reforms". The report is clear of the key objectives and tentative timeline set for open competition. Two issues in the March 2009 ICT report are worthy of note. First, the licensing responsibilities were taken away from ICCC and given to NICTA. The licensing procedures were to be transparent and consistent with regulatory barriers to market entry reduced. The role and contribution of ICCC as far as the telecommunications sector is concerned is sidelined. Second, the last stumbling block from the previous ICT policies that went against competition was the regulation of the international gateway. The March 2009 Report set a tentative deadline for October 2009 (as early as practicable) for the liberalization of the international gateway. This stumbling block , though, still remained as of January 2010.

The Tongan case also shows the significance of WTO telecommunications commitments on telecommunications reform. However, the motives of the stakeholders may differ since the Tongan telecommunications reform program has progressed in the same direction as its WTO commitments. The pursuance of a liberal stance on trade in services was historical due to Tonga's islandness and limited resources. Being a small island economy, it depends heavily on the global economy for trade in goods and services. The Tongan Government recognized this challenge and therefore pursued a relatively liberal trade-in-services regime. [17] It should also be noted that the policy input of certain domestic actors was equally instrumental in setting a clear objective for liberalization. The most noticeable factor was the political commitment from the government of Tonga and the Crown Prince (now King) to the telecommunications reform process.

---

[17] See 'Ofa (2008) for discussion on WTO and trade in services regime in Tonga.

The incumbent state-owned telecommunications providers in both PNG and Tonga lacked experience and financial capacity to operate in a competitive environment. The privatization programs adopted in both countries had only advanced halfway—to corporatization. Limited finance was made available to both incumbents for modernization and rehabilitation, yet they were given short transitional period to prepare for competition. On top of this, the incumbents continued to struggle with their universal commitments in rural and remote areas.

4.2 Telecommunications Operators: Behaviors and Performances

The state-owned incumbent telecommunications operators in both countries behaved like classical monopolists. While both incumbents recognized the importance of telecommunications reform—competition—both relied on government for protection during the transition period. Since the introduction of competition, both incumbents have had to adapt or risk losing market share. Telikom adapted by selling 50 per cent of the equity in its mobile service (B-Mobile) for K$130 million. The 50 per cent equity investment was contributed by a consortium of companies including US-based Trilogy International Partners LLC (20 per cent), GEMS Ltd (20 per cent), PNG's National Superannuation Fund (5 per cent) and Nambawan Super Ltd (5 per cent) (Telikom PNG 2009). With separate ownership and management of the mobile service, the PNG Government anticipated that B-Mobile could compete with new entrant Digicel.

The heightened competition in PNG and Tonga is due to the entrant of Digicel to the Pacific. The private operator Digicel is one of the most influential telecommunications investors operating in the Pacific. Since establishment in April 2001 in Jamaica, Digicel has opened operations in 31 countries and territories throughout Latin America, the Caribbean and the Pacific as of March 2008. [18] Digicel finished the 2008 fiscal year with 6.54 million customers, representing a 39 per cent increase compared to the same quarter in 2007 (Digicel Group 2009). It is reported that Digicel employs more than 5,500 people with major sponsorship of national sport

[18] Including Anguilla, Antigua and Barbuda, Aruba, Barbados, Bermuda, Bonaire, the Cayman Islands, Curacao (Netherlands Antilles), Dominica, French Guyana, Grenada, Guadeloupe (French), Haiti, Jamaica, Martinique, St. Kitts and Nevis, St. Lucia, St. Vincent and the Grenadines, Trinidad and Tobago and Turks and Caicos Fiji, PNG, Samoa, Tonga and Vanuatu.

teams and community programs. It has in excess of 1,000 retail stores with a total investment exceeding US$ 3.4 billion (Digicel Group 2009).

Digicel is estimated to have invested an approximate US$ 92 million long-term package in PNG. [19] Digicel employs more than 400 people in PNG and has contributed around 0.7 per cent to GDP growth in 2007 (AusAid 2008[a]:43). Digicel Tonga in May 2008 reported to have invested TOP$20 million (about US$10 million) in building its infrastructure network with branches opening in the main island groups of Tongatapu, Vava'u, Ha'apai and 'Eua. Digicel employs more than 100 people in Tonga.

The Digicel expansion strategy in PNG and Tonga (and the Pacific) can be characterized into four strategies. First, Digicel has exploited international funding sources—International Funding Corporation (IFC); and Export Development Canada (EDC)—to fund some of its expansion strategies in the Pacific. The PNG network expansion was primarily funded through World Bank's private sector arm, IFC. This was a totally new concept to state-owned telecommunications operators in PNG and Tonga although both countries are members of the IFC and could have exploited these financial opportunities. [20] However, the lack of a proven track record for successful telecommunications expansion projects and lack of financial capacity to implement multi-million dollar projects may have deterred small local incumbent operators in Pacific from exploring this option.

Second, Digicel in the initial stages was investing heavily in social and community programs as a strategy to build close connections with social and cultural assets in PNG and Tonga. The Digicel Foundation Program focuses on funding the social development of communities in PNG and elsewhere. The Digicel Foundation is a non-profit organization that distributes and utilizes funds on a charitable basis for the sole purpose of building communities. The Digicel Foundation work closely with governments and NGOs to support and implement projects in several Caribbean countries and PNG. The Digicel Foundation consist of Digicel employees who volunteer to work in communities, promoting values of respect, hard work and responsibility.

---

[19] International Finance Corporation (IFC) finance US$40 million, Export Development Canada (EDC) finance US$25 million and s local commercial bank to fund US$ 17 million.

[20] PNG joined in 1975, Tonga in 1985.

Digicel Foundation PNG has launched several key projects since its inception in 2008 with the opening of a new school in Baraku, mobile learning centers for several communities and free distribution of school stationery to children in "8 Miles" Province.[21] Digicel has also sponsored national sporting teams in PNG and Tonga including the national rugby union team, the national rugby league team and other major sports. This strategy is extremely effective in connecting with the grass-root level people in the communities, which encourages acceptance, local support and loyalty.

Third, the expansion of Digicel in the Pacific shows that Digicel is expanding mainly in markets which are predominantly closed, with no experience of competition. Although this involves substantially high investment risks, "cream-skimming" is achieved.[22] The dynamic advancement in technology through telecommunications has given Digicel a cost effective tool to overcome geographical isolation.

Fourth, Digicel has exploited mass commercial advertisement at unprecedented levels in PNG and Tonga. Upon entrance to one of the international airports in PNG or Tonga, a welcome billboard by Digicel is usually among the first advertisements international passengers notice (Figure 5-11). Almost every retail shop in PNG and Tonga has Digicel signs (small oval billboards for prepaid cards) and in the case of Nuku'alofa, Digicel painted the national market's roof—Talamahu—with Digicel's logo (Figure 5-12). The Digicel logo on Talamahu market's roof is easily recognizable by passengers on most daylight flights. The physical settings inside the main branches that serve customers throughout Nuku'alofa and Port Moresby are identical, almost to McDonald's international standardization. As a result of competition, the mobile service network in PNG has expanded significantly. The two main operators have rolled out mobile services in new areas, including remote areas, attracting significant numbers of new subscribers.

---

[21] For more information, visit Digicel Foundation PNG <http://www.digicelpngfoundation.org/en/projects>

[22] Picking markets controlled by slow-reacting former monopoly firms with high market prices, and so large potential benefits.

Figure 5-11: Digicel Advertisements in Papua New Guinea

Advertisements inside the immigration area upon arrival at PNG's international airport.

Digicel billboard outside the airport at the taxi stand.

A Digicel branch in Port Moresby.

Source: Author's pictures (September 2008).

Figure 5-12: Digicel Advertisements in Tonga

Digicel logo in Nuku'alofa on the roof of Talamahu Market.

A Digicel branch in Nuku'alofa.

Signed Jerseys of Digicel's sponsored Tongan Rugby Teams ('Ikale Tahi and Sevens National Team).

Source: Author's pictures (November – December 2008).

The Digicel coverage in Tonga is almost nationwide (90 per cent plus). By mid-2007, competition in Tonga had increased mobile phone ownership from 3.4 per cent to 30 per cent. In the same period, there has been a sharp increase in coverage and a doubling of mobile phone services in PNG (AusAid 2008[a]: 43). Figure 5-13 illustrates the network coverage area for Digicel in PNG and Tonga.

Figure 5-13: Digicel Network Coverage Map[23] - PNG and Tonga

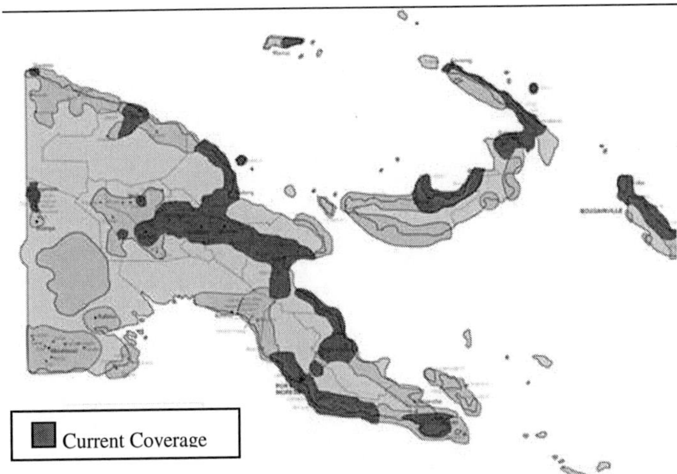

Network Coverage in PNG (as of February 2009)

Source: Digicel Papua New Guinea

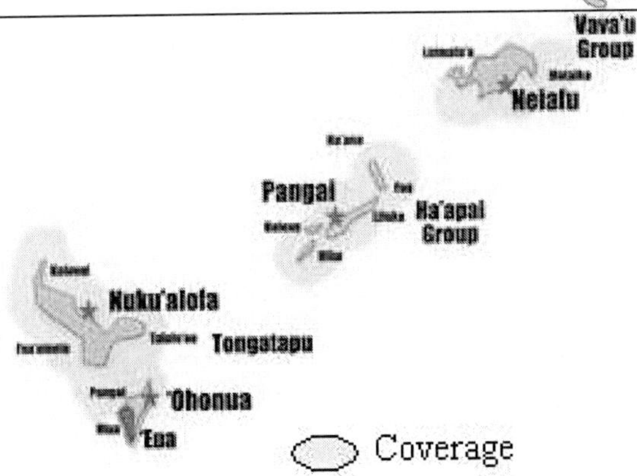

Network Coverage in Tonga (2008)

Source: Adapted from Digicel Tonga Coverage Map

[23] Maps are not drawn to scale.

A comparison of Digicel network coverage to incumbents Telikom (PNG), see Figure 5-14, shows that network coverage (measured by the number of stations established around the country) is relatively smaller in B-Mobile's case. The higher network coverage in Digicel for both countries shows the depth and the magnitude with which Digicel has invested. A comparison with incumbent TCC (Tonga) was not possible due to lack of public information/graphs on the incumbent's network coverage, but a similar relationship could be true for Tonga.

Figure 5-14: B-Mobile Network Coverage (Telikom PNG)

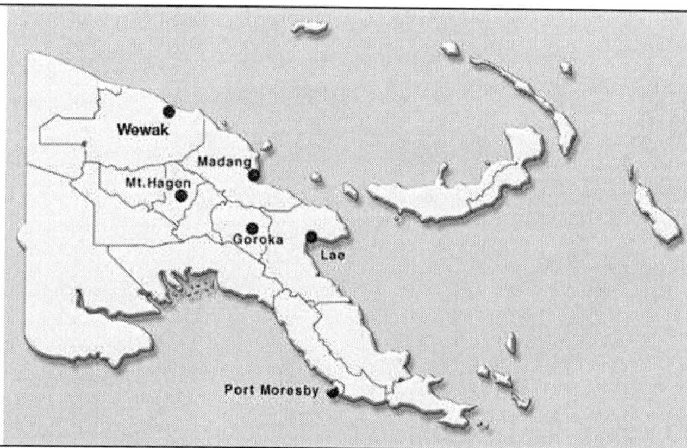

B-Mobile Coverage is solely within the six cities labeled.

Source: Pacific Mobile Communications Ltd (B Mobile) 2009

The overall responses from key telecommunications policy experts participated to the series of interviews conducted were predominantly positive on the outcome of telecommunications reform in PNG and Tonga. The two responses best capturing the positive feedback in relation to competition stated;

> "PNG's experience with introduction of competition into the Telco sector is no different to that experienced by other countries where Telco markets have been liberalized. Prices have fallen, service standards have risen, and the network coverage has risen" (Respondent 1, fieldwork interviews, 08 September 2008).

> "Competition has reduced the prices of international calls dramatically…I now call my relatives in New Zealand more often" (Respondent 26, fieldwork interviews, Nuku'alofa, 4 December 2008).

Three issues commonly appearing in many of the interview responses towards Digicel's entrance to the market are worthy of note. First, the price of mobile services has fallen sharply since the introduction of competition. Second, the quality of services—network coverage and after-hour services—has improved significantly compared to pre-competition times. Third, the interconnectivity gap between urban and rural (and isolated areas) areas has been reduced. Nevertheless, a few responses also raised some concerns on competition. One response stated:

> "Yes, introduction of competition in the telecommunications sector increased network coverage. However, one must think of the challenges encountered when attempting to increase coverage. This includes availability of electricity in remote and rural areas and non-economical [economic] areas of the country for investment" (Respondent 5, fieldwork interviews, Port Moresby, 27 September 2008).

The challenges of electricity may have been addressed by Digicel. Upon launching its mobile services in PNG, Digicel gave out free solar-powered chargers for each handset sold. This effectively dealt with the concern in rural areas about limited access to electricity. The PNG Government through the licencing agreement remedied the investment in non-economical areas, with specific provision for a universal-service fund. One of Digicel's licensing arrangements in PNG was to roll out their network to all four main centers (Port Moresby, Lae, Mount Hagen and Kokopu), 8 minor centers, all districts, plus 229 locations—communities of 1,000 people based on electoral data. The requirement ensures that new entrant Digicel deploy its network throughout the country (nationwide coverage target).

4.3 Politicians, NGOs and the General Public

Opposition to the liberalization of the mobile services[24] sector in Tonga was remarkably muted, considering that several NGOs, the Public Servants Association, the Pro-democracy Movement, the Tongan Small Business Association, Friendly Islands Teachers Associations (FITA) and Tongan Women's Action for Change (TWAC) and several Members of Parliament actively protested against the terms of membership and eventual membership of Tonga to the WTO. The opposition to free trade is widespread throughout the Pacific. Duncan (2008) suggested that within the Pacific, opposition to open markets is very strong and supported by

[24] Either the entrance of TONFON in 2003 or Digicel in 2008.

vested interests, ideology, and cultural beliefs. Economic issues also constrain the response to changes in the terms of trade through trade liberalization, such as insecurity of land tenure and poor access to credit.

The core arguments from NGOs on anti-WTO protests in Tonga can be characterized into four main concerns raised in public forums in Tonga and abroad. These issues included the public concern that Tonga's membership to the WTO meant a loss of government revenue, the financial capacity of government to meet costs of compliance was limited, and their concerns about the limited financial capacity of government to meet costs of compliance. Tonga's ability to implement subsidies for domestic industries would be eliminated and claimed that government would lose control of vital public services including education and health.

Oxfam New Zealand was proactive in the release of briefing notes, which lobbied for public support in Tonga, resulting in an unprecedented public protest towards the Tongan Government against Tonga's finalization of its WTO membership process (Oxfam New Zealand n.d. and 2005)

The discussion in the Tongan Parliament in the lead-up to the December 2005 WTO signing also reflected anti-free trade concerns. However, the Parliamentary minutes at the time do not show any specific opposition to the liberalization of the mobile service sector. The remarkably small degree of concern towards the liberalization of the mobile service sector prompts one fundamental point. Since TONFON entered the market in 2003 and Digicel in 2008, the general public, including rural and remote islands, has benefited from this wireless technology. The interconnectivity gap between the five major island groups in Tonga was dramatically reduced, as was the linkage between Tonga and the outside world. Competition provided incentives for the state-owned incumbent to improve efficiency. Hence, it was unlikely that any political pressure against the development of this sector would have been supported by the general public. Similarly, as reflected in the PNG case, once the wireless technology benefited rural and isolated areas, the general public's support for the liberalization of the mobile service sector increased dramatically.[25] Therefore, the liberalization policy directly

[25] Based on direct observations from the field and numerous hours of conversations with random people, business operators and government officials, there was a general support for increased telecommunications connectivity in PNG. Also, other public institutions reflected this general support including the first NEC Decision

addressed the disadvantages of small isolated islands ensuring public support towards the liberalization of the telecommunications sector.

5.0 Conclusion

The telecommunications regulatory reforms in PNG encountered challenges that the independent regulator dealt with to the best of its ability. The frequent policy changes over the last five years point to the limited ability of the domestic independent regulator in providing credibility to the reform process. Nevertheless, actions instigated through various channels by the Irish-owned Digicel operator, including the European Union communication reminding the PNG Government of its WTO telecommunications obligation, provide evidence that multilateral policy restraints can provide credibility to the telecommunications reform process. In response, the Papua New Guinea ICT policies in late 2008 and early 2009 show that the government recognizes and respects its WTO obligations. The relatively muted public opposition to the liberalization of mobile services in Tonga and PNG provides evidence that once an economic reform program directly addresses the challenges of being small and isolated, policy adoption encounters less political pressure.

These findings provide two important policy insights into the early stages of telecommunications reform in the Pacific islands. First, the liberalization of the telecommunications market to open competition increases sector performances even among one of the smallest markets in the Pacific. Further, the improvement in telecommunications infrastructure increases interconnectivity between urban and rural areas; and between island states and the outside world. The role therefore of telecommunications infrastructure and in particular telecommunications technology to overcome the challenges of small island developing states is of utmost importance. Second, to ensure investment confidence in the sector is enhanced, the multilateral policy restraints provided by the WTO telecommunications commitments provide significant credibility when domestic restraint policies fail.

---

to liberalized telecommunications in 2005 by PNG Government. Also, the assurance of the PNG Government's commitment to competition by PNG's Prime Minister Somare to Digicel in March 2007 and the PNG Government to Irish Ambassador in September 2007, reflect indirectly the PNG people's support for competition and interconnectivity throughout PNG. Further, despite conflicting pressures on telecommunications reform, as of September 2010, the PNG Government is still committed to telecommunications liberalization.

One of the main lessons from the PNG case study is that regulatory capture provides incentives for government to renege on commitments to telecommunications reform. The incentive may be explained by political and economic motives. Politically, the liberalization of the mobile sector was set for March 2007, three months before the June 2007 national election. Several media agencies—Islands Business and The National—and interviewees claimed that the competition date might have been set purposely to coincide with the national election. In addition, the eventual "internal reform" of the ICCC since its involvement in the telecommunications reform process in 2005, culminating in the removal of its autonomous power to grant licences and reverting back to the Minister responsible for telecommunications, shows the vulnerability of this domestic policy restraint to vested political interests.

Economically, Telikom needed significant rehabilitation time and funding to prepare for open competition. The Government may not have been clear about the needed rehabilitation following the 2005 NEC decision. Since the December 2005 Decision, seven national ICT policies had been passed in the time span of about three years. The frequent policy amendments have created significant uncertainty and confusion about the investment regulations.

The Tongan case provides equally important evidence to support the role of multilateral policy restraint and the credibility of telecommunications reform. Although the reform encountered lesser policy uncertainty in Tonga, the WTO telecommunications commitment strengthened Tonga's unilateral reform initiative by locking in its liberalization policy intension. In addition, the crucial political support from Tonga's King provided a stabilizing mechanism for its telecommunications reform whereas PNG's more democratic political system inhibits less stability. The less pronounced role of a democratic system in PNG, though, could have been partly due to weaker institutional and regulatory rules. Lastly, there was no evidence from the two case studies that signing up to bilateral investment treaties was effective in providing credibility to the reform. This is predominantly based on the fact that Digicel's home government has not signed any bilateral investment treaties with the two country case studies.

CHAPTER SIX

INDEPENDENT REGULATOR AND THE CREDIBILITY OF TELECOMMUNICATIONS REFORM[1]

1.0 Introduction

As discussed in Chapter 2, the establishment of an independent regulator in the financial and banking sectors, is a common policy prescription for instilling credibility. The literature on telecommunications reform in developing countries and, more recently, small island developing states, seems to follow this common practice. However, the regulatory capture literature shows that government policies can be captured by interest group pressures (see previous discussion in Chapter 2).

This chapter examines the regulatory capture hypothesis on telecommunications reform in small island developing states. The focus, however, is the examination of the vulnerability of independent regulators—which is well established from the finance and banking literature—in trying to provide a credible policy environment. This chapter, therefore, poses questions about the commonly accepted independent regulators, as independent entities fit to regulate an industry sector—immune from political and interest group pressures.

The analyses of the process of terminating monopoly rights from the case studies of Samoa, Vanuatu and Fiji provide crucial insights into the role and effectiveness of independent regulators during the reform process. The case studies provide evidence that the effectiveness of independent

[1] An earlier version of this chapter was published as 'Telecommunications reform in Fiji, Vanuatu and Samoa and the credibility problem: the impact of independent regulators', *Pacific Economic Bulletin*, Volume 25, Number 1, pp. 96-108, 2010, visit <http://peb.anu.edu.au/pdf/PEB25_1_Ofa.pdf>

regulators in providing policy credibility in the early stages of reform has been limited.

The reasons are twofold. First, the independent regulators had limited technical capacity and financial resources. Second, the independent regulators were vulnerable to political influence. On the other hand, the case studies of Vanuatu and Fiji give support to the crucial role of contractual agreements—deeds of settlement—in providing immediate credibility in the early stages of the reform. A deed of settlement is a contractual legal agreement commonly used when parties (usually government, incumbent telecommunications operators and competitors) negotiate and agree to end the monopoly rights of incumbent telecommunications operators. The deed of settlement usually sets out the legal principles and detailed guidelines on the new rules and legal responsibilities of each party under a competitive market.

The long-term sustainability of such a legal mechanism compared to a comprehensive and permanent legislated framework is, however, unclear. Vanuatu liberalized its telecommunications sector by means of a strong legal contract without modern telecommunications legislation between government and operators. The telecommunications legislation was passed in December 2009 (about 24 months later) with key provisions of the legal contract reflected in the Act.

The structure of this chapter proceeds as follows. Section 2 discusses the context and nature of the independent regulators in Samoa, Vanuatu and Fiji. Section 3 critically examines the role of independent regulators and the deeds of settlement in the negotiations for terminating monopoly rights. Section 4 examines the impact of independent regulators and the deed of settlement on the credibility of the telecommunications reforms. Section 5 concludes the Chapter.

2.0 Independent Regulators: Samoa, Fiji and Vanuatu

2.1 Samoa

One of the fundamental components of Samoa's telecommunications reform was the implementation of a comprehensive telecommunications legislation—the Telecommunications Act 2005. The new telecommunications legislation set out the key regulatory components of a competitive market—in particular, the establishment of a new office to oversee the regulation of a competitive telecommunications sector.

The role of the regulator is defined in Part II, Sections 6-11 of the Act. Section 6 of the act provides the right for the head of state, acting on the advice of Cabinet, to appoint a regulator for a term of three years (with possible extension to a second term). Section 7 provides for the independence of potential candidates considered for the regulator's position, who may not be involved in or have proprietary interest in a service provider, manufacturer or supplier of telecommunications equipment. Section 8 outlines 22 responsibilities, functions and powers of the regulator. The regulator's basic role is to: provide advice to the minister responsible for telecommunications on relevant policies; issue, amend or revoke licences; monitor and enforce compliance; regulate interconnection agreements between operators; resolve disputes; and institute and maintain appropriate measures to prevent dominant operators from anti-competitive behaviors.

Section 9 provides the rights to establish the office of the regulator. The regulator's budget is appropriated from the Government's national budgetary expenditure. The Regulator is also required to conduct its affairs and provide information to the general public in an open and transparent manner. Section 10 provides the authority for the regulator to propose a regulation to establish licence fees, radio spectrum usage fees and telephone numbering fees. A telephone numbering system is used in telecommunications to allocate and route telephone numbers in a telephone network. The number of digits varies between network providers although a higher number of digits reflects a bigger telephone network (more subscribers) and vice versa. Section 11 provides for the rights of appeal and review of the orders of the regulator.[2] This section provides the right for operators to take disputes directly to the Supreme Court with regard to any order made. An amendment to the Act in 2008, however, amended this clause by referring any dispute to a telecommunications tribunal rather than the court system.

The office of the regulator was established in 2005 with seven officers. An interim regulator was appointed to act in the position while a permanent appointment was sought. In 2008, another interim regulator

---

[2] Section 11 of the act was amended and replaced by a new Section 11 in 2008. The new amended Section 11 is discussed in the credibility problems section.

was appointed who lasted about 12 months. On 16 February 2009, a permanent regulator was appointed. A legal analyst and three technical officers operate under the direction of the regulator. The office's fund for the financial year 2008/2009 was WS$ 1,402, 230 (approximately US$ 526,000), of which 54 per cent was for wages (Legislative Assembly of Samoa 2009).

2.2 Fiji

The regulation of the telecommunications sector in Fiji is shared in principle by two independent statutory authorities: the Commerce Commission and the Telecommunications Authority of Fiji (TAF), which was enacted by promulgation in 2008. The Commerce Commission, established under the Commerce Act 1998 (and subsequent amendments), is the independent statutory authority regulating competition and price-control policies on monopolies. Section Eleven of the Act states that the "commission is not subject to the control or direction of the Minister or to any referring authority in the performance of its functions." This provision arguably provides for the independence of the Commerce Commission from ministerial or governmental interference. The commission consists of three and not more than five commissioners with a chairperson, all appointed by the Minister. The commission's budget is appropriated by Parliament. The Minister reserves the right to remove from office any member of the commission for misbehavior, incompetence or incapacity.

TAF was created by the Telecommunications Promulgation Act 2008, approved in January 2008 by the interim military government. The 2008 promulgation aimed to provide a regulatory framework for telecommunications, promoting fair competition, consumer protection and efficient investment measures. TAF is to be responsible for licensing arrangements, spectrum management, the telephone numbering system, universal services, and a Telecommunications Appeal Tribunal. The appeal tribunal body is to be comprised of a chairperson and four other members. Division 2, Section 4 of the promulgation gives legal rights to the independence of TAF, stating that members are to be independent and impartial in the exercise of their functions and represent the public interest. The minister has the right to remove any member on the grounds of misconduct, conflict of interest, inefficiency, fraud or dishonesty or incapacity to perform duties. The funding of TAF is to be appropriated by Parliament. As of February 2010, TAF was not yet operational. However, once TAF is operational, the two authorities in theory should complement each other's objectives with competition and pricing policies regulated by the Commerce Commission while licensing, spectrum management, numbering and universal-service are to be handled by TAF.

2.3 Vanuatu

The office of the regulator was established due to an amendment (Telecommunications Amendment Act No. 15 of 2007) to the Telecommunications Act 1989. The amendment grants two fundamental powers to the Minister to regulate (or delegate to appropriate people the power to regulate) the telecommunications sector and the power to make determinations over disputes relating to interconnection between operators. An interim regulator was appointed in February 2008, supported by two permanent staff and two part-time technical staff.

Unlike Samoa, PNG and Fiji, the regulator's responsibilities in the early stages of the telecommunications reform in Vanuatu were not reflected in the Telecommunications Act 1989 (and subsequent amendments). This unconventional move may have been necessary to swiftly facilitate the telecommunications reform process by limiting the period for political debate—since a comprehensive telecommunications bill could involve public consultations and eventually political debates in Parliament. However, a new Telecommunications and Radiocommunications Regulations Bill (2009) was drafted shortly after competition was introduced, to consolidate the key responsibilities of the regulator. Other telecommunications regulatory aspects such as universal-service funds, anti-competitive behavior, spectrum management, interconnection agreements and the numbering system were not addressed in the previous Telecommunications Act 1989 (and subsequent amendments). These key regulatory principles were addressed in the draft bill. As a regulatory official in Port Vila explained:

> "We are operating under the Telecommunications Act 1989 (as amended). The government is planning to introduce a new Telecommunications Bill, which will include several changes. Since it was drafted 17 months ago [2007], the government has already made a number of changes to its policies. For example, in the settlement agreement and licences for TVL and Digicel, there are certain provisions that are in conflict with the Bill, so that needs to be harmonized. It is a bit odd making the laws consistent with the licence rather than the licence consistent with the laws. The consumer protection and anti-competitive measures have been written into the licences instead of the law. So that is the environment that we are operating

from at the moment [up to November 2009]" (Respondent 45, fieldwork interviews, 11 August 2008).

Hence, the independent regulator's responsibilities were dictated by three fundamental, legally binding documents. First, the regulator's employment contract outlines key responsibilities and other duties delegated by the Minister for Infrastructure and Public Utilities. Second, the deed of settlement—which ended the exclusive state monopoly and was signed by operators and the government—outlined the regulator's role in monitoring, licensing, spectrum management, the numbering system, interconnections agreements and mediation in the case of disputes. Third, the new licences granted to Telecommunications Vanuatu Limited (TVL) and Digicel also reflected the specific rights and powers of the regulator.

Overall, evidence from the telecommunications regulators in Samoa, Vanuatu, and Fiji shows limited technical and financial capabilities. Further, the regulator's office in Vanuatu relies heavily on donor funding, while in Samoa and Fiji, the offices are funded by government. Nevertheless, Samoa and Fiji (and most recently, Vanuatu) have enacted modern, comprehensive telecommunications legislation, including clear responsibilities of regulators.

3.0 The Credibility of Telecommunications Reform

This section discusses the early policy motivation in terminating the monopoly rights of state-owned telecommunications operators in the three Pacific cases, the role of the telecommunications regulator in the credibility of these processes, and the economic and political consequences of terminating the monopoly rights of each key stakeholder—as reflected in the deeds of settlement.

3.1 Samoa: The Independent Regulator and the Interconnection Dispute

Three mobile service operators won licences to operate in Samoa after the public bidding in early 2006: Digicel, SamoaTel and Telecom Samoa Limited (TSL). Digicel was granted a licence in April 2006 but, through a business move, it acquired 90 per cent ownership of TSL, effectively inheriting TSL's licence and entitlements.[3] The mobile sector was set for competition when Digicel launched in November 2006 and SamoaTel's "GoMobile" launched two months later.

One of the contentious issues for the two operators was establishing an interconnection agreement. Dr. John Philip Small, a consulting economist who was an expert witness for Digicel in the interconnection dispute, best captured the definition of interconnection by stating that "When a SamoaTel customer calls a Digicel customer, both networks are used to provide the call service. In this case SamoaTel will charge its customer for the call, and pay some of that money to Digicel in consideration for its help in completing the call. The amount paid will be the interconnection rate" (Supreme Court of Samoa 2008:2).

Preliminary discussions between the two operators were not fruitful. In October 2006, the two operators informed the interim regulator that they were unable to reach an agreement on interconnection rates and requested that the interim regulator set interim interconnection charges. The interim regulator issued interim interconnection rates for fixed and mobile services effective from 31 October 2006.

The interim interconnection rate was imposed for four months and two weeks. During that time, the two operators were required to undertake individual, cost based interconnection studies, to be submitted by March 2007.[4] During the interconnection dispute, the general counsel for Digicel explained that "cost based" "implies that the interconnection charges of a dominant provider shall be based on their costs of providing interconnection services and shall be economically viable" (Supreme Court of Samoa 2008:3). Any service provider whose gross revenues in a specific telecommunications market constitute 40 per cent or more of the total gross revenue of all service providers in that market is designated by the Regulator as dominant service provider (Section 26 (1), Telecommunications Act 2005). A UK consulting firm (Intercai Mondiale Limited, IML) was contracted by the government of Samoa to assist the interim regulator in determining interconnection rates.

---

[3] With the remaining 10 per cent ownership by Communications Services Limited (CSL), a state-owned enterprise.

[4] The basis for determining interconnection rates by the Regulator is outlined in Section 36 (1) of the Telecommunications Act 2005 which prescribed, that determination shall be cost-based.

The operators might, however, have ignored the interim interconnection rates order (2006/4) (see actual mobile rates on 1 March 2007, Table 6-13). An Education, Science, Communication and Information Technology Committee review into the interconnection rates of the two operators on 1 March 2007 noted some inconsistencies between the tender prices and the real mobile rates. One of the committee's findings noted the "concern with the increase in cell phone charges per minute by Digicel and SamoaTel. They both are not complying with amounts they tendered for when they applied for a licence to provide cell phone services' (Lesa 2007:4). As reported in the Samoa Observer (11 July 2007), the Chairman of the Committee and Opposition MP, Levaopolo Talatonu, 'accused both companies of misleading the Tenders Board by submitting tender rates cheaper than what they currently charge."

Table 6-13: Interconnections Rates – Samoa (2006-2008)

	SamoaTel pay Digicel	Digicel pay SamoaTel
Interim Interconnection Rates 2006/4 (31 October 2006 – March 2007)[a]		
Mobile Terminating Rates	25 sene per minute (off-peak) 45 sene per minute (peak hours)	
Fixed Terminating Rates		8.2 sene per minute
Actual Mobile Rates (1 March 2007)[b]		
Mobile Terminating Rates	25 sene per minute (off-peak) 70 sene per minute (peak hours)	
Fixed Terminating Rates		75 sene per minute
(Order 2007/4): 16 May 2007[c]		
Mobile Terminating Rates	22.8 sene per minute	
Fixed Terminating Rates		11.8 sene per minute
(Order 2008/3): 26 September 2008[d]		
Mobile Terminating Rates	35 sene per minute	35 sene per minute
Fixed Terminating Rates		0.082 sene per minute

Source: [a] - Extracted from the Office of the Regulator 2006, "Order of the Regulator – Number 2006/4"; [b] - Office of the Regulator Figures, reported by Mata'afa K Lesa, Samoa Observer, 11 July 2007; [c] – Extracted from the Office of the Regulator 2007, "Order of the Regulator Number 2007/4"; [d] – Office of the Regulator 2008, "Order of the Regulator – Number 2008/03".

The Chairman was also reported as saying that "the licences granted to these companies were given because of the rates they submitted. We all know that both companies are charging rates far off the mark" (Lesa 2007:1). It was also reported that a comparison of mobile call rates as of 1 March 2007, compiled by the Office of the Regulator on 6 March 2007 revealed a different story.

The actual terminating rates based on the regulator's review were higher for both fixed and mobile services compared to the interim connections rates set by the regulator. No public action was recorded to have been conducted by the interim regulator in conjunction with these price discrepancies.

The interim regulator, Digicel and SamoaTel communicated frequently during November and December 2006 on the details of the cost model. The regulator collected information from both parties through submission of comments on the regulator's cost-based modeling proposals and the operators' modeling. The regulator issued a cost study outline, Samoan Guidelines, on 11 January 2007, prescribing the key ingredients of the cost studies that each operator should address (Samoa Office of the Regulator 2007).

Having in mind the deadline for the cost studies of 11 March 2007, the regulator consistently pressured the two operators to submit their cost studies. SamoaTel submitted its cost model on 19 March 2007 and a revised version on 22 March 2007. Digicel submitted on 27 March 2007. The UK consulting firm, (Intercai Mondiale Limited, IML), required further supporting documents from Digicel's cost study, and background information was sent to the regulator on 4 April 2007. The Regulator, however, was not satisfied with the supporting documents.

In an email by the Regulator on 20 April 2007, the regulator advised Digicel's General Counsel, Mr. Dillon, that "his [Mr. Dillon's] comment in his email of 17 April 2007 about considerable effort in preparing a model seems a bit out of place as the model supplied [by Digicel] referred to Trinidad in the main body. The Regulator also pointed out that the three-page document provided by Mr. Dillon three weeks or so before was hardly in keeping with international practices for supporting such a model…the regulator was also critical of the lack of co-operation by Digicel in providing information for the analysis of their cost model" (Supreme Court of Samoa 2008:8).

The Regulator instructed IML to construct its own cost model of Digicel's costs, based on a different model from the one in the Samoan Guidelines. The Regulator says in his affidavit of 8 August 2007 that he had instructed IML to resort to using its own model rather than the model provided by Digicel because of Digicel's failure to provide adequate information despite his requests (Supreme Court of Samoa 2008:9). On 15 May 2007, the final report with recommended interconnection rates was submitted by IML to the regulator and on 16 May 2007, the regulator sent the new interconnection rates (Order 2007/4) to both operators (Table 6-14). Digicel was not satisfied with the new rates.

The new rates anticipated revenue loss for Digicel. Digicel sought an appeal in the Supreme Court against the interim regulator's order (2007/4). Digicel argued that, it "would be expected to receive WS$2,856,000 per annum or WS$238,000 per month less in mobile termination charges for calls originating on SamoaTel's fixed network and terminating on Digicel's mobile network" (Supreme Court of Samoa 2008:9). This alleged amount is based on the decline from 45 sene per minute (peak hour)[5] prescribed by the (2006/4) interim interconnection to 22.8 sene per minute, a 22.2 sene reduction or 49 per cent decrease in price for Digicel. On the other hand, Digicel was required to pay SamoaTel 11.8 sene per minute for calls originating on Digicel's network and terminating on SamoaTel's fixed network. This is an increase of 3.2 sene per minute compared to the 2006/4 interim interconnection rate or approximately 43 per cent rise in price for SamoaTel.

The main argument used by Digicel to argue its case was the failure of the interim regulator to accord procedural fairness to Digicel when conducting the process of establishing the interconnection rates. The Supreme Court's judgment was announced on 30 March 2008, ruling that Digicel's appeal against the regulator's interconnection order 2007/4 was allowed and the order was declared unlawful. The cost of the litigation imposed on the regulator and subsequently paid by the government was quoted at WS$1 million (about US$385,000). An agreement between the regulator and the two operators to revert to the interim interconnection rates (2006/4) was reached, with the two operators to make further submissions to the regulator. By September 2008, the regulator approved a new interim interconnection charge (2008/03).

---

[5] This is the highest amount of revenue it can possibly forgo compared to off-peak rate.

The outcome of the interconnection dispute favored Digicel, although the regulator's intention was to ensure prompt decisions on interconnection rates in the public's interest. The urgency of the regulator could, however, have been the result of pressure from a third party. The interconnection dispute reflected the limited technical capacity of the regulator's office and its inexperience in handling disputes of this nature.

3.2 Vanuatu: The Independent Regulator and the Deed of Settlement

Pre-competition regulatory framework

One year before Vanuatu's independence in 1980, VANITEL was established as a private operator delivering international telecommunications services, while the government-owned Vanuatu Post and Telecommunications provided the domestic services. [6] When developing countries in the 1980s and 1990s reformed their telecommunications sectors by way of privatization, Vanuatu adopted similar policy directions. In 1992, Vanuatu adopted a privatization program for telecommunications, whereby VANITEL and Vanuatu Post and Telecommunications merged and formed an incorporated company namely TVL. TVL was granted exclusivity to provide all telecommunications services. A 20-year franchise agreement was signed with the Vanuatu Government, that is, the two colonial powers—Cable and Wireless (UK) and France Telecom—having equal shares. TVL initially established its infrastructural network in the main towns, including Port Vila and Luganville. Copper wire (fixed lines network) was the primary communication channel and cross-subsidization of the main urban area network enabled limited expansion to rural areas. A telecommunications operator official in Vanuatu stated that "the main aspect of the agreement was the exclusivity allowing TVL to run on a commercial basis and make a profit out of Port Vila, Luganville…the main towns, and cross-subsidize the rural areas" (Respondent 51, fieldwork interviews, 20 August 2008).

TVL, however, soon encountered challenges that hindered its rural development program. A telecommunications Operator Official in Vanuatu stated:

[6] Jointly owned by Cable and Wireless (UK) and France Telecom.

> "In the beginning it was alright, but as the economy grew, the population grew. The burden on TVL increases, particularly in the urban areas where we had to support the increasing demand, and at the same time trying to expand rural network via cross-subsidization. TVL's rural development program was further deterred by the lack of access to electricity and roads in the rural areas. We encountered challenges on land ownership[7] issues and we had to negotiate with each and every customary owner on accessing land needed for the establishment of our network facilities. The general population at the time was highly dependent on subsistence farming and generating less cash economy. It was simply not economically viable to invest in laying copper wires throughout the islands" (Respondent 51, fieldwork interviews, 20 August 2008).

A closer look at the historical trend in network deployment (proxy by fixed lines per 100 people) since 1980, shows a sluggish increase in fixed-lines teledensity but large under-investment (noticeable in the period 1980-1999) compared to Vanuatu's economic growth (proxy by GDP per capita constant 2000) trend (Figure 6-15). The sharp increase in network deployment in the 2000-01 period can be attributed to the threat to TVL in a liberalized telecommunications market, when Vanuatu offered to liberalize the telecommunications sector in the WTO.[8] Also, the sharp increase in network deployment in 2007-2008 can be attributed to TVL's response to the imminent threats of planned competition in the sector.

A comparison of network deployment against the percentage of the total population living in urban areas, shows a noticeable similar trend throughout the 30-year period (Figure 6-15). In 1982, 15 per cent of the total population lived in urban areas with a national network coverage of 1.3 fixed lines per 100 people. Within a 25-year period (1982-2007), the urban population only grew to about 24 per cent of the total population, with a coverage of about 3.3 fixed lines per 100 people. In other words, by 2007, about 76 per cent of the total population of Vanuatu (rural population) was largely underserved with basic fixed line services.

---

[7] The issue of land ownership was also raised by another telecommunications operator, as a key deterrent to the progress on network deployment, more than fifteen years later.

[8] Vanuatu however withdrew its accession package in 2001. Nevertheless, the policy direction in liberalizing the sector was reflected in Vanuatu's WTO services offer.

Figure 6-15: Telephone Fixed Lines per 100 People versus GDP per capita constant (2000) US$

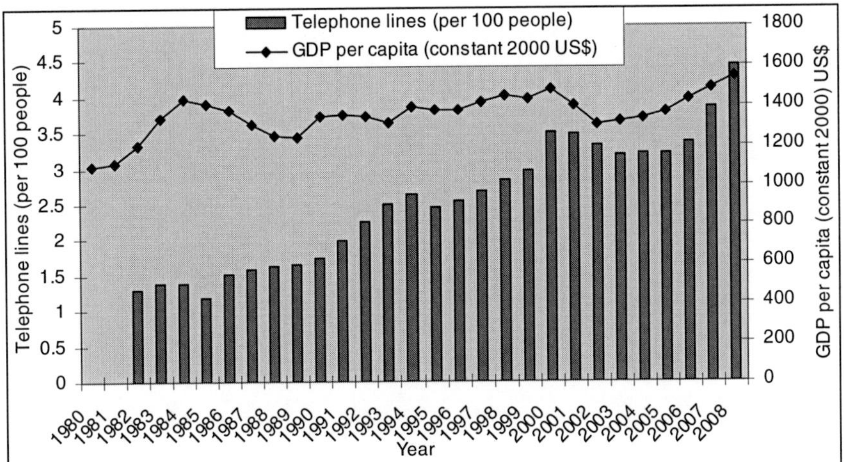

Source: World Development Indicators, 2009.

These trends provide anecdotal evidence for TVL's statement on focusing its early network deployment in Port Vila and other main towns. A telecommunications operator official in Port Vila stated that,

> "in the last two years [2006/2007], the government has changed direction. They decided that it is about time to introduce competition. There are number of reasons for that but most noticeable were pricing and rural [fixed lines] coverage" (Respondent 51, fieldwork interviews, 20 August 2008).

A government official in Port Vila described the public's sentiments towards the low network coverage in rural areas by recalling that:

> "People in the rural area used to complain about TVL. They used to walk for 3 kilometers or more to access a landline. TVL normally put a landline phone [public phone booth] in areas with concentration of settlement, so outer and smaller scattered rural settlements had to walk long distances to access the phone line…when they reach the landline, they find out that the land line is not working, so what a waste of effort and time" (Respondent 52, fieldwork interviews, 20 August 2008).

Figure 6-16: Vanuatu Telephone Fixed Lines per 100 People versus Urban Population (% of Total)

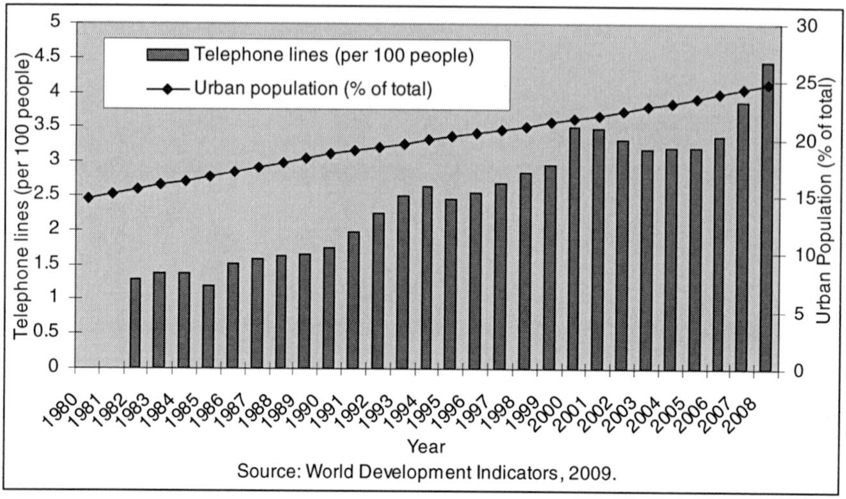

Poor coverage was not the only issue. The prices of telecommunications services in Vanuatu historically have been extremely high. For example, a mobile call at peak hours in Vanuatu per minute approximately cost over US$0.40 in September 2007, see (Figure 4-5). This tariff rate was among the highest in the Pacific countries at the time.

Evidence from the field also provides support to the high prices charged for telecommunications services in Vanuatu before competition was introduced. A telecommunications operator official in Port Vila recalled that, "a few years ago, a SIM card pack used to cost VT$ 5,000 (about US$52.00). A SIM card is not an expensive input but this is obviously a huge mark up on those. It has gone down, before Digicel launch, it was VT$ 1,000 with VT$ 1,000 of free credit. Digicel launched with a VT$ 500 SIM card and VT$ 500 free credit" (Respondent 47, fieldwork interviews, 12 August 2008).

Breaking exclusive rights: Negotiations versus Court settlement?

The public's pressure to reform the sector grew over time. Three incidents deserve further discussion. First, when Vanuatu withdrew its WTO accession package in 2001, several reasons—mainly political—were cited (Gay 2005). One of the fundamental issues, however, was the issue of committing the telecommunications sector in Vanuatu's services offer ('Ofa 2008[a]). Grynberg and Joy (2000:171), discussing Vanuatu's terms of WTO accession, write that, "the United States has added a further demand for the opening of the telecommunications sector. In Vanuatu this is not legally possible as with the condominium arrangement, France has an ironclad gateway monopoly until 2012." The Vanuatu Government at the time considered the cost of opting out was extremely high, although the policy direction was towards liberalizing the sector.

Second, the "ironclad" gateway monopoly was legally tested between October 2005 and September 2006 when the government granted a private company (Pacific Data Solution) a telecommunications licence to operate an electronic-gambling service to a closed-network client (Supreme Court of the Republic of Vanuatu 2006). State-owned monopolist, TVL, legally challenged the government's decision to grant a licence on the basis that the franchise agreement granted exclusive rights to TVL to operate all telecommunications services in Vanuatu. The court ruled otherwise, however, stating that the government's decision was legal since the licence given to Pacific Data Solution was to a restricted electronic-gambling network rather than the general public. A government official in Port Vila stated that, "at that time and through that process of the initial decision and the appeal, the question of the whole future of the telecommunications sector came to a head" (Respondent 48, fieldwork interviews, 14 August 2008).

The third and probably most crucial incident was the government's 2006 ICT policy paper and the amendments to the Telecommunications Act 1989. Through its policy paper, the government signaled its intention to liberalize the market A government official in Port Vila recalled that "the policy paper was discussed in Parliament. When we were involved with the court case, revision was undertaken to the Telecommunications Act 1989 to allow granting of licences to new operators" (Respondent 52, fieldwork interviews, 20 August 2008).

Part 3, Section 16, (6) of the Telecommunications Act 1989 states that the Minister has the right to grant a licence for the provision of public domestic and public international telecommunications services provided that at one time in Vanuatu there shall be no more than one telecommunications system in operation to provide public international telecommunications service and no more than one telecommunications system in operation for the public national telecommunications service. Condition 2.1 (Supreme Court of the Republic of Vanuatu 2006) of the franchise agreement between the Government of Vanuatu and TVL stated that:

> "Subject to the terms and conditions of this licence, the Minister hereby grants to the company [TVL] the sole rights…to provide, operate and develop, and the company shall provide, operate and develop, the public telecommunications system of Vanuatu and further to be the exclusive provider of public telecommunications services in Vanuatu".

It was apparent that to terminate the exclusive rights enjoyed by TVL, all stakeholders had to negotiate the terms of the franchise agreement that legally bound the government, Cable and Wireless (UK) and France Telecom. Negotiating to end the franchise agreement, however, as indicated earlier by the experience of Vanuatu's 2001 WTO accession package, was extremely costly for the government. A government official in Port Vila stated that;

> "the prevailing wisdom was that TVL's monopoly was contractually solid. It was thought that because of the franchise agreement, there was absolutely nothing the country could do to liberalize telecommunications unless with the consent of TVL" (Respondent 48, fieldwork interviews, 14 August 2008).

TVL initially requested monetary compensation for any loss of exclusivity. The limited public funds to pay compensation could have compelled the government to pursue negotiation of a deed of settlement. It might not, however, have been the only stakeholder to favor such an option. The other two stakeholders, Cable and Wireless (UK) and France Telecom, could have also incurred risks if they had attempted to protect their exclusive rights through the courts. The franchise agreement was not as "ironclad" as previously thought. A 2000 Privy Council decision from Dominica's Court of Appeal, known as the "Marpin decision", ruled that an exclusive telecommunications monopoly held by Cable and Wireless Dominica Limited infringed on Dominica's freedom of speech as guaranteed by Dominica's Constitution (Court of Appeal 2000). A government official in Port Vila recalled that:

> "Because telecommunications is such a prevalent means of communicating whether business level or personal through faxes or internet, any inhibition amounts to in fact an infringement of the freedom of speech which is guaranteed by the Vanuatu Constitution and very similar to Dominica's

> Constitution. There were also other previous and subsequent court decisions from Europe, Zimbabwe, Canada and the United States which all contributed to a fairly credible argument. Cable and Wireless was on the Marpin Case so they knew the consequence and how the argument would be run" (Respondent 48, fieldwork interviews, 14 August 2008).

A similar defense was arguably possible for the Vanuatu government to exploit if it had to go through the court system.

3.3 Fiji: The Radisson Accord

Pre-competition regulatory framework: 2005 road map

The move for comprehensive regulatory reform in the telecommunications sector was a long-term policy direction tracing back to 2003. A World Bank mission in 2003 and a case study of Fiji's telecommunications sector by the International Telecommunications Union (ITU) in 2004 indicated that the major impediment to the telecommunications sector's performance was exclusive rights (Fiji Ministry of Information, Communications and Media Relations 2005:7). The Laisenia Qarase government's Minister for Information, Communications and Media Relations, Marieta Rigamoto, in a workshop in Suva on the Road Map for Telecommunications Sector Reform in December 2005 acknowledged that:

> "[s]everal analyses indicate that the current sector structure and rigid licensing regime, with technological restrictions—operators with exclusivity in particular market segments such as domestic fixed, international fixed, mobile, and internet—have hampered service provision. The rigid structures impede beneficial use of emerging and quickly changing technologies, and do not take account of convergence between telecommunications, internet and media" (Ministry of Information, Communications and Media Relations 2005:2-3).

Minister Rigamoto also added that the exclusive rights model has "well-known problems of high prices, lack of alternatives and serious deficiencies in service provision in rural areas".

The 2005 Road Map for Telecommunications Sector Reform outlined the updating of the 1998 Telecommunications Policy, establishment of TAF and ending of exclusive licences. The Telecommunications Policy Statement 1998 was the basis for the creation of Amalgamated Telecommunications Holdings (ATH) and the sale of ATH shares to Fiji National Provident Fund (FNPF) and private investors. The policy was also the basis for the Telecommunications Bill 2006 (now passed as Telecommunications Promulgations 2008).

The roadmap for ending exclusive rights in the telecommunications sector encountered two regulatory challenges. First, the structure of the market in Fiji was artificially dissected so that each key sub-sector held exclusive rights: FINTEL held international services, Vodafone held mobile services and TFL held domestic services). Any deregulation plan would therefore involve three different sets of negotiations for the three operators, rather than one. Figure 6-17 illustrates the Fiji market and ownership structure in pre-reform time.

Figure 6-17: Market and Ownership Structure of Fiji's Telecommunications Sector (pre-reform)

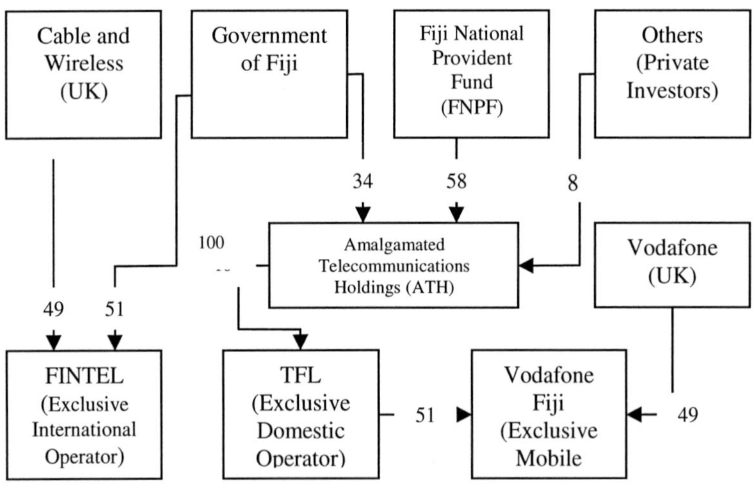

Source: Adapted from International Telecommunications Union 2004:24.

Note: Fiji Government's share in FINTEL is managed by ATH.

A legal dispute ignited in December 2005 between the Government and Vodafone, based on the roadmap's direction for the Government to grant mobile licences to new competitors (High Court of Fiji 2005). Vodafone challenged these plans based on the argument that it had inherited (sub-leased) the exclusive mobile licence from its parent company, TFL. The High Court was, however, unsure about the legality of the inherited exclusive rights as the Telecommunications Act 1989 authorized only the minister to grant a licence. Similar to the Vanuatu negotiations, the Fijian Government used the Marpin case in Dominica (though it was not exploited to its full potential) in the attempt to justify its deregulation roadmap. The High Court's decision of 20 December 2005, and also the Court of Appeal decision of 28 July 2006 both granted decisions favoring Vodafone maintaining its exclusive licence (Court of Appeal 2006).

Deed of settlement: Radisson Accord

The *coup d'etat* led by Commodore Bainimarama in December 2006 catalyzed the progress of the reform. A telecommunications policy expert in Suva recalled that, "when the coup happened, the interim government came in and all of a sudden the process of deregulation was really fast and how the transition took place". (Respondent 54, fieldwork interviews, 14 November 2008). Digicel had expressed interest in entering the market and had been negotiating with the ousted Qarase government. The interim government reopened a tender process. Together with the exclusive rights holders of telecommunications services, the interim government arranged for a conference to negotiate the details of the deregulation. The series of meetings between the stakeholders was held at the Radisson Fiji Resort in Nadi.

The interim government was in no position to grant monetary compensation for prematurely ending the monopoly rights, and hence chose to pursue the negotiations path. The complexity of the market structure meant that a negotiated resolution was going to be difficult to achieve. The deed of settlement was a complex set of arrangements to end the exclusive rights of monopolies and in return, received short transitional periods to prepare for open competition. Vodafone Fiji's exclusive licence for mobile service was to end by 30 September 2008 (about nine months transitional period). Vodafone Fiji in return was to receive a 15-year open licence to operate in any of the sectors (subject to the transitional periods granted to FINTEL and TFL). TFL also received a 15-year open licence but would not be allowed to operate in the mobile service sector "as long it has direct economic interests in Vodafone Fiji Ltd to avoid potential abuse of market dominance" (Baselala n.d). TFL was allowed to establish its own international gateway, but subject to an 18-month transitional period granted to FINTEL, which ended in July 2009. FINTEL also received an open licence and was allowed to operate in all sectors. The new entrant,

Digicel, was granted an open licence to operate in the mobile service sector from October 2008 onwards, subject to the transitional period restrictions offered to the incumbents.

Overall, the Radisson Accord achieved it first objective, which was to end monopoly rights in the telecommunications market. The Radisson Accord is crucial as it sets forth the legal arrangements and responsibilities for all operators and stakeholders in the market to follow for the next fifteen years. The 15-year licence, coupled with other telecommunications principles outlined in the deed of settlement, provided some certainty to the telecommunications sector.

The next section discusses the impact of the telecommunications regulator and the deed of settlement on the credibility of telecommunications regulatory reforms in Samoa, Vanuatu and Fiji.

4.0 The Impact of Independent Regulators and the Deed of Settlement

4.1 Samoa: The Independent Regulator

The outcome of the court dispute[9] did not go down well with government. A government official in Apia hesitantly commented that, "although we did not get the outcome from that case we [wanted]…the regulator acted independently and tried his best in resolving the differences between the two operators" (Respondent 40, fieldwork interviews, 22 July 2008). The WS$1 million court cost was a major blow to public funding, but the fact that a private foreign company took a statutory arm of government to court and won convincingly created some bitterness. A telecommunications operator in Apia recalled that, "there was a bit of bitterness after the court case when we won and the government had to put in money to pay for the court case of WS$1 million. I think that was one of the things that caused bitterness after the court case" (Respondent 42, fieldwork interviews, 23 July 2008).

A regulator official in Apia best captured the general sentiments towards the outcome of the court case by commenting that, "the government

[9] Dispute settlement between the Samoan Government on behalf of the Telecommunications Regulator and Digicel. Digicel appeal's was upheld by Court on the Regulator's decision on interconnection and termination rates.

was concerned about Digicel's appeal against the [Regulator's] Office because it was a cost to government and they [government] wanted to make sure that the services were given at a rate that was affordable to consumers" (Respondent 32, fieldwork interviews, 17 July 2008). Another regulator official in Apia said that "the question of the case... was one of procedure and also I think one of transparency...the government has every right to be shaken up because it is not just Digicel that can take them to court but any entity or player within the sector can take them to court" (Respondent 33, fieldwork interviews, 15 July 2008).

The prospect of potential future litigation against the regulator, indirectly affecting the government, could have forced some consideration of key provisions in the Telecommunications Act 2005 legislation. As one telecommunications operator official in Apia explained, "they [government] are always behind the eight ball, they are always on the back foot, suddenly Digicel litigate, suddenly they won, suddenly it cost the government a WS$1 million debt. Now, they [government] are doubly shy, they don't want to do anything in case there is litigation...they are trying to change the act but it is a little bit too late" (Respondent 34, fieldwork interviews, 15 July 2008).

Amending the Act, however, might not be the ideal solution to the problem as a regulator official in Apia explained:

> "Even if you try to put all these regulatory policies—establish an independent regulator, set up universal funds; competition policy; interconnection agreement; and so on—in place before the market is liberalized, it is only when the market starts to operate that you observe how operators react to the policy framework put in place [and] that you understand how the sector is developing. The principle may be sound but the application of how they are actually designed to work may not yield the outcome that was originally envisaged" (Respondent 34, fieldwork interviews, 15 July 2008).

Nevertheless, Parliament passed an amendment to the Telecommunications Act 2005 in June 2008. The 2008 amendment is important in four fundamental ways. First, an appeal to the order of the regulator may only be made to a Telecommunications Tribunal (Section 11 of Telecommunications Act as amended). The original Section 11 states that an appeal from an order of the regulator may be made only to the Supreme Court. A Telecommunications Tribunal was also to be set up, with a judge or lawyer, to be appointed by the Chief Justice, and two other members. Second, the government was to be exempted from the payment of any costs associated with any tribunal proceedings. Third, the decision of the tribunal is final and binding on all parties. Further, any appeal of the tribunal's decision may not be filed in any court. Fourth, the regulator's discretion in determining interim interconnection charges was further refined to grant more powers to the regulator to determine and impose interim interconnection rates on operators in the case of operators failing to reach an agreement on interconnection within two weeks.

The amendments ensured that any future dispute case against the regulator (and government indirectly), must be settled via a telecommunications tribunal—out of court; the government was exempted from financial penalties; the telecommunications tribunal was final and binding, which limits the possibility of pursuing other legal channels for an appeal; and, the regulator's authority was further strengthened in determining interconnection rates. It is worth noting that Fiji, PNG and Vanuatu adopted a similar line of policy via their telecommunications legislations, as a consequence of the Samoa experience. New entrant Digicel was concerned about the amendments as raised by a telecommunications operator in Apia:

> "Unfortunately, the latest amendment passed by government…we [Digicel] feel that we have been treated unfairly, because we were never approached or given a chance to have an input into the new amendment. The amendment basically gave more power to the independent regulator in determining decisions like interconnection agreements, if the parties cannot resolve it themselves…there is a lot of unhappiness in our company especially at higher management. What we are trying to do now is mend our differences with government as we are not very popular with government at the moment before we proceed forward" (Respondent 42, fieldwork interviews, 23 July 2008).

The outcome of the interconnection dispute highlights three fundamental issues: first, the susceptibility for policymakers to make changes in policies and legislation in order to avoid future litigation costs. The political and fiscal consequences of incurring a WS$1 million public debt for a small island state like Samoa is higher compared to a similar situation in a larger economy.

Second, the dispute highlighted weaknesses in the process of setting up and implementing the regulatory framework in the appropriate sequence—the powers of the regulator could have been clarified and strengthened in the legislation before competition was introduced. A regulator official in Apia explained that:

> "Timing matters. I think that from the experience shown, the political will to liberalize the market often at times overtakes a lot of the regulatory steps that probably needed to be put in place before. So what you often find happening is that legislation needed to liberalize the sector happens and almost as an afterthought, the details of the policy reforms" (Respondent 33, fieldwork interviews, 15 July 2008).

A telecommunications operator official in Apia also echoed similar views:

> "Sometimes policies are implemented before they are finalized. Because there is enthusiasm to get the result—which is to earn some money for government, introduce competition, or reduce prices—they [government] don't even wait for the policy to be properly formulated" (Respondent 34, fieldwork interviews, 15 July 2008).

Third, the capacity of the office of the regulator to deal with complex issues—such as determining interconnection rates, spectrum management, numbering systems, setting up competition policies and to be able to justify the regulator's position during negotiations with operators—was evidently limited but crucially important for its effectiveness. A telecommunications operator official in Apia stated that, "to regulate the telecommunications sector in Samoa, you need a person with great breadth of skills and it is very difficult to find anyone who is willing to come and live in Samoa and do that work" (Respondent 42, fieldwork interviews, 23 July 2008).

The interconnection dispute also highlighted a fundamental challenge of being small, common in all Pacific case studies, which was the limited technical capacity from government to effectively deal with telecommunications issues during and after reform. Vaai (2008) highlighted that:

> "One of the key challenges for the government and the regulator on the telecommunications reform in Samoa is not having enough manpower on the ground, particularly at the ministerial level. There is a limited number of chief executive officers, who deal with several public sector reform programs on top of the telecommunications reform. And retaining their attention to specific issues from the telecommunications sector is a very difficult exercise".

Vaai (2008) also identified the lack of technical expertise which the telecommunications industry can recruit —in the case of Samoa, there was a significant loss of technical level officials from the local telecommunications operator, who were "headhunted" and employed by Digicel. The experience from Samoa highlighted a wider supply-side constraint, of a limited number of skilled people across the industry sectors, common in many other Pacific islands states.

Overall, the case of Samoa shows that regulatory policies have been changed such that they could hamper a private investor's ability to seek legal justice through the court system. Further, I find evidence that the strong political will of the government to move swiftly towards a liberalized market could have come at the cost the independent regulator's office lacking technical experience and financial resources. The resulting uncertainties could lead to more frequent disputes and litigation.

4.2 Vanuatu: The Independent Regulator and the Deed of Settlement

The World Bank facilitated the negotiations over the deed of settlement in Vanuatu. The negotiations took more than 12 months (2006-07). The deed of settlement covered five key principles on regulating telecommunications. First, it was required that TVL forgo the remainder of the term of its protected licence (2008-12). In return, the government agreed to transfer its shares (33.33 per cent) equally between Cable and Wireless (UK) and France Telecom and establish TVL as a private ownership with a 50-50 partnership. Second, the deed of settlement provided for the establishment of a regulator. Third, a universal service fund was to be established from the contributions of all operators, based on a percentage of their annual revenues. Fourth, certain commercial concessions would be made available to all operators—for instance, import duties were to be exempted for all capital goods imports. Fifth, an interconnection agreement was to be established before operations began.

Four issues in the deed of settlement require further discussion. First, both telecommunications operators, particularly the incumbent, were keen on establishing a regulator. A telecommunications operator in Port Vila explained that, "we negotiated aggressively with the government to ensure the establishment of an independent regulator. We wanted a very good referee and a level playing field. Without that, TVL would not have given up its exclusivity rights" (Respondent 51, fieldwork interviews, 20 August

2008). TVL saw the establishment of a regulator's office as protection for them in a competitive environment. Also, TVL was anticipating intense competition from a multinational telecommunications operator, committed to establishing its operational footprint in the Pacific region. A regulator official in Port Vila explained that, "TVL wanted to see a regulatory framework in place, based on fair trading practices. It is unusual for a monopoly to seek that kind of protection, because normally the monopoly is the player that can abuse its dominant market position" (Respondent 45, fieldwork interviews, 11 August 2008).

According to fieldwork respondents, the new competitor also valued the establishment of an independent regulator. A telecommunications operator in Port Vila stated that,

> "setting up a regulatory body the way it has done, making it an independent body has been positive. I think what also is positive in Vanuatu is [the independence of the Office of the Regulator in Vanuatu] there is a danger that a small country may take people to the regulatory body from the current incumbent [state-owned telecommunications operator]. I think that makes the [independent regulator] body less impartial. Whereas here, there is currently an interim regulator but they are training a local one and a very impartial one, which is very positive from our perspective" (Respondent 47, fieldwork interviews, 12 August 2008).

The interim regulator has been effective in areas such as building the office's technical capacity (two local, part-time employees with technical expertise in radio licensing and radio spectrum have been recruited). A website (http://www.telecommunicationsregulator.gov.vu) for the regulator has been established, providing crucial information to the general public on the regulator's policies and decisions. The office has also been effective in providing mediation in negotiations between the incumbent and the new entrant.[10]

Second, the Government drew up an interconnection agreement for the operators to sign before any licence was granted. Normally, the interconnection agreement is negotiated between operators after licences have been granted and is usually a point of dispute between the dominant market player and the new entrant. The Government's initiative in drawing up its own interconnection agreement does appear to minimize

[10] For a full account of the Interim Regulator's operational milestones for 2008, see Vanuatu Interim Telecommunications Regulator's Annual Report 2008.[a]

future disputes between operators. A regulatory official in Port Vila best captured the dynamics of the government's intentions:

> "The Government did something that was quite smart in the process of setting up the licence and the settlement agreement...the government offered the interconnection agreement to TVL and Digicel as part of their commitments in the deed of settlement. Since government compensated TVL by giving up its shares, it asked TVL to be willing to sign the interconnection agreement. Similarly with Digicel, it wanted a licence...and so government was very careful not to grant Digicel a licence until they also agreed to sign this interconnection agreement. There was never a negotiation between TVL and Digicel on the interconnection agreement" (Respondent 45, fieldwork interviews, 11 August 2008).

The pre-setting of an interconnection agreement as part of the deed of settlement was one of the successful regulatory initiatives in the Vanuatu reform. It provided certainty to the market by ensuring that both licensees were aware of the interconnections tariffs to be used. The new telecommunications operator shared this point by saying that:

> "If you did the commercial arrangements as part of the deed of settlement then that would remove any potentially thorny issues and quite difficult negotiation, which can delay on the liberalization process. So I think having put that out of the way removes any potential problems later on. So with that certainty, we invested. On the day of our launch [25 June 2008], we had full connection on voice that provided a level playing field for Digicel to compete with TVL on voice except SMS, but was resolved on 1 July 2008" (Respondent 47, fieldwork interviews, 12 August 2008).

Third, there was opposition to the Government's decision to give up its shares in TVL. As reported by the Vanuatu Daily Post (2 April 2008), "... the decision to give away VT$1 billion shares in TVL was bad business. The opposition questioned the sort of agreement was negotiated with TVL for the acquisition of government interest. They also said that the divesting state assets from highly profitable entities for nothing or negligible benefit is without doubt bad business."

Perhaps crucial to the government's general revenue was the immediate loss of revenue from its shares in TVL. A government official in Port Vila explained that:

> "The government seriously considered the implication of revenue loss from foregoing the shares. However, when we did our analyses, the government found that we would actually be earning more due to the two

telecommunications operators' payment of value-added tax. The licence alone would generate roughly VT50 million. The Deputy Prime Minister [now Prime Minister] presented the Bill and everyone supported it, even the opposition" (Respondent 26, fieldwork interviews, 20 August 2008).

A closer look at the Government's TVL dividend payments, however, reveals a different story (Table 6-14). From 2000 to 2006, TVL paid the government an average of VT$48 million annually. The highest dividend payment recorded was in 2006: VT$103 million. Further, in comparison with the government's general revenue in the period 2000-06, the average revenue contribution by TVL's dividend was a mere 1 per cent of the total annual government revenue.

Table 6-14: Dividends Paid from Telecommunications Vanuatu Limited to Vanuatu Government 2000-2006, (Million Vatu)

Year	Government of Vanuatu's total revenue	TVL dividend paid	TVL Dividend (% of total revenue)
2000	7423	44	0.59
2001	7366	75	1.02
2002	7082	54	0.76
2003	7056	15	0.21
2004	8075	16	0.20
2005	9193	32	0.35
2006	10009	103	1.03
Average over 2000-06	8029	48	1
Percentage value of 7 years average	100	0.6	

Source: Vanuatu National Statistics Office (2009) and Vanuatu Department of Trade (2008).

Further, several stakeholders within government thought that signing a cashless deal was a well-negotiated deal. A government official in Port Vila recalled that:

"Returning the shares was a price of escaping the monopoly, which was disadvantageous to consumers and massively restrictive of national development. So some might think it was a very small price to pay. There

> has been some political comment about the terms of the settlement. In my respectful opinion, those political comments were uninformed. It has to be pointed out that initially, TVL sought monetary compensation for any deregulation of the industry. So to have signed a deal that does not involve any payment by government might be thought to have been well negotiated" (Respondent 48, fieldwork interviews, 14 August 2008).

The Minister responsible for telecommunications, Edward Natapei also played a crucial role in the reform program. A regulatory official in Port Vila stated that Natapei "is the champion of the telecommunications reform in Vanuatu. I don't think that it was widely held in government that telecommunications reform was [necessarily the] right path to go [down] but he held [the] necessary power and commitment to bring it through" (Respondent 45, fieldwork interviews, 11 August 2008).

Fourth, the World Bank and AusAID were instrumental in the reform process. The government had limited technical capacity to negotiate the termination of monopoly rights in telecommunications. AusAID provided valuable assistance in funding legal expertise and capacity building on telecommunications reform—AU$6 million was secured to fund the universal service fund and long-term capacity building and another AU$1.85 million for funding the office of the regulator and supporting staff (Respondent 49, fieldwork interviews, 14 August 2008). The World Bank gave strategic advice on how to approach the reform process and provided assistance on mediation to get the parties talking.

Overall, the negotiations that led to the deed of settlement for ending the monopoly rights of TVL were the vital instruments in providing certainty to the regulatory reform process. From the introduction of competition in March 2008 to enactment of the new telecommunications Act in December 2009, the key responsibilities of the independent regulator were determined by the deed of settlement. The motivation for this unprecedented regulatory move could be well justified, as it allowed instant and ample flexibility for the operators and government to terminate exclusivity and allow competition to flourish without prolonged political debate. The regulatory vacuum, however, could pose institutional uncertainty in the long term when market operators play in a market that is based largely on contractual rather than a mainstream regulatory framework. Further, the problem of supply-side constraints—particularly technical expertise and financial means by government to establish and maintain an independent regulatory body—should be flagged. The effectiveness of the independent regulator depends on the capacity of the office to undertake in-depth economic analyses and modeling of price and cost structures of operators, and its ability to validate price structures and coverage. The financial and technical assistance provided facilitated this process, its long-term sustainability is unclear.

4.3 Fiji – The Independent Regulator and the Deed of Settlement

As mentioned earlier, TAF is not yet operational and the Commerce Commission continues to provide a majority of the regulatory functions in the telecommunications sector. The effectiveness of the Commerce Commission during and after the telecommunications reform has been mixed. One of the early contributions by the Commerce Commission in the move to deregulate the telecommunications market was the determination of the prices of telecommunications services in 2005. A regulatory official in Suva recalled that:

> "Over the years, the operators were never regulated [on prices]; no-one determined the prices of their services. There were a lot of complaints from foreign investors who wanted to come in [but could not], because of the cost of establishing a business was very high and telecommunications [costs] contributed significantly to that high cost. So that triggered the commission to look at the prices of telecommunications charges across the sector and to some extent [it] did manage to reduce the prices of telecommunications overall" (Respondent 57, fieldwork interviews, 20 November 2008).

Mr. Sayed-Khaiyum, Attorney General, Minister for Justice and Acting Minister for Industry, Tourism, Trade and Communication's opening statement on Fiji's WTO Trade Policy Review on 25 March 2009 in Geneva also acknowledged that "the monopoly of this [telecommunications] sector increased the cost of doing business in Fiji and discouraged potential investors from investing in Fiji" (Fiji Government Online 2009[a]:1). A further price review was undertaken in 2008 that resulted in a further reduction in prices.

These reviews, however, raised two fundamental challenges for the commission. First, the financial information made available to the commission by the incumbents on which to base its price determinations was limited. Second, the commission did not have the technical capacity to deal with the complex exclusive arrangements of the three monopoly operators in the price review processes. A regulatory official in Suva described the situation as follows:

> "[The] three operators were interlinked – FINTEL, Vodafone and TFL [sic] on how they operate termination of call charges. So policies were complex and we [Commerce Commission] did not have the technical capacity because when we looked at one of the operator's price lists, we had to look at the other two operator's price lists as well because it affects their profitability too" (Respondent 57, fieldwork interviews, 20 November 2008).

Furthermore, anecdotal evidence from the fieldwork and regulatory policies implemented suggests that political influence hampered the independence of the regulatory body. For example, whether intentional or not, the Telecommunications Promulgation 2008 has not operationalized one fundamental component, the establishment of an independent regulatory body, TAF (as of February 2010). The reasons for the delay were based on administrative and logistical challenges. A government official in Suva explained that "it is in the process of being established with four board members have [sic] been appointed while the chairman remains to be appointed…now that we have a change of minister, the new minister is looking at it" (Respondent 55, fieldwork interviews, 15 November 2008). Perhaps the slow progress is understandable as the powers granted to the independent regulator under the Promulgation are significant—in particular, the power to grant telecommunications licences that was previously held by the minister responsible for telecommunications.

Further, in the period 2008-09, the Commerce Commission encountered internal controversies, including the Chairman's (Mr. Charles Sweeney's) contract being prematurely terminated by the government. The Fiji Times Online reported that Sweeney claimed that his removal from office is "linked to the commission's inquiry into the telecommunications industry. The commission was reported to have conducted an inquiry "on a reference from Mr. Sayed Khaiyum [interim Attorney-General] under section 33[11] of the Commerce Act 1998, in relation to whether the price control order [price determination of 2008] which governs telecommunications should be amended, varied or revoked" (Singh 2009[b]). The chairman claimed that his removal from office appeared to be an attempt by

---

[11] Section 33 deals with the requirement for the commission to report to the minister on 'whether a [price] order should be extended, amended, varied or revoked'.

government to prevent him from "expressing a view in that report whether upon competition in telecommunications was limited, including by reason of any arrangements between ATH, TFL and VFL [Vodafone Fiji Ltd]" (Singh 2009[b]).

The chairman also reportedly disputed his removal from office on legal grounds, claiming "that the Minister had no power to remove a member of the commission except for misbehavior, incompetence, incapacity or failure to comply with obligations not to participate in a decision where a member has a pecuniary interest" (Singh 2009[a]). In a letter to the interim Attorney-General dated 1 March 2009, the Chairman reportedly claimed that "it is clear that your letter [removal letter dated 27 February 2009] does not identify any of the above grounds…it is also clear that none of these grounds exist…your letter is therefore not an exercise of the power of removal" (Singh 2009[b]). Fijilive (2009) quoted the interim Attorney-General saying in response to the reasons for the chairman's departure that, "under the Commerce Act the Minister is authorized to remove anyone in the commission and that is what has happened". The Government has since appointed a new chairperson to the Commerce Commission.

The interim Government's heavy influence on the regulatory body is no surprise since the regulatory body is heavily reliant on public funding. The Commerce Commission was temporarily closed in September 2008 due to lack of funding. The Fiji Times Online (Singh 2009[b]) reported that the commission has "closed down because it does not have funds to pay its staff". It was reported that the commission contacted the Permanent Secretary for Industry, Tourism, Trade and Communications and later the Ministry of Finance but was told that "the commission needed to have a further audit". The ousted chairman of the commission was reported as saying that "the commission has been audited by the Audit Office…using [the] audit process as a means of intimidation of an independent statutory body is unacceptable" (Singh 2009[a]). The heavy reliance on public funding though was solved to some extent when an amendment to the Commerce Act 1998—Commerce (Amendment) Promulgation 2009 passed in January 2009—provided the legal rights for the commission to operate on a self-funding basis and for that purpose to charge fees in respect of the performance of its functions.

About three weeks later, on 16 March 2009, the Telecommunications Price Determination Order 2008 was revoked. "The interim Attorney-

General and Minister responsible for telecommunications signed a notice revoking the price control that was put in place last year after a report was received from the commission" (Fiji Government Online 2009[a]). The interim Attorney-General commented that the market itself will decide on the prices that are to be set within the market. The stakeholders' submissions on the review of the telecommunications pricing order were made between February 2009 and June 2009. Publicly available reports and those in the media provided mixed signals. While government and Vodafone Fiji [12] publicly supported the move, based on pro-competitive economic principles, the Consumer Council of Fiji (2009) and Fiji Daily Post (7 July 2009) had reservations.

The Consumer Council of Fiji (26 February 2009) held the general view that "since the Ministry of Communications has opted for controlled competition by restricting the number of players entering this sector, it is therefore crucial that price control on telecommunications service must remain." Also, the report stated that, "the council would like to see that there was a fair competition and a level playing field. There must be a price ceiling for basic services such as call charges and text messages. The price cap would allow competition within the range. We had seen how promotion by Vodafone Fiji Limited was charging FJ$ 1.98 for a text message despite the price order being put in place by the Commerce Commission". Further, the report stated that:

> "The council believes strongly that companies who are objecting to price control has the intention to increase the price of product gradually, otherwise they would not be objecting to price control. With visibly two major competitors in mobile industry [referring here to Vodafone and Digicel specifically as council is not convinced that Innkk Mobile is a real competition to Vodafone], there is a danger that these companies may be susceptible to price collusion in order to sustain profit margins or survival of the industry" (Consumer Council of Fiji 2009:2-3).

Innkk Mobile is a subsidiary of Vodafone predominantly selling mobile services (handsets, SIM cards and refill cards) using Vodafone's mobile network.

---

[12] Vodafone Fiji Ltd was reported to have filed legal proceedings for judicial review of the price control order (see Vodafone Online Source, 16 March 2009.)

The Fiji case study shows evidence supporting the vulnerability of independent regulatory bodies to political influences. Further, I also find evidence of the credibility of the telecommunications reform in Fiji being supported by the Deed of Settlement (Radisson Accord), the interim military government and the Attorney General.

5.0 Conclusion

Overall, as I have demonstrated, the case study of Samoa provides evidence that political influences through legislative amendments undermined the integrity of the independent regulator and overall credibility of the reform. Similarly, the case study of Fiji provides evidence of capture problems affecting the independence of the regulator. The sources of such capture—the heavy involvement of the Attorney General in the sacking of the Regulator in 2009 and the interim government's lack of urgency to implement the 2008 approved telecommunications legislation with a comprehensive set of responsibilities for the regulator—are unclear, although two examples of anecdotal evidences in the case of Fiji provide useful hints.

First, encountering competition for the first time, it is plausible that one of the incumbent operators (particularly Vodafone Fiji, which enjoyed a monopoly on the mobile service sector) could have pressured the government to "slow down" on its ambitious telecommunications liberalization plan. Second, the military government in Fiji has a history of removing persons speaking against it. The most recent cases are the expulsion of one Australian and two New Zealand journalists in April 2009 for the international coverage against Fiji's military government leader, Commodore Frank Bainimarama (Ligauila 2009). In November 2009, the military government expelled the Australian High Commissioner in Fiji (and also his New Zealand counterpart) arguing that Australia and New Zealand "interfered with Fiji's internal affairs". Hence, the removal of the Chairman (an Australian) of the Commerce Commission for commenting (most probably against) about a government report on telecommunications is potentially a rationale behind his premature job termination. Furthermore, I also find evidence from all Pacific case studies on the limited technical and financial capacity of independent regulators, undermining their overall effectiveness.

The case studies also shed light on six important issues in the early phases of telecommunications reforms worth noting. First, the legislative amendments in Samoa and the design of the new regulatory body in Fiji, TAF, show that these island governments may have moved away from delegation of regulatory powers to independent entities. The heavy political influences in Fiji and specific amendments to the telecommunications act in Samoa indicate a move back to centralizing power back to policymakers—in this case, it is the Minister responsible for Communications. This seems contrary to the commonly accepted regulatory practice prescribed by the literature on telecommunications, finance and banking.

Second, although it is generally recognized by the telecommunications literature that the role of an independent regulator provide some certainty to the reform process, its effectiveness can be hampered by lack of technical and financial capacity. Samoa and Vanuatu initially set up an interim regulator staffed by foreign experts. Vanuatu's regulator relies predominantly on the long-term financing of international donors for its sustainability. All three regulators' offices rely to a great extent on budgets appropriated by parliaments (and donors funding assistance). Given the lack of technical and financial capacity therefore, coupled with susceptibility to regulatory capture, the role of independent regulators in providing credibility is limited.

Third, it is worth noting that donor agencies and international institutions play an important role in facilitating the reform process through providing technical expertise and funding. Through the sharing of information between development agencies, regulatory lessons from each country have been exchanged, which will benefit future reform programs. This is clear from the interconnection dispute in Samoa (which was the first country to reform with World Bank and AusAID involvement), which has provided regulatory lessons for the other countries. The establishment of the interconnection agreement by the Government of Vanuatu prior to granting of a licence as part of the deed of settlement, avoided the interconnection disputes that Samoa initially encountered. The global private telecommunications operator Digicel may also be sharing its local information internationally, as shown by the reluctance to "headhunt" top management officials of incumbents to markets opened later—Papua New Guinea, Tonga, Vanuatu and Fiji—following strong criticism in Samoa.

Fourth, the political will from all governments to intensify and speed up the liberalization process in the early phases of the reform could have led to the bypassing of some regulatory steps that could have been established before opening up of the market. The early regulation of the newly liberalized market in Vanuatu, based predominantly on the legal provisions of the deed of settlement, is a case in point. Another example is Fiji's proposed telecommunications authority—TAF—which was legalized as part of the Telecommunications Promulgation 2008 in January 2008, but had not yet been established (as of February 2010).

Fifth, an issue closely connected to the political commitment by governments to liberalize markets quickly was the use of legal contractual agreements—deeds of settlement—identifying the rights and responsibilities of each stakeholder. The use of contractual agreements was effective in two ways. First, the terms and conditions, including compensation, for breaking exclusive rights of incumbent operators were outlined in the deeds, which legally bound all parties. Second, the responsibilities and legal functions of incumbent operators, competitors and the regulator and other key regulatory principles on telecommunications, such as competition policy, interconnection agreements, numbering systems and spectrum management, were outlined in the deed of settlement. The deed of settlement therefore provided a legal framework within which the sector could operate in the absence of legislation. Vanuatu is a case in point. The use of the deed might have been favored by key stakeholders due to its industry-specific effects; the flexibility for all parties to negotiate and; most importantly, less vulnerability to political debate prolonging the reform process.

Sixth, all three Pacific case studies did not sign a bilateral investment treaty with Ireland. In fact, Fiji's commercial and foreign trade policy does not promote adoption of bilateral investment treaties, predominantly due to the costs imposed on the host state. With no bilateral investment treaty signed between the Pacific case study countries and Ireland, the applicability and future usage of such legal dispute mechanisms is quite limited to Digicel specifically.

The next chapter triangulates through quantitative analyses of the two main variables examined in Chapter 5 (Multilateral Policy Restraint, WTO telecommunications commitments) and Chapter 6 (Domestic Policy Restraint, Independent Regulator). The quantitative chapter not only provides preliminary statistical evidence on the effects of the main variables of the study, but also merges the five case study analyses from Chapters 5 and 6 by allowing comparison between the two main variables through statistical means.

CHAPTER SEVEN

THE CREDIBILITY OF TELECOMMUNICATIONS REFORM: AN EMPIRICAL APPROACH[1]

1.0 Introduction

Taking one step further in the comparative case analyses in the Pacific Islands, this chapter interrogates the impact of WTO telecommunications commitments (multilateral policy restraints) adopted by small island states on the credibility level of telecommunication's regulatory reforms. Based on a revised panel of 160 developing countries, including 26 small island developing states covering the period of 1995-2006, I ran multiple regression analyses to test for the robustness of the impact of WTO telecommunications commitment (multilateral policy restraint) and independent regulator (domestic policy restraint) on the credibility of telecommunications reforms. Bilateral investment treaty (bilateral policy restraint) was also controlled for in the regression analyses. The aim of this chapter is to provide a robust statistical triangulation based on a larger data set sample to substantiate the comparative case studies findings.

The study fundamentally provides a statistical triangulation on the impact of multilateral policy restraints on the credibility level of telecommunications regulatory reforms in small island developing states. The main findings of the statistical analyses reaffirm the empirical propositions observed in the five Pacific Islands case studies results. The study found that controlling for telecommunications reform policy and socio-political, economic and technological factors, there is evidence of a

[1] An earlier version of this Chapter was published as 'The WTO's telecommunications commitments and the credibility of telecommunications regulatory reforms in small island developing states', *Pacific Economic Bulletin*, Volume 24, Number 3, pp. 39-57, 2009, visit
<http://peb.anu.edu.au/pdf/PEB_24_3_Ofa.pdf>.

positive relationship between WTO telecommunications commitment and the credibility of telecommunications reform in small island developing states. In particular, the impact of WTO telecommunications commitment is positively stronger and statistically significant on improving the credibility level of telecommunications regulatory reforms in both developing countries and small island developing states compared to independent regulators. In addition, the study found evidence that being a signatory to a bilateral investment treaty has a statistically significant positive impact on the credibility level of telecommunications regulatory reforms in the larger 160 developing countries, but found no evidence for an impact when 26 small island developing states were controlled.

The analysis in this chapter is divided into three sections. Section 2 discusses the analytical framework, data collection, and variable definitions, followed by Section 3—a discussion on the empirical results and analyses. The last section concludes this chapter.

2.0 Data, Analytical Framework and Variables

2.1 Data

Plagued by lack of statistical data and out-of-date or conflicting data, studying small island states are a challenge for empirical research. In recent years however, improvements in the availability of statistics has led to some progress – most notably, the World Bank's (online) World Development Indicators, the International Telecommunications Union's World's ICT Indicators 2007 and the World Bank's (online) Good Governance Indicators have made several useful policy and economic data sets available for time-series analysis.

This study updates and revises an earlier panel data set on telecommunications policy and regulation compiled by the ITU and World Bank in 2003. Fink et al. (2003) used the data set for analysis of 86 developing countries for the period 1985-99. The data set covered key indicators of telecommunications regulations, market structures and the presence of an independent regulator.

The data set was expanded for the period 1995-2006.[2] Updates of key telecommunications variables were sourced from ITU[3] and World Bank.[4] Missing observations were sourced from government websites, telecommunications operators and national telecommunications regulatory authorities. Other economic, institutional, technological, social, and geographic variables were sourced online from the ADB, IMF, the Commonwealth Secretariat, Freedom House, UNCTAD, and the Fraser Institute.[5] The ADB dataset (accessed online at <http://www.adb.org/Economics/>), provides updated social-economic statistics for most Pacific Islands. Similarly, the IMF (online) provides socio-economic statistics but with a larger coverage in terms of countries included. The IMF statistics can be accessed online via <http://www.imf.org/external/data.htm>. The Commonwealth Secretariat provides statistics and key information about the political economy of small island states (accessed online at <http://www.thecommonwealth.org/Internal/181889/resources/>).

There are more than 60 states[6] with a population of 1.5 million (see Chand 2006:73-74 for a list of 60 "microstates" including some non-sovereign islands states). Due to lack of statistical data on telecommunications and the regulatory variables required for this chapter, the number of the small island developing states sample is limited to 26. The data set contains 160[7] developing countries of which 26 are categorized as small island developing states.[8] Small island developing states are defined based on adaptations from UNCTAD's unofficial list of small island developing states and Commonwealth Secretariat definitions of small states. These are archipelagos with a total population of less than 1.5 million. An exception is made here for the inclusion of Jamaica and PNG. PNG's and Jamaica's foreign and trade policies claim themselves to

---

[2] The PNG, Vanuatu and Fiji telecommunications reform occurred outside this timeframe, while Tonga and Samoa's telecommunications reform took place inside this timeframe. The case study analyses (Chapters 4,5 and 6) however, compensate by analyzing the telecommunications reform from 2006 onwards.

[3] ITU World Telecommunications ICT Indicators 2007 Data set and ITU Telecommunications Report 2006.

[4] World Bank (2009).

[5] Economic Freedom Index Data set.

[6] Although not all 60 states are self-governing and sovereign.

[7] The use of a large developing countries sample is important to ensure the accuracy of measurements used (Monroe 2000:68-69).

[8] Adapted from UNCTAD's unofficial list of small island developing states and Commonwealth Secretariat's categorization of small states.

suffer from the disadvantages of small island developing states. Also, they have traditionally been categorized as small island states by UNCTAD (unofficially); World Bank; WTO and the Commonwealth Secretariat although their populations are more than 1.5 million.

Given the natural challenges of small island states, one is always suspicious of regression results from large scale developing countries studies. Many of these quantitative studies seldom do justice to the special circumstances of small island developing states and how they can affect regression estimates. Understandably, the lack of data on small island developing states means that many are excluded from empirical studies, thereby rendering less information. With the necessary data available to include 26 small island developing states in the panel data set, it was possible to test the credibility of telecommunications reforms via island-interacted variables.

Of the 26 small island developing states, 15 had established independent regulatory bodies to oversee the regulatory and implementation aspects of the telecommunications sector by 2009. Nine island states have signed a telecommunications commitment under the WTO framework while 16 have signed to one or more bilateral investment treaties. Twenty-one island states had introduced competition into the telecommunications sector as of 2009. The key policy characteristics of the 26 small island developing states are outlined in Table 7-15.

Small island developing states in terms of GDP per capita (constant US$ 2000) seem to outperform low and middle income countries as categorized by the World Bank's World Development Indicators (World Bank 2009). However, when divided by geographic regions, the Pacific Islands are by far the smallest in terms of population and smallest economies in terms of GDP per capita.

Table 7-15: Selected Key Telecommunications and Economic Characteristics of Small Island Developing States (2008)

Country name	Region	Population, total	Urban population (% of total)	Land area (sq.km)	GDP per capita US$ constant (2000)	WTO telecom commitment	Independent regulator	Bilateral investment treaty	Competition (controlled2 or 3 players)
Bermuda	North Atlantic	64,000	100	50	..	NO	NO	YES	YES
Marshall Is.	Pacific	66,508	70.7	180	2,066	NO	NO	NO	NO
Dominica	Caribbean	72,793	73.6	750	4,775	YES	NO	YES	YES
Antigua and Barbuda	Caribbean	84,814	30.5	440	10,754	YES	NO	NO	YES
Seychelles	Indian Ocean	85,032	53.9	460	7,408	NO	NO	YES	YES
Tonga	Pacific	100,599	24.5	720	1,621	YES	NO	YES	YES
Kiribati	Pacific	101,860	43.8	810	552	NO	NO	NO	NO
Grenada	Caribbean	108,111	30.8	340	4,313	YES	YES	YES	YES
Micronesia, Fed. Sts.	Pacific	110,961	22.5	700	2,003	NO	NO	NO	NO
St. Vincent and the Grenadines	Caribbean	120,325	46.7	390	3,734	NO	YES	NO	YES
St. Lucia	Caribbean	167,975	27.8	610	4,759	NO	YES	YES	YES
Samoa	Pacific	186,759	22.8	2,830	1,607	NO	YES	NO	YES

Vanuatu	Pacific Region	225,898	24.3	12,190	1,275	NO	YES	YES	YES
Barbados	Caribbean	293,942	39.4	430	8,454[c]	YES	YES	YES	YES
Maldives	Indian Ocean	305,340	36.5	300	3,668	NO	YES	NO	YES
Bahamas, The	Caribbean	331,140	83.5	10,010	15,858[c]	NO	YES	NO	YES
Malta	Mediterranean	409,198	94	320	10,322[a]	NO	YES	YES	YES
Solomon Islands	Pacific Region	495,362	17.6	27,990	731	NO	NO	NO	NO
Cape Verde	Africa	530,269	58.9	4,030	1,447	NO	YES	YES	YES
Comoros	Africa	625,834	28	1,861	371	NO	NO	YES	NO
Bahrain	Middle East	752,789	88.5	710	14,776[b]	NO	YES	YES	YES
Fiji	Pacific	838,205	51.8	18,270	2,246	NO	NO	NO	YES
Mauritius	Indian Ocean	1,262,722	42.4	2,030	4,700	YES	YES	YES	YES
Trinidad and Tobago	Caribbean	1,333,050	12.9	5,130	10,974	YES	YES	YES	YES
Jamaica	Caribbean	2,677,170	53.1	10,830	3,400	YES	YES	YES	YES
Papua New Guinea	Pacific	6,324,097	12.6	452,860	656	YES	YES	YES	YES
Small Island Developing States		679,798[d]	46[d]	21,355[d]	2810[d]				

Low income	21,216,891	31.7	1,295,73 6,911	415
Middle income	74,923,175	48.1	4,259,96 9,264	1,997
High income	33,504,521.1 5	77.5	1,056,33 4,218	28,777
World	129,644,587. 20	49.5	6,612,04 0,394	5,964

Sources: World Bank, various years. World Development Indicators, The World Bank, Washington, DC. Regulatory Variables sourced from ITU, World Bank and respective government sources (online).

Note: [a] most recent available data from 2006, [b] most recent available data from 2005, [c] most recent available data from 2002 respectively, [d] simple average estimate, .. not available

2.2 Analytical Framework

Two restraint policies (multilateral and domestic) were employed to proxy for the credibility of unilateral telecommunications reform. Restraint policies were tested on their own to account for the respective effects on the 160 developing countries. This approach crosschecks the research findings against the literature. To ensure that the particular features of small islands are controlled for, two methods have been adopted. First, a dummy variable for islands was included to proxy for the 26 small island developing states. Second, the restraint policies were interacted with the island dummy to isolate any spurious effects the island dummy might have picked up due to other factors. The use of island-interacted variables cross-checks the estimate results of the larger data set.[1]

Relationships between each of the two policies were tested using ordinary-least-square (OLS) estimates and generalized least squares (GLS) methods. The use of simple OLS was to address outliers within the data set, given that economic, social, political and institutional characteristics of developing countries were large. The use of the GLS method effectively controls for country-wise heteroscedasticity (Fink et al. 2003:453). The efficiency of GLS method compared to OLS was also raised by Greene (2003:217) saying that, "as might be expected, the greater is the dispersion [residuals] across observations [higher heteroscedasticity], the greater the efficiency of GLS over OLS". Greene (2003:217) however argued that even "in the presence of heteroscedasticity, the [ordinary] least squares estimator is still unbiased, consistent, and asymptotically normally distributed." The only problem with heteroscedasticity is increasing residuals when the value of the dependent variable increases. A linear regression model (similar to the model in this research) assume that the residual remain constant.

An initial check using a scatterplot graph of performance variables' residuals indicate a potential heteroscedasticity problem exists for Performance variable 2 is illustrated in Figure 7-21 (Appendix G). Under linear regression assumption, the variance of the dependent variable is expected to be constant. Heteroscedasticity problem exists when the

[1] An '*' is use to denote 'interacted variable'. For example, Islands*Multilateral restraint denotes that the variable 'islands' was interacted with the variable 'multilateral restraint', creating a new dummy variable 'island*multilateral restraint variable'.

variance of the dependent variable is not constant. In other words, the residual values of each performance variable from the regression line differ for every independent variable's value. Hence, we can expect to see the residual errors for a dependent variable increases as the values for an independent variable increases. Through using graphical method, the potential heteroscedasticity problem exists when the scatterplot of residual errors for a dependent variable (performance variables in this case) shows a "triangular residual spread".

The Econometric model

The equation explaining the credibility of telecommunications reform in small island developing countries assume the following basic model specification:

(Equation 1)

$$y_{i,t} = \alpha + \delta year + \beta_1 X_{1i,t} + \varepsilon_{i,t}, \quad i = 1,2,\ldots,N; t = 1,2,\ldots,T,$$

where $y_{i,t}$ is the natural logarithm of performance variable 1 (total number of subscribers per employee) and performance variable 2 (total number of fixed and mobile subscribers per 100 people) in country "i" at time "t". The coefficient α is the constant term while δ coefficient represents time-trend proxy for technological progress. The independent variables "$X_{i,t}$" include all predictor and control variables. The "β_1" is the slope (beta coefficient) for independent variable "$X_{1i,t}$". The "ε" is the error term represent the effect of the variables that were omitted by model. The number of countries included are N=160 countries with number of time-series T=12 years.

A further look at the main predictor and control variables assume the following model specification:

(Equation 2)

$$y_{i,t} = \alpha + \delta year + \beta_1 X_{1i,t} + \beta_2 Islands * X_{2i,t} + \beta_3 C_{3i,t} + \varepsilon_{i,t}$$

where $\beta_1 X_{1i,t}$ is the main predictor variable—multilateral policy restraint (WTO Telecommunications commitment). The $\beta_2 Islands * X_{2i,t}$ show the interacted variable between the islands dummy variable and the main predictor variable (island-interacted variables were also included for two other control variables—independent regulator and bilateral investment treaties). The $\beta_3 C_{3i,t}$ include the following control variables: independent regulator, bilateral investment treaties, competition, institution, interest group, geography, islands, population size and economic standard. The dependent, independent and control variables are discussed further below. Descriptive statistics and sources of each variable are listed in Table 7-16. The inclusions of all other variables therefore assume the following specification:

(Equation 3)

$$y_{i,t} = \alpha + \delta year + \beta_1 WTO_{1i,t} + \beta_2 Islands * WTO_{2i,t} + \beta_3 Ireg_{3i,t} + \beta_4 Islands * Ireg_{4i,t} + \beta_5 Bit_{5i,t}$$
$$+ \beta_6 Islands * Bit_{6i,t} + \beta_7 Comp_{7i,t} + \beta_8 Inst_{8i,t} + \beta_9 IntG_{9i,t} + \beta_{10} Geo_{10i,t} + \beta_{11} Islands_{11i,t}$$
$$+ \beta_{12} Popu_{12i,t} + \beta_{13} GDPPC_{13i,t} + \varepsilon_{i,t}$$

The credibility level of telecommunications regulatory reform is the dependent variable ($y_{i,t}$). If the regulatory reform process is credible, we should see better telecommunications sector performance and vice versa. The credibility level is therefore roughly measured by telecommunications sector performance. The study adopts similar variables to those used in the earlier study by Fink et al. (2003). Sector performance is proxied via internal (productive) efficiency within operators and allocative efficiency across the whole sector.[2] Productive efficiency (Performance variable 1) is proxied by the total number of subscribers per employee. This measure provides a limited indicator of the internal efficiency of rendering quality services subscribers. We therefore expect that a higher number of subscribers per employee roughly indicate that efficiency is higher.

Allocative efficiency (Performance variable 2) is measured by a crude, commonly used measure – namely, the total number of fixed and mobile subscribers per 100 people. This ratio roughly indicates the network allocations for expansion throughout a country. We would therefore expect

[2] See Flacher and Jennequin (2008) for a recent discussion on the efficiency concept in telecommunications.

that a higher ratio indicates a higher resource allocation to network expansion and investment. The use of this measure ensures that the major part of the telecommunications sector's activity is accurately reflected. Added-value services (internet services) were not included due to acute lack of up-to-date and consistent country data, particularly for small island developing states.

Obviously, these two performance variables have limitations, which Fink et al. (2003:445) have touched on. Nevertheless, the two proxies are available as time series for a large number of countries. Fink et al. (2003) used 86 developing countries for the period 1985-99 while I use 160 developing countries for the period 1995-2006. In addition, by no means do the two performance indicators mirror performance.[3] Pair-wise correlations between the two restraint policies and the two performance variables show that Performance variable 1 (0.41 for multilateral restraint and 0.34 for domestic restraint) denotes higher pair-wise correlations of the two variables. [4] The analyses from this chapter therefore emphasize the OLS and GLS estimates for Performance variable 1 while using Performance variable 2 estimates to crosscheck the results.

---

[3] Refer to the bivariate scatterplots/kernal density graph (Figure 7-18) for comparison of pair-wise correlations.

[4] Pair-wise correlations for Performance variable 2 show 0.35 for multilateral restraint and 0.14 for domestic restraint.

Table 7-16: Descriptive Statistics for Dependent and Independent Variables

Variable name	Variable description	Obs.	Mean	Standard deviation	Min.	Max.	Source
Dependent Variables							
Performance Variable 1	Total number of subscribers per employee (log)	1520	4.8	1.09	1.90	7.79	World Bank online and ITU (2007)
Performance Variable 2	Total number of fixed and mobile subscribers per 100 population (log)	1832	2.30	1.74	-3.28	5.22	ITU (2007)
Independent Variables							
Multilateral restraint	1 = WTO commitment on telecommunications sector, 0 = no commitment	1920	0.36	0.48	0	1	WTO online source.
Islands*Multilateral Restraint	1 = WTO commitment on telecommunications and islandness, 0 = otherwise.	1920	0.03	0.19	0	1	UNCTAD; WTO; Commonwealth Secretariat; World Bank online

Control Variables							
Domestic restraint	1 = independent regulator, 0 = no independent regulator	1878	0.50	0.50	0	1	Fink et al. (2003); World Bank online; ITU (2007)
Islands*Domestic Restraint	1 = independent regulator and islandness, 0 = otherwise.	1878	0.04	0.21	0	1	UNCTAD; ITU; Commonwealth Secretariat; World Bank online
Bilateral restraint	Total Aggregate number of Bilateral Investment Treaties (log)	1573	2.03	1.12	0	4.45	UNCTAD online source.
Islands* Bilateral restraint	Total aggregate number of bilateral investment treaties (log) signed and islandness	1573	0.13	0.47	0	3.40	UNCTAD; Commonwealth Secretariat; World Bank online
Competition	1 = Competition in mobile and/or local services; 0 = no competition (Fink et al, 2003 and World Bank)	1915	0.46	0.49	0	1	Fink et al. (2003); ITU (online) and World Bank Regulatory Source

Institution (Corruption Free)	Perception of corruption in business and government environments: 100 = most corrupted, 0 = free from corruption (log)	1497	1.82	0.40	-0.51	2.30	Index of Economic Freedom (online source)
Interest group pressure	Percentage of total population in urban areas (square root)	1920	6.84	1.74	2.68	10	World Bank online
Islands	Small island developing states	1920	0.16	0.36	0	1	UNCTAD; Commonwealth Secretariat; World Bank online
Geography	Absolute (latitude of capital)/90	1920	0.24	0.16	0.01	0.66	CIA Factbook (online)
Population (Country Size)	Total population per year (log)	1875	15.30	2.20	3.28	20.99	World Bank online
Time Dummy (Technological Progress)	Year (1995-2006)*Country	1920	0.08	0.27	0	1	Fink et al. (2003)
GDPPC (Economic Standard)	GDP per capita US$ constant 2000 (log)	1768	7.16	1.34	4.03	10.44	World Bank online

The hypothesized explanation for the varied performances of telecommunications sectors is the use of multilateral policy restraints ($\beta_1 WTO_{1i,t}$). Multilateral policy restraints impose regulatory restraints that limit the policy discretion of policymakers, thereby establishing a credible policy environment for investment. While independent regulators have been used to establish credible telecommunications reform, I argue that through WTO's telecommunications commitments, governments can provide a more credible reform policy than the domestic independent regulator in small island developing states. The legal effects of WTO commitments therefore strengthens unilateral reforms in island states. Independent regulators on the other hand are governed by domestic legislation which can be amended by policymakers if sufficient incentives exist. A multilateral commitment that is legally binding is difficult to renege on and costly[1] for smaller island states. I also included a variable indicating that where a country has signed on to a bilateral investment treaty this is included as another control variable since it poses similar international legal obligations to the WTO commitments.

The WTO commitment on telecommunications agreements ($\beta_1 WTO_{1i,t}$) made by member countries in the telecommunications sector since 1997[2] was quantified based on a dummy variable for which 1 = country made a commitment in the telecommunications sector and 0 = no commitment (Keck and Djiofack-Zebaze 2009:11; Buthe and Milner 2008:748). Countries that are not WTO members or are currently undergoing the accession process were marked with "no commitment". Information on years of commitment was sourced online from the WTO.[3]

To account for the effects of other factors, five categories of control variables were used: domestic telecommunications reform policy, bilateral policy restraint, socio-political factors, economic and technological development and a geography variable.

Domestic policy restraint ($\beta_3 Ireg_{3i,t}$) is a measure of the impact of domestic regulatory institutions on telecommunications sector

---

[1] International reputation, financial and political costs vary across countries.

[2] First round of telecommunications sector negotiations was launched at the WTO.

[3] See WTO's Telecommunications Service, <http://www.wto.org/english/tratop_e/serv_e/telecommunications_e/telecommunications_e.htm>

performance. Domestic credibility is realized when governments grant independent entities authority to regulate telecommunications policies outside the government's policymaking boundaries. A dummy variable for the establishment of an independent regulator therefore has a value of 1, while the existence of a regulator that is not independent = 0, as in Maiorano and Stern (2007:169). This dummy variable is a proxy for "strong country institutions" (Maiorano and Stern 2007:168). Information on the independence of regulators was extracted from Fink et al. (2003) and updated based on the ITU's online sources, and the online sources of respective regulators.

To control for bilateral policy restraints ($\beta_5 Bit_5$) on telecommunications sector performance, the cumulative number of bilateral investment treaties (Bilateral investment treaties) signed by a country at the end of a given year (Buthe and Milner 2008:748) was chosen. The use of cumulative numbers reflects the signaling effect of bilateral investment treaties for a safe investment environment (Kim 2006; Tobin and Rose-Ackerman 2005; Neumayer and Spess 2005). The log of the total aggregate number of bilateral investment treaties signed was taken to normalize data set distribution. The information on the bilateral investment treaties indicator was sourced online from UNCTAD.[4]

The introduction of competition ($\beta_7 Comp_{7i,t}$) in the telecommunications sector is another important control variable for telecommunications regulatory reform. The choice of this particular reform policy is based on the fact that it has consistently been found to influence strongly and positively telecommunications sector's performance (Maiorano and Stern 2007: 165-181; Armstrong and Sappington 2006[a]: 325-366; Fink et al. 2003:443-466). In addition, unlike privatization, developing countries have adopted competition policy more willingly (see Chapter 2 for discussion on telecommunications literature).[5] Privatization policy, on the other hand, has been partially adopted (corporatisation) in many developing countries (Fink, et al. 2003:2). Competition is therefore presently the most influential reform policy and therefore the most appropriate indicator for telecommunications regulatory

[4] See UNCTAD Investment Instruments Online at <http://www.unctadxi.org/templates/DocSearch____779.aspx>

[5] The other major telecommunications policy reform vigorously analyzed in the telecommunications policy literature.

reform in small island states. Furthermore, the experience of telecommunications regulatory reforms in the Pacific shows that introduction of competition has been the major policy focus while privatization seems to be less forthcoming. The Competition dummy therefore is quantified with 1 = introduced competition in the telecommunications sector and 0 = otherwise. The competition variable reflects competition in both mobile and /or fixed-line services. The objective is to control for any effects of introduced competition.

Two socio-political factors were included. The first is the extent of corruption[6] taken as a proxy for institutional quality ($\beta_8 Inst_{8i,t}$). It is well documented that corruption hinders foreign direct investment (Cuervo-Cazurra 2006; Wei 2000; Kaufmann 1997). Moreover, corruption results in the inefficient allocation of resources towards areas that are more prone to bribery (Mauro 1998, cited in Cuervo-Cazurra 2006:808). A "Freedom from Corruption" indicator was sourced online from the Heritage Foundation[7] - Index of Economic Freedom. The Index of Economic Freedom is constructed from 10 "freedoms" including freedom from corruption. The Freedom from Corruption Index is derived from Transparency International's Corruption Perceptions Index (CPI).[8] The CPI is scaled so that a score of 10 indicates very little corruption and a score of 1 indicates a very corrupt government. The freedom from corruption index also adopts this scaling; however, the raw CPI data are multiplied by 10 to obtain the freedom from corruption score (Beach and Kane 2008:52).[9] The quantitative analyses in this chapter revert to the original CPI score and, to avoid confusion on reading the regression

---

[6] Corruption understood as the 'abuse of public office for private gains'

[7] <http://www.heritage.org/Index/Default.aspx> , a US research institute founded in 1973 to undertake policy research on issues pertinent to the American principals and values.

[8] For further information on CPI, visit Transparency International's website, < http://www.transparency.org/policy_research/surveys_indices/cpi/2009>

[9] The Index of Economic Freedom contain 10 components of which freedom from corruption index is one of them. Hence, as a methodological approach to granting equal weights between the 10 components, each component's raw CPI index was multiplied by 10. Beach and Kane (2008) justification was to ensure that no one component dominates the overall index for a particular country as the objective is to provide a general snapshot of each country's economic freedom but not an indicator for economic growth.

coefficients, I have recoded the corruption measure to show that a high corruption index number means little corruption and vice versa.[10]

Second, whether telecommunications sector performance was influenced by domestic business interest group ($\beta_9 IntG_{9i,t}$) lobbying. The square root of urban population as a percentage of total annual population is used as measure of interest group pressure on telecommunications infrastructure deployment.[11] The more urbanized a country, the higher are the pressures from interest groups (business interest groups) for telecommunications reform (Henisz and Zelner 2006:266-268; Li et al. 2005:1309).

It is argued that geography ($\beta_{10} Geo_{10i,t}$) negatively affects economic development.[12] Nearly all countries geographically located at 23 degrees north and south of the equator are poor, while almost all countries in the higher latitudes are rich (Sachs 2001:1; Gallup et al. 1999:180). The "cursed" tropical regions are often disadvantaged by distance from major markets, scarcity of natural resources and high transportation costs due to populations being concentrated inland rather than on the coast (including landlocked countries). Sachs (2001:10-19) argues that geography negatively affects labor productivity through tropical infectious diseases, low soil fertility for farming (due to heavy precipitation), large numbers of tropical pests and diseases that affect farming systems and acute shortages of water for agriculture.[13] Almost all 26 small island developing states in the sample are located in the tropics. Geography is quantified by absolute latitudinal location of capital cities from the equator (Rodrik et al. 2004).

The technological nature of the telecommunications sector does, however, alleviate some of the geographic challenges of small island states

---

[10] See Wei (2000:3) for similar methodology adopted.

[11] The data for urban population is not in a normal distribution and tend to skew to the left side, hence, square root of data is used to normalized the distribution. This is considered extremely important to the validity and accuracy of the overall estimation and model specifications.

[12] See Easterly and Levine (2003) for discussion on the geography hypothesis. For geography hindering growth prospects, see Gibson 2007; Armstrong and Read 2006; Easterly and Kraay 2000.

[13] Refer to Acemoglu et al (2001) in Chapter 2 for discussions on the impact of diseases on colonization, institutional structure and development. Also, see Barro (2001) for cross-country study and the determinants of economic growth.

granted that the appropriate regulatory policies ensure universal access. In addition, an island dummy variable ($\beta_{11}Islands_{11i,t}$) is included for small island developing states, with 1 = island while 0 = otherwise. This is a necessary control variable for "islandness". To isolate any spurious effects, the island dummy variable might pick up in the regressions, interacted variables between the island dummy and the main predictor policy variables are also included (($\beta_2 Islands * WTO_{2i,t}$),($\beta_4 Islands * Ireg_{4i,t}$),($\beta_6 Islands * Bit_{6i,t}$)).[14]

Technological development is a key ingredient for the development and effectiveness of telecommunications services. It is therefore crucial to control for technological development in the estimates. A time dummy[15] ($\delta year$) is included to account for the effects of technological developments and diffusion in the telecommunications sector (as in Maiorano and Stern 2007; Fink et al. 2003). It is expected that its effect will be positive and strong.

Two economic control variables were included. First, the natural logarithm of total population per country ($\beta_{12}Popu_{12i,t}$) was included to control for country size (Frankel and Romer 1999). Second, the natural logarithm of GDP per capita (constant US$ 2000) was used as a measure of economic performance ($\beta_{13}GDPPC_{13i,t}$), (as in Maiorano and Stern 2007; Cubbin and Stern 2006; Estache et al. 2006; Waverman, Meschi and Fuss 2005).

3.0 Empirical Results

The relationships between multilateral ($\beta_1 WTO_{1i,t}$), domestic ($\beta_3 Ireg_{3i,t}$) and bilateral ($\beta_5 Bit_5$) policy restraints on telecommunications sector performance ($y_{i,t}$) was first checked through

---

[14] Much of the literature on telecommunications policies has focused on developing countries or LDCs but none have systematically isolated and estimated small island developing states grouping.

[15] Each year was allocated with a time dummy. For full specification and coefficient's estimates of time dummies, refer to Table 7-24, Appendix I.

the use of simple scatter plots/kernel density graphs.[16] Figure 7-18 shows correlations between restraint policies and the two performance variables. As indicated by the kernel density graphs, there is a noticeable difference between the means when the multilateral policy restraint (x) is not present ($mean(y \mid x = 0)$) compared with when it is present ($mean(y \mid x = 1)$).

The kernel density graph therefore provides a useful graphical display of the positive correlation between multilateral policy restraint and performance variables, when multilateral policy restraint is present (mean (y | x=1).[17] The kernel density graph for domestic policy restraint shows similar positive correlations with the performance variables, when domestic policy restraint is present.

One noticeable difference in the pair-wise correlations between the two sets of independent variables (multilateral and domestic policy restraints) and the two performance variables is that the two sets of independent variables are highly correlated with Performance variable 1, as shown by the distinct difference of the two (dotted and solid) lines. On the other hand, the pair-wise correlations between the two sets of independent variables and Performance variable 2 are much weaker, as shown by the difference between the two lines. This suggests that Performance variable 1 reflects sector performance better than Performance variable 2. Moving on from comparison of uncontrolled bivariate scatter plots, I undertook first stage multiple regression analyses. Table 7-17 encapsulates simple multiple OLS (Models 1 and 3) and GLS (Models 2 and 4) estimates on the two performance variables.[18] Models 1 and 2 are regression estimates on Performance variable 1 while Models 3 and 4 are estimate results on Performance variable 2.

---

[16] The multilateral and domestic restraints variables are best depicted using kernel density graphs since both indicators are dummy variables. When a data contain non-sequencing order or does not assume normal distribution (nonparametric statistics), for instance—dummy variable with yes or no values or categorical variables with properties such as city names, ethnic background or gender—the commonly used histogram graph to showing data distribution is redundant. Kernel density graphs are effective with nonparametric statistics as they smooth samples and provide a smooth probability function which in general reflect better the underlying variable.

[17] Depicted by the solid line shifting to the right of the kernel density graph, when multilateral policy restraint is present.

[18] For a panel dataset, correcting for Heteroscedasticity.

Figure 7-18: Bivariate Correlations Kernel Density/Scatterplots Graphs – 160 Developing Countries

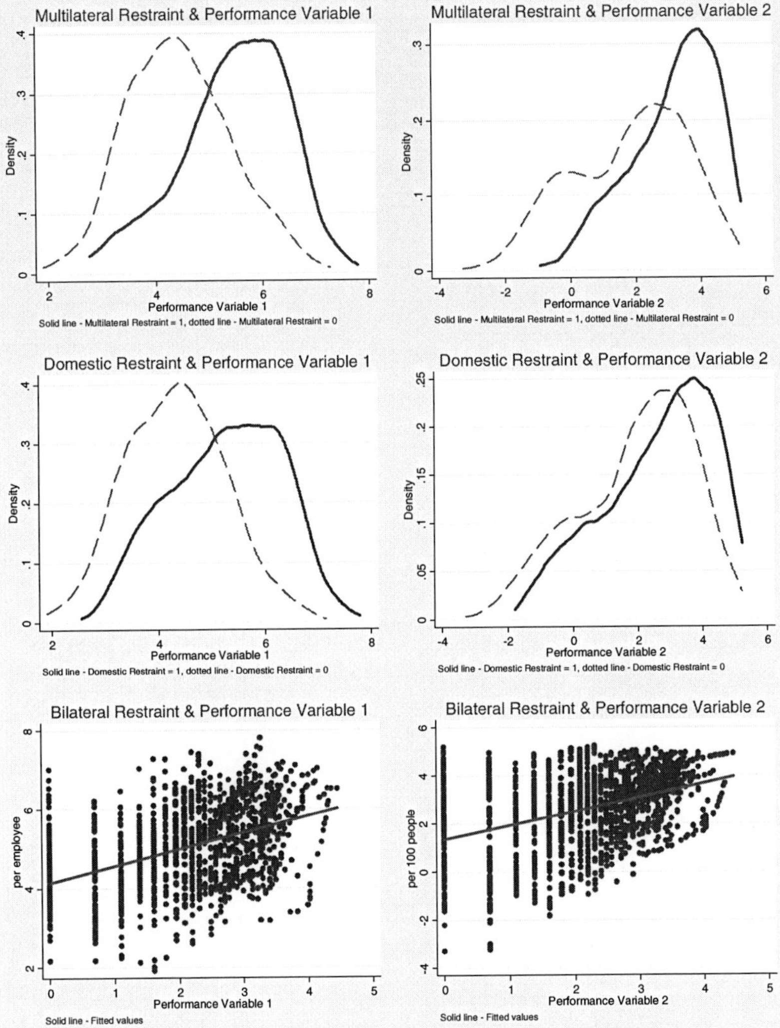

Source:Panel dataset compiled from World Bank (2003) & ITU online sources

Table 7-17: OLS and GLS Regression Results (160 Developing Countries)

	Performance variable 1		Performance variable 2	
	(1) OLS	(2) GLS	(3) OLS	(4) GLS
Multilateral policy restraint	0.18 *** (0.04)	0.17 *** (6.61)	0.27 *** (0.04)	0.22 *** (8.35)
Multilateral policy restraint*Islands	0.20 (0.16)	0.13 (1.53)	0.57 *** (0.18)	0.53 *** (4.83)
Domestic policy restraint	0.15 *** (0.04)	0.16 *** (6.32)	0.21 *** (0.05)	0.16 *** (6.07)
Domestic policy restraint*Islands	0.11 (0.17)	0.04 (0.37)	-0.18 (0.20)	-0.23 ** (-2.14)
Bilateral policy restraint	0.08 *** (0.02)	0.11 *** (7.43)	0.17 *** (0.03)	0.18 *** (12.27)
Bilateral policy restraint*Islands	-0.19 *** (0.09)	-0.13 *** (-3.05)	-0.44 *** (0.10)	-0.37 *** (-6.98)
Competition	0.26 *** (0.05)	0.21 *** (7.83)	0.06 (0.05)	0.06 ** (2.09)
Institution	0.17 *** (0.06)	0.16 *** (5.52)	0.18 *** (0.07)	0.20 *** (5.19)
Business Interest group pressure	0.04 ** (0.02)	0.04 *** (4.57)	0.15 *** (0.02)	0.15 *** (13.06)
Geography	-0.52 *** (0.12)	-0.60 *** (-8.38)	1.98 *** (0.15)	1.97 *** (26.56)
Islands	0.05 (0.18)	0.03 (0.39)	1.24 *** (0.21)	1.14 *** (11.90)
Population	0.06 *** (0.01)	0.06 *** (9.31)	-0.03 *** (0.01)	-0.04 *** (-4.97)
GDPPC	0.39 *** (0.03)	0.38 *** (23.40)	0.64 *** (0.03)	0.49 *** (0.11)

Constant	-0.24	-0.01	-4.56 ***	-4.51 ***
	(0.28)	(-0.09)	(0.32)	(-23.80)
Wald Chi-squared	n/a	7637.80	n/a	18801.55
Observations	1051	1051	1232	1232
Adjusted R-squared	0.72	n/a	0.82	n/a
VIF (Mean)	2.84	n/a	2.99	n/a

Sources: Panel data set compiled from World Bank, 2003, World Development Indicators, The World Bank, Washington, DC; ITU online sources and respective government data sources.

Notes: * significant at 10 per cent; ** significant at 5 per cent; *** significant at 1 per cent; time dummy is included in the regressions but not reported; n/a: not applicable; Robust standard errors in columns 1 and 3 in parentheses; GLS corrected z-statistics in columns 2 and 4 parentheses.

To begin with, the multilateral policy restraint ($\beta_1 WTO_{1i,t}$) coefficient is consistently positive and statistically significant at 1 percent across robust OLS and GLS estimates in both Performance variable 1 (0.18 and 0.17) and Performance variable 2 (0.27 and 0.22).

In comparison, the domestic policy restraint ($\beta_3 Ireg_{3i,t}$) coefficients are positive and significant but weaker coefficients (0.15 and 0.16 for Performance variable 1; 0.21 and 0.16 for Performance variable 2).[19] As expected, WTO's multilateral agreements with their legal obligations strengthen domestic telecommunications reforms by locking in policies. On the other hand, the domestic policy restraint coefficients show a positive and statistically significance relationship for the two performances variables. The weaker coefficient estimates for the domestic policy restraint show its vulnerability to regulatory capture on instilling credibility when compared to multilateral policy restraint coefficients.

As expected, bilateral policy restraint variable ($\beta_5 Bit_5$) positively influences the performance of the telecommunications sector in developing countries. This result is in line with the literature on the positive impact of bilateral investment treaties on foreign direct investment inflows. While the bilateral policy restraint variables have

[19] The regression coefficients for the main predictor including the other two policy restraints were standardized for easy cross-comparisons. The standardized beta weights (not reported) indicate that the Multilateral Restraint consistently reflects the strongest unique contribution compared to the other two policy restraints.

statistically significant regression coefficients for both performance variables, they are, however, lower than for the other two restraint variables' coefficients (0.08 and 0.11 for Performance variable 1; 0.17 and 0.18 for Performance variable 2).

A further examination of the main explanatory variables yields two important results. First, there is a strong positive relationship between the external policy restraints—WTO commitments and bilateral investment treaties adopted by developing countries—and their telecommunications sector performance under competition. Second, the impact of domestic policy restraints adopted by developing countries (establishing of an independent regulator) is diminished (as reflected by regression coefficient "r") when the two external policy restraints are added to the model specification. These anecdotal results suggest that external policy restraint plays an important role in establishing stronger credibility.

The islands interacted multilateral policy restraint ($\beta_2 Islands*WTO_{2i,t}$) estimates show positive regression coefficients for the two performance variables. Performance variable 1 show positive coefficients (0.20 and 0.13) while Performance variable 2 shows positive coefficients (0.57 and 0.53) and are statistically significant at 1 per cent. This estimated result provides an important cross-check and control for the independent effects of the island variable within 160 developing countries. Looking closer into the two independent variables, the OLS and GLS estimates for the island-interacted multilateral restraint variable show stronger regression coefficients (0.20 and 0.13 for Performance variable 1; 0.57 and 0.53 for Performance variable 2) compared to the island-interacted domestic restraint variable ($\beta_4 Islands*Ireg_{4i,t}$) with lower regression coefficients (0.11 and 0.04 for Performance variable 1; -0.18 and -0.23 for Performance variable 2).

The island interacted policy variables coefficients are generally similar to the 160 developing countries policy restraints variables. As expected, the estimated results show positive relationships between the multilateral policy restraints (in the 160 developing countries and the islands-interacted policy restraints coefficients) and the credibility of unilateral telecommunications reforms in small island developing states. The domestic policy restraint coefficients produced a statistically significant result at 1 per cent level, although were dramatically lower than the multilateral policy restraints coefficients.[20]

The island interacted bilateral policy restraint variable ($\beta_6 Islands * Bit_{6i,t}$), interestingly, shows a negative relationship (-0.19 and -0.13 for Performance variable 1; and -0.44 and -0.37 for Performance variable 2) on performance. By contrast, the bilateral policy restraint variable estimates show positive and mostly statistically significant results at 1 per cent level (0.08 and 0.11 for Performance variable 1; 0.17 and 0.18 for Performance variable 2). This preliminary result is contrary to the literature on bilateral investment treaties and its positive effect on foreign direct investment in developing countries.

This preliminary results show that signing of bilateral investment treaties by small island developing states may not adequately provide credibility for unilateral telecommunications reforms. Three probable causes come to mind in explaining this contradictory result. First, small island developing states signatory to bilateral investment treaties is extremely low compared to larger developing countries (refer to discussions in Chapter 2, Section 4.3 Bilateral Investment Treaties). The participation and therefore reflection of small island developing states in bilateral investment treaty's dataset is insignificant. Hence, it is highly likely that empirical studies, which comprehensively control for small island developing states will result in 'negative' signs coefficients for bilateral investment treaties.

Second, the costs of signing to Bilateral investment treaties are extremely high for small island developing states (Aisbett 2007, 2008). Hence, several small island developing states are reluctant to sign bilateral investment treaties which usually impose costs of protection on the host country. Third, small island developing states are hampered with "supply-side constraints" (refer to discussions of the characteristics of smallness in Chapter 2). There are very few feasible domestic investors that are capable of competing in the international market or specifically in another developed market. Hence, there is always reluctance to sign bilateral investment treaties that may only protect a developed country's investments in a small island developing state (with all costs of protection borne by the host), while small island developing states have limited or no foreign direct investment in the developed country's market (Fiji is a good

[20] Coefficients were standardized for comparison.

example of not signing any bilateral investment treaty based on this rationale). Hence, the benefits of such treaty are "one-way" towards the developed country's investment interests.

The contradictory result on bilateral investment treaties call for greater consideration on the empirical treatment, analyses and generalization of large n-samples of developing countries findings to small island developing states. Two important issues stem from the bilateral investment treaties estimated results. First, the overall contribution of bilateral investment treaties to providing credibility on telecommunications reform is, at best, minimal in larger developing countries. Second, the island interacted variable estimates did not show any evidence of positive impact of bilateral investment treaties on telecommunications sector performance.

Looking at the overall effect of the simple ($\beta_1 WTO_{1i,t}$ = 0.22) and island-interacted ($\beta_2 Islands * WTO_{2i,t}$ = 0.53) coefficients from the GLS estimation for Performance variable 2 in Equation 4, we would predict the impact of multilateral policy restraint[21] to be (0.22 + 0.53) = 0.75. On the other hand, while we expect domestic policy restraint to work for developing countries overall ($\beta_3 Ireg_{3i,t}$ = 0.15), when controlling for islandness—the island-interacted domestic policy coefficient ($\beta_4 Islands * Ireg_{4i,t}$ = -0.22)—the overall impact is less pronounced (0.15 + -0.22) = -0.07. Hence, it provide anecdotal evidence that the present of domestic policy restraint (independent regulators) in small island developing states is less effective in imposing telecommunications reform credibility.[22] Evidence from the Pacific cases studies discussed in Chapter 5 and 6 provide support and possible explanations to the inadequacy of independent regulators.

Addressing the other control variable in the model, the fitness of the estimates is fairly robust as indicated by the statistical significance of many control variables across OLS and GLS estimates. The

---

[21] Controlling for islandness.

[22] Performing a similar exercise to the Bilateral restraint policy overall estimate shows a less pronounced result (($\beta_6 Islands * Bit_{6i,t}$) = -0.37 + ($\beta_5 Bit_5$) = 0.18) = -0.19, compared to the multilateral policy restraint overall estimate.

telecommunications reform policy indicator ($\beta_7 Comp_{7i,t}$) is positive (0.26 and 0.21 for Performance variable 1; 0.06 and 0.06 for Performance variable 2) and mostly statistically significant at the 1 per cent level. This result is expected, as unilateral competition policy introduces private operators to the market, which results in better sector performance.

The Socio-political variables (Institution and business interest group pressure) show positive relationships with performance. Freedom from corruption ($\beta_8 Inst_{8i,t}$), as a limited indicator for integrity of governments (institutional quality), has positive and statistically significant coefficients for both performance variables (0.17 and 0.16 for Performance variable 1; 0.18 and 0.20 for Performance variable 2). This result aligns with the literature on corruption and investment—lower corruption leads to higher foreign direct investment in telecommunications.[23] Similarly, the business interest group pressure variable has positive and statistically significant results (0.04 and 0.04 for performance variable 1; 0.15 and 0.15 for performance variable 2)—all statistically significant at the 5 per cent level. This result is in line with the literature on the positive impact of interest group pressures[24] (proxy by the higher urban population ratio) on telecommunications infrastructure deployment.

The economic control variable ($\beta_{13} GDPPC_{13i,t}$) is positive and statistically significant (0.39 and 0.38 for Performance variable 1; 0.64 and 0.49 for Performance variable 2). The high regression coefficients, compared with most other variables in the model, are understandable, as income and sustainable economic activities generally determine private telecommunications operators' investment strategies. Population as a proxy for country size ($\beta_{12} Popu_{12i,t}$), is also positive and statistically significant for performance variable 1 (0.06 and 0.06), suggesting economies of scale. Although not reported, the proxy variable for technological development a time dummy ($\delta year$) is positive and statistically significant on both of the performance variables. As expected,

---

[23] The assumption is that, if there is a credible telecommunications reform policy environment, it is expected that performance increases (increase network deployment—coverage and total subscribers per 100 people). Increased number of subscribers and coverage indirectly reflects increased investment on capital investment and infrastructure by telecommunications operator in the sector.

[24] Specifically for business interest groups.

"geography"($\beta_{10}Geo_{10i,t}$) has a negative relationship with performance (-0.52 and -0.60 for Performance variable 1). The estimated results suggest that geographical disadvantages may provide less incentive for foreign direct investment.

3.1 Robustness Checks

With respect to the overall significance of the statistical estimates, three issues are worthy of note. First, examining the significant of the model as a whole shows that overall—we can reject the null hypothesis, at 1 per cent significance, that the effects of the independent variables did not happen by chance. The F Test was used to test the significance of the whole model. That is, the model is considered statistically better than would be expected by chance. Hence, we reject the null hypothesis of no linear relationship of "Y" to the independent variables within the model.

Also, multiple OLS estimates explain a high percentage of the variation of Performance variable 1 (adjusted-R^2 = 0.72) and Performance variable 2 (adjusted-R^2 = 0.82). Second, multicollinearity is of minimal concern, as shown by the low variance inflation factors (VIF) of the OLS estimates from 1.31 to 5.84 (mean VIF = 2.84) for Performance variable 1, and 1.26 to 6.29 (mean VIF = 2.99) for Performance variable 2. As a general rule, an individual VIF level of more than 10 requires attention (Castillo 2007:146-147; Szmrecsanyi 2006:215; Der and Everitt 2002:85).

Controlling for islandness—which effectively reduces the number of observations in the study sample from 160 to 26—comes with some statistical challenges. The total number of observations potentially available for an empirical study of small island developing states is quite low (60 micro-states, half of which are non-sovereign states). The relatively small number of island states within the data set therefore can be considered as outliers. Further, only nine small island developing states out of 160 Developing countries made a telecommunications commitment to the WTO and 15 out of 160 established independent regulators. Therefore, the relative impact of such small numbers in the sample may be minute.

Cross referencing of the regression estimate results over the data set, I find statistically significant results on both robust OLS and GLS regression estimates. In addition, the low multicollinearity of regression estimates and significance of the overall estimates strengthened the case for an appropriate estimate specification. Nevertheless, five systematic issues warrant attention. First, the OLS and GLS estimates predict coefficients with differing signs indicating the overall model is somewhat volatile. The magnitude of the coefficients vary between one model and another, suggesting that the overall model specification may be volatile and therefore interpretation of higher and lower coefficients should be treated with caution.

Second, it is possible to further refine the independent variables (domestic and multilateral restraint policies) from a dichotomous variable to ordinal with three options. For example, domestic policy restraint can be further refined to include 0 = no independent regulator, 1 = regulator but not independent and 2 = independent regulator. This should produce further detailed insights on the nature of independent regulators and how they impact on performance.

Third, the model may not adequately control for important political variables. The high diversity in terms of geo-political and economic development among developing countries hindered new potential political variables.

Similarly, the main predictor—multilateral policy restrain—could be further improved by refining the dummy variable to a nominal variable. For example, within the telecommunications sector commitment of countries, commitments could be further categorized into more detailed sub-sectors – 0 = no telecommunications commitments under the WTO; while 1 = commitment on voice telephone services (fixed lines and mobile services)[25], 2 = electronic mail (email services); and 3 = on-line information and database retrieval (internet services). This approach could clarify the individual impact of telecommunications sub-sectors on performance. Again, the attempt to increase the number of observations over a longer time period constrained this possibility.

Fourth, since the research design is based on a correlation design, it is difficult sometimes to establish time-order conditions[26] for causality. Monroe (2000:40) argued that "since no difference is required in the point in time when the independent and dependent variables are collected, we can never be sure that one must be the cause and the other the effect".

---

[25] See 'WTO's Services Sectoral Classification List' (MTN.GNS/W/120, 10 July 1991), for detailed classifications (CPC) listings.

[26] See Monroe (2000:31-46) for discussion on the concept of causality.

Fifth, the theoretical model developed operates under two inflexible assumptions. The model assumed that WTO telecommunications commitments are always respected and observed by all WTO members. This is not always the case. The effect of the multilateral trading system in the WTO can only be triggered if any other WTO member has a problem with such non-compliance and raises it in the WTO. The WTO's Trade Policy Review, which most members periodically undertake, can highlight cases of non-compliance. Furthermore, the WTO telecommunications commitments variable in this study generally reflects the commitment of a member to any sub-sector in the telecommunications sector. There are two limitations on this proxy variable. First, the proxy variable used failed to account for the specific impact of specific telecommunications sub-sectors on the domestic reform. The WTO's telecommunications sector classification contains numerous sub-sectors including mobile and fixed-line among many. Second, the use of this proxy does not adequately reflect the real depth in the level of commitment between a member's multilateral commitments (ceiling commitments) and unilateral commitments (actual commitments). The objective of this chapter however, is to explore any controlled effects signaled by the WTO telecommunications commitments on the credibility of domestic telecommunications commitments.

4.0 Conclusion

The empirical approach in this chapter shows evidence to support the claim that multilateral policy restraint signals predictability and certainty for unilateral telecommunications reforms in small island developing states. The overall estimated results from 160 developing countries (with 26 small island developing states controlled) show that a 1 percent increase in the multilateral policy restraint would yield 0.75 percent increase in the telecommunication's reform credibility level. By contrast, the more traditional independent regulator overall estimate show a reverse effect when controlling for islandness, a 1 percent increase in domestic policy restraint yields a -0.07 percent decrease in the telecommunication's reform credibility level. The estimates provided by the model highlight the importance and effectiveness of a multilateral policy restraint (WTO) on imposing credibility on telecommunications reform (even in small island developing states). Further, the estimates provide empirical evidence contributing to the broad policy debate on the costs and benefits of WTO commitments in small island developing states.

Further, the regression result from the bilateral restraint variable is worthy noting. The overall bilateral restraint variable's coefficient estimated on a 160 developing countries data set produces positive relationships with performance; while controlling for islandness show a 1 percent increase in bilateral policy restraint yields -0.19 percent decrease in telecommunications reform credibility level. This finding raises two fundamental issues. First, it emphasizes the need to study small island developing states as a special grouping within developing countries and that research findings in larger developing countries need to be cross-checked within the small island developing states context. Second, although bilateral investment treaties contain similar legal provisions to the WTO telecommunications commitments, their effect (credibility level produced) is less pronounced since the scope of legal coverage is far narrower, there is a low rate of signatories from small island developing states and costs of implementation are higher.

CHAPTER EIGHT

CONCLUSIONS AND POLICY IMPLICATIONS

1.0 Research Problem Revisited

Introduced competition in the telecommunications sector increases network coverage and increases quality of services, while leading to lower prices in small island developing states. If regulatory capture undermines the credibility of telecommunications sector reforms, the policy challenge therefore for governments is how to draft a framework that ensures investment credibility. With the recent telecommunications reform initiatives in the Pacific Islands, the policy debate has increasingly emphasized the form of regulatory policy and institutional framework in place. Despite best-intentioned government reforms, regulatory amendments resulting in uncertainties continue to undermine the credibility of telecommunications reforms. While the literature on the telecommunications policy offers an explanation of the important regulatory and institutional demarcation between policymaker and regulator, the existing explanation is deficient in addressing the domestic political pressures that affect the ability of independent regulators to operate outside policymakers' political reach.

The five case studies from the Pacific Islands provide fresh insights for examining telecommunications regulatory reforms in a small island developing states context. The regulatory reform processes adopted by each Pacific case study were unique, although regulatory amendments and ICT policy changes predominantly existed in most case studies, allowing for the examination of causal hypotheses.

2.0 Research Findings

The overall findings of this study provide a counterargument to the mainstream policy debate on the telecommunications policy debate. That is, the commonly accepted discretionary policy mechanism—independent regulators, described by the telecommunications and the banking literature to be immune to capture—could still be vulnerable to the political influence of governments. This research has introduced the literature strand on multilateral trade agreements as the main fixed-policy mechanism proposed to instill credibility on domestic sectoral reforms.

From the case study analyses in Chapter 5, I have argued the case for the effective use of a fixed multilateral policy restraint imposed to consolidate unilateral telecommunications reforms. The lock-in mechanism lessens the opportunities for frequent policy reversals to occur. In contrast, I demonstrated in Chapter 6 the limited effectiveness of independent regulators, vulnerable to regulatory capture, in imposing a credible telecommunications reform.

The evidence from Tonga and PNG showed that WTO telecommunications commitment provided certainty to an unpredictable ICT policy environment. The case for multilateral policy restraints, as argued in Chapter 6, stems from the fact that compliance to WTO obligations provided predictability to the reform. The case of Tonga showed how its WTO telecommunications commitments consolidated domestic telecommunications reform, which provided certainty to foreign private investors. The case of PNG, on the other hand, showed evidence of how the national government observed its WTO telecommunications commitments (which was triggered by another WTO member), thereby consolidating a pathway[1] for competition. Also, the PNG case highlighted the vulnerability of the independent regulator to regulatory capture.

On the other hand, the case studies of Samoa, Fiji and Vanuatu highlighted the limited effectiveness of independent regulators, susceptible to political influence. The amendment to the regulator's principal legislation to "redefine" the scope of responsibilities after competition was introduced in Samoa, and the lack of comprehensive implementation of the regulator's responsibilities, mandated by legislation in Fiji, provided support for a regulatory capture proposition. Further, the case of Vanuatu showed that the legal responsibility of independent regulators was based on legal contract and not on legislation. The policymakers played "catch-up" through the development of a regulator's piece of legislation after competition had been introduced. Also, the research found that newly established regulators' effectiveness in the Pacific cases was undermined

[1] Within three years of introduced competition, the ICT policy was amended seven times. The pathway for reform through each respective ICT policy was not necessarily in one direction.

due to resource constraints—financial and technical capacity—to perform their duties independently and competently. Further, the research found evidence from the case of PNG, Samoa, and to a lesser extent Fiji, of pressures from incumbent telecommunications operators (and other ICT-related services which stood to lose rent from monopoly protection) on a government's liberalization policy.

The effect of WTO telecommunications commitments (compared to independent regulators) on the credibility of telecommunications reform in small island developing states was also tested empirically and found to be positive and significant. The multiple regression analyses in Chapter 7 provided empirical evidence to support in general the important role of WTO in the credibility of telecommunications reform in small island developing states. In triangulating fieldwork findings, estimation from the panel data set of 160 developing countries including 26 sovereign small island developing states showed that multilateral policy restraint (WTO telecommunications commitment) provided the most consistent explanation for the credibility of telecommunications reform in small island developing states. Overall, the empirical results triangulated provided an important validated cross-check to the main arguments outlined by the qualitative case study analyses.

Across all five Pacific cases, I found two important common aspects. First, advancement in technology behind telecommunications played an important role in the competitiveness of Digicel, and, enabled high network coverage across Pacific cases with wireless telephony. The latter also enabled Digicel to increase connectivity of isolated rural communities. The case of Samoa showed that Digicel (and later on, the state-owned SamoaTel) preferred to invest in wireless telephony instead of copper-wire telephony, based on financial costs and effectiveness. Also, the case of Tonga showed that Digicel expanded to cable television—DigiTV, as part of its acquisition deal of domestic operator TONFON, to utilize the opportunities offered by technology in the entertainment services.

Second, contrary to the established role established in the literature on bilateral investment treaties providing certainty to the investment environment in larger developing countries, the evidence from the comparative case study analyses in Chapters 5 and 6, and the regression analyses in Chapter 7 showed that the impact of bilateral investment treaties was insignificant in small island developing states. The reasons identified from the preliminary findings are twofold. First, small island developing states have signed to lower number of bilateral investment treaties compared to larger developing countries. Second, the costs implied for host countries are high, thereby discouraging most small island states from pursuing any such treaties.

The comparative case analyses from Chapters 5 and 6 found three regulatory factors, not anticipated earlier by the scope of this research, but considered to be important contributors to the credibility of telecommunications reform in the Pacific case studies. As discussed in Chapter 5, these three factors are political will, legal contractual agreements for breaking monopoly rights, and the role of donor community and international institutions in Pacific island's telecommunications reforms.[2]

Political will for telecommunications reform was identified as an important factor for instilling credibility in telecommunications reform in Chapters 4, 5 and 6. The political will of governments, and in some cases political leaders, has led to the speedy liberalization of monopolistic markets. The motivation for strong political will from governments and political leaders was found to vary across Pacific cases. In the case of Tonga, the close business affiliation of Crown Prince Tupouto'a (now King Siaosi Tupou V) to the new mobile competitor "TONFON" provided the strong political support required from government for the liberalization of the telecommunications market in Tonga. Similarly, the leadership and strong preference of Commodore Bainimarama's interim government for introduction of competition to the Fiji telecommunications market provided enough of a catalyst for eventual competition. The cases of Vanuatu, PNG and Samoa were driven by the political will of governments to address the long-term challenges of high costs and low network coverage of telecommunications. The political will from these respective governments was predominantly driven by pressure from the general public and in particular, the business community.

The influence of political will (and political leaders) may be partly determined by different political systems in the Pacific case studies. Less democratic political systems such as Tonga and Fiji show more credible commitment to telecommunications reform compared to more democratic political systems such as PNG and Samoa. Tonga's constitutional

[2] The consideration granted to these factors is equally important to lessen the threat of omitted variable problems and give justice to the effects of uncontrolled third variables beyond the research boundary.

monarchial system of government provides stability. Political stability with limited changes in the government's domestic and foreign policies provides some certainty for investors. Similarly, the strong support from Commodore Bainimarama's military government in Fiji provided the catalyst needed for reforming the sector.

The regulatory implications of strong political will for swift telecommunications reforms, however, proved to be detrimental to the long-term effectiveness of the reform program. The cases of Samoa and Vanuatu show that political will for swift transition to pro-competitive markets experienced difficulties due to the limited human and financial expertise of the new telecommunications regulator. Further, the principal legislation addressing the institutional reform on telecommunications in Vanuatu was playing "catch-up" with the actual regulatory reforms on the ground.[3]

Second, all four Pacific case studies, with the exception of Tonga, prematurely ended their exclusive terms of monopoly licences. With strong political will from governments to speed up the reform process, complex negotiations between government and monopoly holders ended with the signing of settlement agreements. As discussed in Chapter 5, these settlement agreements paved the legal framework and individual stakeholders' legal rights for a competitive market structure. The settlement agreement in Vanuatu also proved to be instrumental to the harmonious and healthy co-existence of key stakeholders, as the government is currently drafting the key telecommunications bill around the key principles set forth in the settlement agreement.

Third, the active collaboration of the donor community and institutions such as the World Bank and AusAID in Vanuatu and Samoa, and to a lesser extent in PNG, Fiji and Tonga, provided the much needed technical and financial resources to facilitate the unilateral initiatives of these Pacific governments. As discussed in Chapters 4 and 5, the World Bank provided the technical assistance in assisting Samoa's and Vanuatu's government officials to negotiate the terms and conditions of terminating their respective monopoly markets. AusAID, on the other hand, is funding a longer-term operation of the regulator's office in Port Vila. Close collaboration therefore between donor community and international

[3] Until it was passed in December 2009.

institutions through targeted technical and financial assistance is paramount.

The overall finding of the research was that the multilateral policy restraint provided credibility to telecommunications reform in Pacific cases, whereas, domestic policy restraint was vulnerable to capture. While it is crucial to note the limited effectiveness of independent regulators, the main findings from Chapters 5 and 6 and the empirical findings from Chapter 7, confirm a case for implementing the combination of domestic, bilateral and multilateral restraint policies conducive to larger developing countries. The sustainability, though, of imposing such policy combinations in small island developing states may be limited due to their supply-side constraints (technical and financial capacity). In addition, other domestic variables such as strong political will, role of settlement agreements and donor community technical support are important in contributing to a credible reform program.

3.0 Policy Implications

Investments in the telecommunications sector are sensitive to policy uncertainties due to their high sunk costs, the politically sensitive nature of the sector and the non-transferability of its assets. The credibility of the regulatory reform is therefore of utmost importance.

3.1 Implications for the Literature

As discussed in Chapter 2, one of the current policy debates on telecommunications policy involves the establishment of an independent regulator to instill credibility in the sector to improve developing countries' sector performance. (Flacher and Jennequin 2008; Wallsten 2004 and 2003; Fink et al. 2003; Li and Xu 2002; Ros 1997). On the other hand, other scholars have identified the shortfalls of independent regulators in instilling credible policies. Melody (1997:195) argued that the institutional rules and settings that establish independent regulatory bodies are questionable in reflecting the true impartiality of such bodies, for example, members of the board of independent regulators include government ministers and membership is often determined by government or funding is often appropriated by parliament. Further, Etzioni (2009:319-321) stated that as with any other domestic institution, independent regulators are vulnerable to regulatory capture due to economic and political pressures.

This research has provided fresh insights into the behaviors and design of telecommunications regulatory frameworks in small island developing states. The examination of recent telecommunications reform experiences from the five Pacific island case studies renders two crucial implications for the telecommunications policy dialogue. First, telecommunications regulatory policy design needs to address the challenges of small island states. Second, the vulnerability of domestic institutions to regulatory capture, even so-called independent authorities, needs to be recognized

As discussed in Chapter 2, the small island states literature focuses on two main research paths. The first of these examines the "economic vulnerability" argument, which questions whether smallness disadvantages the development prospects of small island states. The proponents of the economic vulnerability argument generally agree that the geographical factors of isolation and smallness (of population and natural resources) hamper the development prospects of small island states. The opponents of the vulnerability argument claim that small island states are just as wealthy as any other developing states and smallness does not matter. Small states have been found to have high incomes, relatively high economic growth, and despite their vulnerabilities and generally not to be in need of assistance and policy advice that is in any way different from that of other developing countries (Easterly and Kraay 2000). Rather than invest in productive activities to finance imports, small islands prefer to be rent-seekers, using sovereignty and related instruments to pursue development goals (Sutherland 2009:5). Some island states have used the concept of vulnerability as a political exercise to gain attention at the international level. Grynberg's (2006) "small vulnerable states trade and development" argument best captures this research path, by arguing for the need for small island states to maintain monopoly rents due to the high costs of smallness.

The second research path focuses largely on the "economic resilience argument, that institutional reform and appropriate policy design for development in small island developing states lessens the effects of natural disadvantages (Briguglio, et al. 2006:13-15). While this economic resilience argument recognizes the smallness concept as an issue, it focuses on developing relevant and effective socio-economic policies for reform, including the respect of intellectual property rights, rule of law, good governance and reforming institutional policies.

In consideration of the two paths of research on small island states, I found evidence from the Pacific case studies that is consistent with the "economic resilience" argument. The introduction of competition in the mobile service sector, as shown from Chapters 5 and 6, increased connectivity between rural and urban areas in PNG and international connectivity between Vanuatu and the outside world. As a result of competition, prices declined, which gave opportunities for grass-roots people to access the communications technology easily.

The second insight focuses on the vulnerability of domestic institutions to regulatory capture in small island developing states—even the so-called independent authorities. Based on the comparative case studies analyses from the Pacific (Chapters 5 and 6) and the multiple regression analyses (Chapter 7), the research provided evidence of the vulnerability of independent regulators to political influences in small island developing states. This systemic weakness is predominantly due to poor governance and weak institutional rules in small island developing states. The weak institutions and corruptions in the Pacific have been identified by Larmour (2005) as historical, and due to unsuccessful policy transfers implanted during colonial periods.

This, however, may not be the only reason. The cases of Samoa, Vanuatu, Fiji and PNG highlighted a supply-side constraint on technical experts as the regulators lacked technical expertise on telecommunications. In the case of Samoa, Vanuatu and Fiji, foreign experts were hired to lead the regulator's office. The handling of the dispute case in Samoa reflected the limited capacity of the regulator's office to handle complex issues. Further, most regulators' budgets depend on government sources, which provides opportunities for government to influence the regulator's tasks. These findings generally support the need for the design of telecommunications regulatory reforms to fit the specific conditions of small island states.

Overall, the comparative case study findings from Fiji, PNG, Samoa, Tonga and Vanuatu provide two vital issues for the telecommunications policy debate. First, that selection of key regulatory policies on telecommunications—widely accepted by the telecommunications literature to be successful in developed and developing economies—may not necessarily be compatible in a small island developing states context. Smallness matters. Therefore, appropriate consideration of the natural challenges facing small island developing states when designing regulatory policies is important. Second, domestic institutions such as independent regulators in small island developing states were found to be vulnerable to capture. Hence, multilateral agreements are needed to lock-in unilateral policy reforms with weak domestic institutional regulation.

3.2 Policy Implication for International Institutions and Aid Agencies

The telecommunications reform in the Pacific case studies highlighted successful sharing of information and close collaboration between development agencies at the international level. The evidence from the case studies of Samoa, Vanuatu and PNG showed the importance of the donor agency, AusAID, and the World Bank collaborating closely on telecommunications reform. The case of Vanuatu highlighted an effective partnership when the World Bank relied on AusAID's local expertise in providing updated information and constant communication with the Vanuatu government on the ground. The World Bank, on the other hand, provided the regulatory advice on reforming the telecommunications sector based on broader regulatory experiences from advising developing countries and other small island developing states.

Also, evidence from the Pacific Islands showed the importance of the World Bank's active participation in providing regulatory advice to governments across the Pacific to reform their telecommunications sector. The lessons from the regulatory dispute between Digicel and the independent regulator (and government) in Samoa in 2006 was recognized by the World Bank and later reformers alike, and drastic steps were taken to avoid a similar case in Vanuatu two years later.

The research findings therefore provide two useful sets of feedback for international aid agencies currently offering funding and regulatory advice in the Pacific islands. First, there is a need to revise the current key regulatory principles that international aid agencies recommend to the Pacific islands. Considering the supply-side constraints of the Pacific islands, the policy advice to establish an independent regulator for telecommunications in each island state may not be sustainable in the long-run. Therefore, a regional approach to regulating the telecommunications sector—through pooling of financial and technical resources—should be considered for the Pacific islands. This regionalizing of resources in the Pacific is not new. Several regional organizations had been established before based on the need to share scarce resources in the Pacific. Some regional initiatives—such as the University of the South Pacific, the Secretariat of the Pacific Community and Forum Secretariat—have been successful in accomplishing the regional pooling of resources for the common good.

Regulatory lessons for successful regional pooling of resources from outside the Pacific also exist. Since 2000, a regional regulator model has been successfully tested in the Caribbean region with the establishment of the Eastern Caribbean Telecommunications Authority, ECTEL. National regulators' offices were therefore established to complement ECTEL (Sutherland 2009:22). Further, a recent study by Kessides et al. (2009) found that regional harmonization of telecommunications regulatory frameworks reduced cross-border transaction costs and improved the performance of backbone infrastructures in West Africa.

Other regional initiatives, however, have not been so successful in the Pacific including the Forum Shipping Line; an unsuccessful bid for common currency, and an unsuccessful bid for a regional airline (Chand 2003). One of the major challenges identified by Chand (2003) was balancing the considerations of minimum service obligations—public service with less concern for profitability—and returning profits to shareholders. Nevertheless, since a regional regulatory authority on telecommunications would generally aim at providing a public rather than a profit-oriented service, political support from Pacific islands could be forthcoming.

Second, while the positive experience from telecommunications reform in the Pacific is atypical, its potential policy implications to other utilities sectors currently under monopoly (for example, electricity and water utilities) could be considered. A replication of such policy experience, however, could only be effective depending on the existence of three key factors—the role of technology in the sector and its potential future usage, presence of a second capable foreign/domestic utility provider, and strong support for reform due to the disadvantages of smallness. Regional regulation of electricity and water, with controlled competition, could lower utility costs and overall lower the costs of doing business in the Pacific.

3.3 Policy Implications for Small Island Developing State Governments

Informed by fieldwork evidence collected from the early telecommunications reform experiences in Fiji, PNG, Samoa, Tonga and Vanuatu, three policy dimensions have emerged, deemed useful for small island developing states consideration.

First, considering the high costs for private investment in telecommunications in the Pacific, governments need to consider an international policy restraint mechanism to instill credibility when domestic institutions are weak. This entails the process of considering regional and multilateral agreements to strengthened weak institutional mechanisms. The case of PNG and Tonga provides support for small island developing states strengthening unilateral telecommunications liberalization at the WTO.

Second, the research findings provide a valuable lesson for small island developing states governments' trade policies. The thesis findings support a sector-by-sector trade liberalization—which is easier for small island states to adopt politically and any policy consequences can be addressed to a great extent—in contrast to the "single undertaking principle" of the WTO. The single undertaking principle is one of the Doha Declaration's principles for negotiations, meaning that "virtually every item of the negotiation is part of a whole and indivisible package and cannot be agreed separately—nothing is agreed until everything is agreed" (WTO 2009). The single undertaking principal has been incorporated into most regional trade negotiations, including the Pacific Economic Partnership Agreement currently being negotiated between Pacific islands and the European Union; the Pacific Closer Economic Partnership Agreement, PACER, currently being negotiated between the Pacific islands and Australia and New Zealand; and the Pacific Island Countries Trade Agreement, PICTA.

Although the single undertaking principal may have been devised as a balancing mechanism to the market access commitment of a country, the principle could also equally impose an overall unnecessary and costly umbrella commitment for small island developing states' narrow-based trade interests. Small island developing states could, therefore, enter into negotiations on trade agreements which are domestically—socially, economically and politically—sensitive due to inherent natural challenges, rendering unnecessary negotiating costs. Evidence from the series of interviews of telecommunications policy experts in the Pacific case studies shows that political and interest group opposition to sectoral trade liberalization and the benefits of telecommunications immediately connected the isolated communities.

Third, evidence from the case of Vanuatu showed that new entrant Digicel identified the land tenure system as a deterrent to the speedy deployment of its mobile service networks, slowing down national coverage targets. Since most of the Pacific islands (with the exception of Tonga) consist of communally owned land, telecommunications network expansion means lengthy negotiations with communal landowners. Pacific governments therefore could consider facilitating the negotiations on land ownership rights by establishing a "one-stop shop" for foreign investors. This focal point should assist tremendously by saving foreign investors negotiation costs spent on negotiating on their own with communal landowners. This policy recommendation, however, could be challenging to implement. Government intervention on common property in the Pacific is frowned upon. Larmour (1997:1) stated that the idea that government should intervene to remedy the defects of common property might sometimes make things worse. Common property is claimed to be part of indigenous people's defense and reaffirmation of political sovereignty. Land reform in the Pacific is also politically sensitive when communities have strong ties to their land. Hence, while it is crucial that a government framework facilitate land tenure negotiations for investment, the ultimate authority and responsibility should be left to landowners.

3.4 Policy Implications for Telecommunications Sector Operators

The discussion of telecommunications operator's experience and business strategies, as discussed in Chapter 5, render two useful feedbacks for operators in the Pacific islands. First, state-owned telecommunications operators in the Pacific—who lacked initial competitive experience—could learn from the four general strategies used by Digicel, discussed in Chapter 5. These were: the ability to source international funding for expansion; heavy investment in social and community programs to promote brand and customer loyalty; a more coordinated sharing of information and collaboration across the Pacific region, through the Pacific Islands Telecommunications Association (PITA); and public advertisement programs of unprecedented level through most media channels to ensure mass market penetration.

Second, the dynamic advancement in technology behind telecommunications could continue to be an important factor in competitiveness in telecommunications, as proven by Digicel. Innovation and early adoption of new technology that connects isolated communities at a reasonable cost should, therefore, be an objective for all operators. The experiences of state-owned telecommunications operators in Samoa, Vanuatu and PNG showed that an outdated telecommunications infrastructure put them in a disadvantaged position—as it required a tremendous effort on funding and restructuring of the management system—when competition was introduced.

4.0 Future Research

The case studies and empirical analysis of the credibility of telecommunications regulatory reforms in small island developing states raises two important issues for future policy research.

First, while the findings of this research have shown that multilateral policy restraint provides credibility in comparison to domestic policy restraint, it would be useful for future researchers to examine other domestic policy restraints—such as property rights and rule of law—which this research did not account for.

Second, as highlighted by the case studies, there is an important role to be played by international institutions (and agreements) in domestic regulatory reform. Further research is therefore needed on an appropriate assistance framework relevant to assisting economic reform programs in small island developing states. The most recent studies on “aid for trade” in addressing the infrastructural needs of small island developing states are likely to play an important role in identifying the regulatory challenges crucial for developing an effective reform program.

APPENDIX A

GEOGRAPHY OF SMALL ISLAND DEVELOPING STATES

Figure 2-19: GDP per Capita (Nominal) (2007)

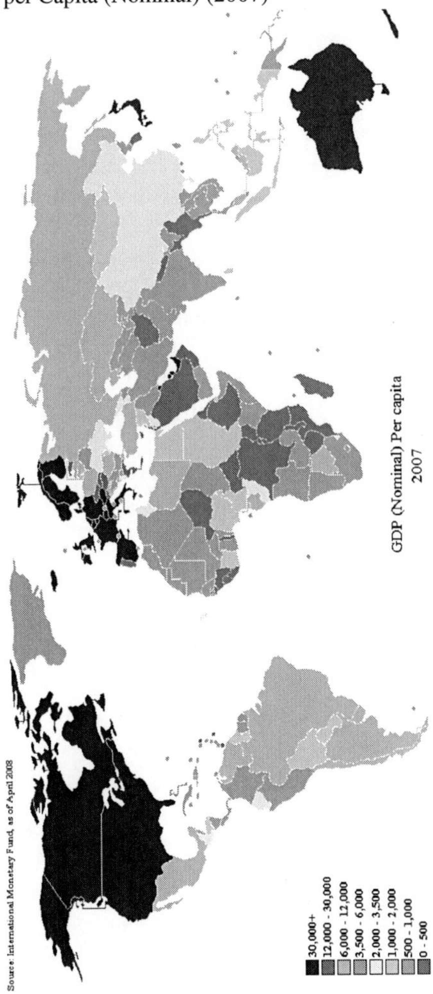

Source: International Monetary Fund, viewed April 2008,

<http://images.google.com.au/imgres?imgurl=
http://upload.wikimedia.org/wikipedia/commons/7/70/GDP_nominal_per_capita_world_map_IMF_2007.
PNGandimgrefurl=http://commons.wikimedia.org/wiki/File:GDP_nominal_per_capita_world_map_IMF_2007.
PNGandusg=__IPlOGFfuwXqudrACdYeGEhJXnlo=andh=625andw=1350andsz=52andhl=enandstart=1andum=1andtbnid=ih1D1XGXG0KiHM:andtbnh=69andtbnw=150andprev=/images%3Fq%3Dgdp%2Bper%2Bcapita%2Bmap%2B2008%26hlDen%26um%3D1>

Figure 2-19 show that countries located in the tropical areas are generally poorer (nominal GDP nominal per capita) than countries located outside the tropics. Figure 2-20 shows that countries located in the tropics generally have higher reported cases of malaria than countries located outside the tropics. A former Chief Economist of the World Bank, Kamarck (1976) cited in Ram (1997:1443) argued that countries located in temperate zones are at a big advantage, and those in the tropics are at a substantial disadvantage. Erratic patterns of rainfall in the tropics can play havoc with agriculture. Also, continuous heat and absence of frost lead to a wide variety of weeds, insects, fungi, and other microbes that affect both crops and human life. Diseases affect human health, which eventually contributes to lower labor productivity and accumulation of human and non-human capital. Further, it is more difficult to find mineral resources in tropical countries.

Figure 2-20: Malaria Risk Areas

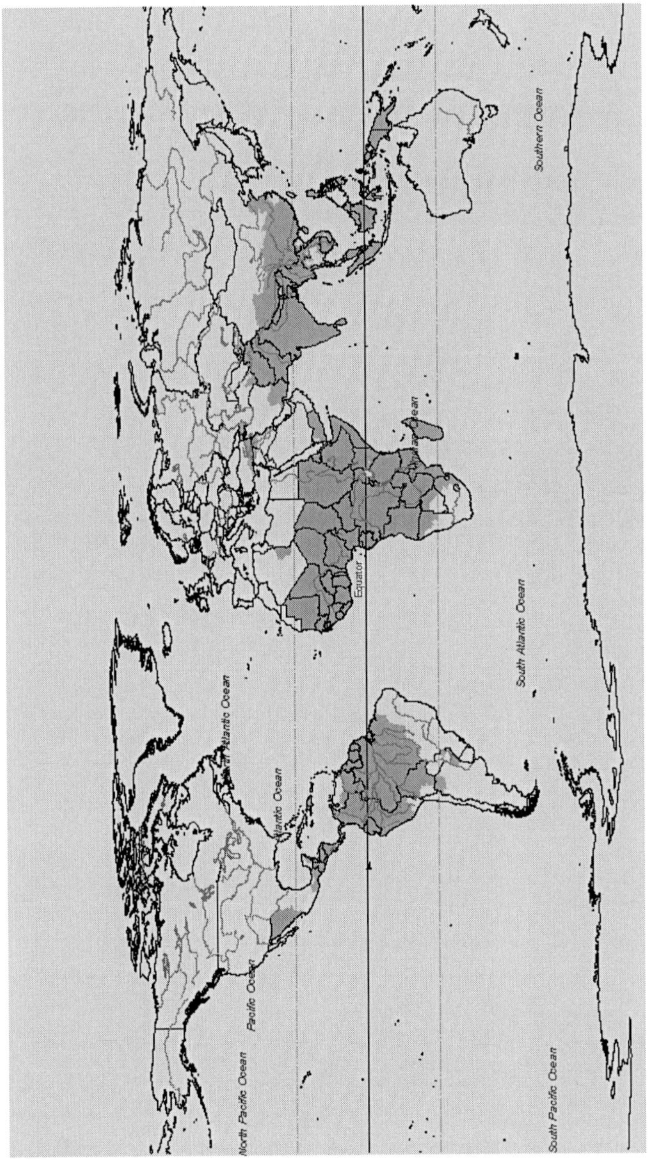

Source: Center for Disease Control and Prevention, viewed 28 October 2008, <http://cdc-malaria.ncsa.uiuc.edu/cdc-malaria/Default.aspx>

Note: ▭ - Malaria cases reported.

APPENDIX B

WORLD'S REGIONAL POPULATION

Table 3-18: World's Regional Population

Region	Mid-year Population Estimates (millions) 2005	Surface Area (km^2) (000s)	Population Density (popu./km^2 of surface area)
OCEANIA	33.4	8564	4
Australia and New Zealand	24.4	8012	3
Melanesia	7.8	541	14
Micronesia	0.5	3	167
Polynesia	0.6	8	75
AFRICA	922	30312	30
Eastern Africa	292	6361	46
Middle Africa	112	6613	17
Northern Africa	190	8525	22
Southern Africa	55	2675	21
Western Africa	272	6138	44
LATIN AMERICA and CARIBBEAN	558	20546	27
Caribbean	40	234	173
Central America	144	2480	58
South America	374	17832	21
NORTHERN AMERICA	332	21776	15
ASIA	3938	31880	124
Eastern Asia	1522	11763	129
South Central Asia	1646	10791	153
South Eastern Asia	558	4495	124
Western Asia	212	4831	44
EUROPE	731	23049	32
Eastern Europe	298	18814	16
Northern Europe	96	1810	53
Southern Europe	150	1317	114
Western Europe	187	1108	168
WORLD	6515	136127	48

Source: Populations Division 2007, "World population prospects – the 2006 revision", Department of Economic and Social Affairs, United Nations, New York.

APPENDIX C

PACIFIC CASE STUDIES: KEY CHARACTERISTICS

Table 3-19: Pacific Case Studies, Key Characteristics

	Papua New Guinea	Tonga	Fiji	Samoa	Vanuatu
Independent Variable					
WTO Telecommunications Agreement Commitment	Yes	Yes	No	No	No
Remarks:	Multilateral Policy Restraint		Domestic Policy Restraint		
Control Variables 1.Telecommunications Institutional Framework					
Telecommunications Reform (Competition)	Yes	Yes	Yes	Yes	Yes
Corporatization of Public	Yes	Yes	Yes	Yes	Yes

	Papua New Guinea	Tonga	Fiji	Samoa	Vanuatu
Telecommunications Operator Independent Regulators	Yes	No	Yes	Yes	Yes
Remarks:	Largely similar				
2. Memberships to Free Trade Agreements					
PICTA	Yes	Yes	Yes	Yes	Yes
PACER	Yes	Yes	Yes	Yes	Yes
EU-EPA	Yes	Yes	Yes	Yes	Yes
WTO	Yes	Yes	Yes	Yes* (Acceding)	Yes* (Acceding)
Bilateral investment treaties	Yes	Yes	No	No	Yes
Remarks:	Largely similar				

3. Socio-economic Factors					
GDP per capita (constant 2000 US$)	630	1,693	2,362	1,572	1,243
Population, total (July 2009 est.)	6,057,263	120,898	944,720	219,998	218,519
Highest age structure (15-64 years) (% of total)	59	62.9	64.9	56.7	65.3
Urban Population (% of total)	13	24	51	23	24
Agriculture, value added (% of GDP)	36	26	15	12	15
Ethnic Groups	Melanesian, Papuan, Negrito, Micronesian, Polynesian	Polynesian, Europeans	Melanesian, Indian and Polynesian.	Polynesian	Melanesian
Health Expenditure, total (% of GDP) (2005)	4.2	5	4.1	4.9	4.3
Life Expectancy at birth, total (2009 est.)	66.34 years	70.73 years	70.73 years	71.86 years	63.98 years
Remarks:			Largely similar		

4. Governance Indicators (2007) (Governance Score (-2.5 to +2.5))					
Voice and Accountability	0.12	-0.08	-0.51	0.67	0.46
Political Stability	-0.76	0.38	0.09	1.11	1.36
government Effectiveness	-0.74	-0.58	-0.52	-0.21	-0.34
Regulatory Quality	-0.51	-0.75	-0.46	-0.08	-0.48
Rule of Law	-0.85	0.5	-0.37	0.93	0.63
Control of Corruption	-1.05	-1	-0.46	0.24	0.21
Remarks:			Largely similar		

Overall Remarks: Most control variables show generally similar characteristics, with the exception of the outlier population size and economic standard of Papua New Guinea.

Source: Institutional Frameworks data from ITU, Free Trade Agreements data from respective government's sources, Socio-economic data sourced from World Development Indicators Online source and CIA Factbook online; Governance data from the World Governance Indicators online source. Give the address?

APPENDIX D

TYPE AND SOURCE OF DATA COLLECTED

Table 3-20: Type and Source of Data Collected

Data Source	Subject	Type of Document	Format
ANU Library	International Trade Telecommunications Policy and Small States.	• Journals (Academic) • Books	Electronic/hard copies
Samoa National Library	Telecommunications and Trade Policy	Media Archives	Hard Copies
Case Studies governments	Telecommunications and Trade Policy	Official Reports and Annual Reports	Hard Copies
Department of Trade, Samoa.	WTO GATs Schedule	Draft copy of WTO GATS Commitment	Hard Copy
Department of Trade, Vanuatu.	WTO GATs Schedule	Draft copy of WTO GATS Commitment	Hard Copy
Ministry of Labor, Commerce and industries, Tonga	WTO GATS Schedule	Copy of WTO GATS Commitment	Hard Copy
Ministry of Foreign Affairs and Trade, PNG	WTO GATS Schedule	Copy of WTO GATS Commitment	Hard Copy
Tongan Parliament	WTO	Annual Reports and Minutes (1999-2005)	Hard Copies
Vanuatu Independent Regulator	Telecommunications	Copies of Telecommunications Reports, Contracts, and Licences.	Electronic Copies
Samoa Independent Regulator	Telecommunications	Copies of Telecommunications Reports	Hard Copies

PANGTEL, PNG.	Telecommunications	Copies of Telecommunications Reports	Hard Copies
ICCC, PNG	Telecommunications	Copies of Telecommunications Reports	Electronic Copies
World Bank	Telecommunications	World Development Indicators	Electronic Copies
ITU	Telecommunications	World Telecommunications/ICT Indicators Database 2008 (11th Edition)	Electronic Copies
UNCTAD	Trade Policy	Official Reports	Electronic
WTO	Trade Policy	Schedules of Telecommunications commitment	Electronic

APPENDIX E

LIST OF INTERVIEW RESPONDENTS

Table 3-21: Interview Respondents

Interviews in Port Moresby, Papua New Guinea

Respondent	Sector	Date	Duration (minutes)
1	Small Business Association of PNG	08 September 2008	58 minutes
2	Manufacturing Council of PNG	09 September 2008	21 minutes
3	Government Official	09 September 2008	41 minutes
4	Government Official	09 September 2008	55 minutes
5	Business Operator	10 September 2008	27 minutes
6	Telecommunications Policy Expert	10 September 2008	47 minutes
7	Telecommunications Policy Expert	11 September 2008	52 minutes
8	Business Operator	11 September 2008	19 minutes
9	Telecommunications Policy Expert	13 September 2008	155 minutes
10	Business Operator	16 September 2008	22 minutes
11	Business Operator	17 September 2008	35 minutes
12	Government Official*	6 May 2009	-
13	Telecommunications Policy Expert*	7 May 2009	-
14	Telecommunications Policy Expert*	8 May 2009	-
15	Government Official*	8 May 2009	-

Interviews in Nuku'alofa, Tonga

Respondent	Sector	Date	Duration (minutes)
16	Government Official	27 November 2008	32 minutes
17	Government Official	28 November 2008	58 minutes
18	Government Official	28 November 2008	37 minutes
19	Telecommunications Policy Expert	24 November 2008	49 minutes
20	Telecommunications Policy Expert	24 November 2008	53 minutes
21	Telecommunications Policy Expert	23 November 2008	50 minutes
22	Telecommunications Policy Expert	25 November 2008	24 minutes
23	Telecommunications Policy Expert	26 November 2008	32 minutes
24	Business Operator	2 December 2008	34 minutes
25	Business Operator	4 December 2008	17 minutes
26	Business Operator	4 December 2008	29 minutes

Interviews in Apia, Samoa

Respondent	Sector	Date	Duration (minutes)
27	Telecommunications Policy Expert	10 July 2008	24 minutes
28	Telecommunications Policy Expert	10 July 2008	31 minutes
29	Government Official	11 July 2008	56 minutes
30	Government Official	14 July 2008	45 minutes
31	Government Official	14 July 2008	59 minutes
32	Regulatory Official	14 July 2008	67 minutes
33	Regulatory Official	15 July 2008	52 minutes
34	Telecommunications Operator	15 July 2008	71 minutes
35	Telecommunications Operator	15 July 2008	55 minutes
36	Business Operator	18 July 2008	22 minutes
37	Business Operator	18 July 2008	35 minutes
38	Business Operator	18 July 2008	47 minutes
39	Telecommunications Operator	21 July 2008	54 minutes
40	Government Official	22 July 2008	30 minutes
41	Government Official	22 July 2008	26 minutes
42	Telecommunications Operator	23 July 2008	63 minutes
43	Government Official	24 July 2008	27 minutes

Interviews in Port Vila, Vanuatu

Respondent	Sector	Date	Duration (minutes)
44	Government Official	11 August 2008	47 minutes
45	Regulatory Official	11 August 2008	74 minutes
46	Government Official	11 August 2008	25 minutes
47	Telecommunications Operator	12 August 2008	61 minutes
48	Government Official	14 August 2008	47 minutes
49	Donor Agency	14 August 2008	36 minutes
50	Government Official	18 August 2008	46 minutes
51	Telecommunications Operator	20 August 2008	53 minutes
52	Government Official	20 August 2008	71 minutes
53	Government Official	21 August 2008	33 minutes

Interviews in Suva, Fiji.

Respondent	Sector	Date	Duration (minutes)
54	Telecommunications Policy Expert	14 November 2008	62 minutes
55	Government Official	15 November 2008	58 minutes
56	Telecommunications Operator	15 November 2008	47 minutes
57	Regulatory Official	20 November 2008	59 minutes
58	Government Official	20 November 2008	33 minutes
59	Regional Institution	21 November 2008	50 minutes
60	Business Operator	26 November 2008	24 minutes
61	Business Operator	26 November 2008	32 minutes
62	Business Operator	26 November 2008	34 minutes

Note: * - Interview questions and responses communicated via electronic mail.

APPENDIX F

SEMI-STRUCTURED INTERVIEWS

The questions below were used as a guideline for the semi-structured interviews conducted in each respective case study. Apart from a few key questions, the questions asked in each interview session were predominantly determined by the interviewee, based on his/her knowledge of the subject matter.

Guideline Questions:

1	Has introduction of competition improved the overall quality and prices of mobile service in the Telecommunications sector?
2	Has introduction of competition in the Telecommunications sector increased network coverage?
3	Are transparent and predictable regulatory policies important for investments in the sector?
4	Does fair and equal treatment of domestic and foreign Telecommunications operators promote competition and performance in the sector?
5	Do regulatory policies on free repatriation of profits promote investment and performance in the sector?
6	Do independent dispute mechanisms (either domestic or international) that deal with investor-to-state disputes promote predictability and transparency in the sector?
7	Do independent dispute mechanisms (either domestic or international) that deal with investor-to-investor disputes promote investment and performance in the sector?
8	Does regulatory protection of Telecommunications investments against Government expropriation promote investment and thus performance in the sector?
9	Do positive spillovers from the Telecommunications sector promote domestic business performance?
10	Do small businesses in urban areas promote pro-market regulatory reforms in the Telecommunications sector?
11	If yes, how do small businesses pressure policymakers?

APPENDIX G

RESIDUALS OF PERFORMANCE VARIABLES (GRAPHICAL TESTING OF HETEROSCEDASTICITY)

Figure 7-21: Residuals of Performance Variables

Performance variable 1

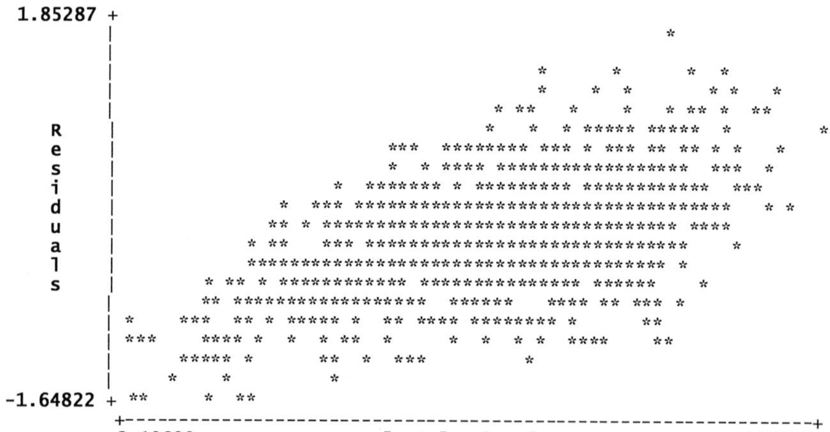

Performance variable 2

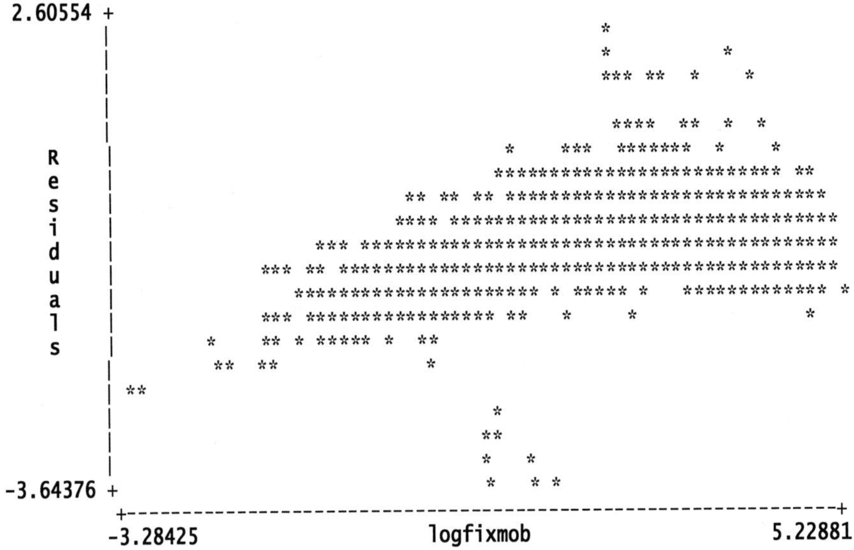

Source: Author's estimations.

APPENDIX H

PAIR-WISE CORRELATIONS

Table 7-22: Pair-wise Correlations Matrix – Performance variable 1

Performance Variable 1	Island* WTO	Island* BITs	Island* Regulator	WTO	BITs	Regulator	Competition	Institutions	Interest Groups	Geography	Islands	Population	GDP per Capita
1.0000													
0.0293	1.0000												
0.0525	0.4343	1.0000											
0.0582	0.6118	0.7968	1.0000										
0.4167	0.1619	-0.0521	-0.0059	1.0000									
0.3499	0.0011	0.1648	0.0756	0.3011	1.0000								
0.4670	-0.0513	-0.0853	-0.0162	0.2825	0.0348	1.0000							
0.5250	-0.0059	0.0123	0.0325	0.3292	0.4441	0.3363	1.0000						
-0.2213	-0.0665	-0.0701	-0.0845	-0.1927	0.0144	-0.0364	0.0252	1.0000					
0.4276	-0.1249	0.0964	0.0279	0.1753	0.0117	0.3205	0.0600	-0.4460	1.0000				

0.0822	-0.0933	-0.0342	-0.0541	-0.0473	-0.2492	0.4651	-0.0367	-0.0191	0.3348	1.0000			
0.0145	0.6026	0.8219	0.8491	-0.0416	0.0423	-0.1528	-0.0492	-0.0855	0.0070	-0.0733	1.0000		
0.0684	-0.1513	-0.2717	-0.2841	0.0514	0.0264	0.2127	0.0826	0.1644	-0.1126	-0.0549	-0.3361	1.0000	
0.5067	0.1007	0.1492	0.1747	0.2840	-0.0165	0.2598	0.0286	-0.6384	0.7696	0.2420	0.2013	-0.2051	1.0000

Table 7-23: Pair-wise Correlations Matrix – Performance variable 2

	Performance Variable 2	Island* WTO	Island* BITs	Island* Regulator	WTO	BITs	Regulator	Competition	Institutions	Interest Groups	Geography	Islands	Population	GDP per Capita
Performance Variable 2	1.0000													
Island* WTO	0.1307	1.0000												
Island* BITs	0.1589	0.4982	1.0000											
Island* Regulator	0.1737	0.6761	0.8053	1.0000										
WTO	0.3613	0.1824	-0.0129	0.0345	1.0000									
BITs	0.1515	0.0005	0.1607	0.0673	0.3171	1.0000								
Regulator	0.5071	-0.0553	-0.0715	-0.0164	0.2626	0.0457	1.0000							
Competition	0.2703	-0.0151	-0.0010	0.0152	0.3050	0.4436	0.3246	1.0000						
Institutions	-0.3612	-0.0756	-0.0785	-0.0975	-0.2196	-0.0178	-0.0585	0.0266	1.0000					

Interest Groups	0.6428	- 0.1592	0.0524	-0.0180	0.1795	0.0185	0.3189	0.0597	-0.4261	1.0000				
Geography	0.3999	- 0.1028	- 0.0384	-0.0611	- 0.0617	- 0.2410	0.4644	-0.0410	-0.0091	0.3250	1.0000			
Islands	0.1751	0.6762	0.8169	0.8683	0.0060	0.0330	-0.1362	-0.0652	-0.1023	- 0.0424	-0.0780	1.0000		
Population	-0.1625	- 0.1636	- 0.2418	-0.2651	0.0298	0.0301	0.1926	0.1057	0.1552	- 0.0912	-0.0377	- 0.3085	1.0000	
GDP Per Capita	0.7495	0.1288	0.1566	0.1904	0.2924	- 0.0147	0.2722	0.0051	-0.6266	0.7490	0.2371	0.2141	-0.2043	1.0000

APPENDIX I

TIME DUMMY COEFFICIENTS

Table 7-24: Time Dummy Coefficients

	Performance variable 1		Performance variable 2	
	(1)	(2)	(3)	(4)
	OLS	GLS	OLS	GLS
Year 1	(dropped)	(dropped)	(dropped)	(dropped)
Year 2	-0.05	-0.07	-0.05	-0.14 **
	(-0.50)	(-1.37)	(-0.50)	(-2.42)
Year 3	0.02	-0.01	0.02	-0.12 **
	(0.26)	(-0.22)	(0.25)	(-2.10)
Year 4	0.09	0.05	0.09	-0.04 **
	(0.88)	(0.93)	(0.89)	(-0.65)
Year 5	0.22 **	0.19 ***	0.22 **	0.11 **
	(2.20)	(3.60)	(2.25)	(1.99)
Year 6	0.31***	0.32 ***	0.31 ***	-0.36 ***
	(3.16)	(-3.05)	(3.15)	(0.05)
Year 7	0.58 ***	0.53 ***	0.58 ***	0.48 ***
	(5.70)	(9.60)	(5.71)	(8.41)
Year 8	0.79 ***	0.73 ***	0.79 ***	0.64 ***
	(7.74)	(12.35)	(7.46)	(11.02)
Year 9	0.96 ***	0.87 ***	0.96 ***	0.77 ***
	(9.22)	(14.51)	(9.00)	(13.26)
Year 10	1.14 ***	1.03 ***	1.14 ***	0.94 ***
	(10.39)	(16.69)	(10.34)	(16.08)
Year 11	1.36 ***	1.26 ***	1.36 ***	1.18 ***
	(11.65)	(19.84)	(12.15)	(19.90)
Year 12	1.55 ***	1.43 ***	1.55 ***	1.40 ***
	(12.13)	(20.97)	(13.20)	(22.49)
Constant	-0.23	-0.01	-0.24	-4.51 ***
	(-0.88)	(-0.09)	(-0.83)	(-23.80)
Wald Chi-squared	n/a	7637.80	n/a	18801.55
Observations	1051	1051	1223	1223
Adjusted R-squared	0.72	n/a	0.82	n/a
VIF (Mean)	2.84	n/a	2.99	n/a

Sources: Panel data set compiled from World Bank, 2003, World Development Indicators, The World Bank, Washington, DC; ITU online sources and respective government data sources.

Notes: * significant at 10 per cent; ** significant at 5 per cent; *** significant at 1 per cent; n/a: not applicable; T-Statistics under columns 1 and 3 in parentheses; GLS corrected z-statistics in columns 2 and 4 parentheses; Year 1 is dropped because of collinearity.

APPENDIX J

VARIANCE INFLATION FACTORS (TESTING MULTICOLLINEARITY)

Table 7-25: Variance Inflation Factors Test – Performance variable 1

Variable	VIF	1/VIF
islands	5.84	0.171116
ibit	4.77	0.209804
loggdppc	4.31	0.232010
ireg	4.17	0.239832
sqrturbanp	3.18	0.314217
y6	3.16	0.316601
y7	3.15	0.317393
y5	3.11	0.321839
y9	3.02	0.331126
y8	3.02	0.331193
y4	2.96	0.337431
y10	2.95	0.339316
y11	2.82	0.354443
y3	2.67	0.374472
y12	2.54	0.393657
y2	2.45	0.408991
logbit	2.26	0.441987
iwto	1.98	0.504776
logcorrupt~e	1.92	0.519770
competition	1.83	0.547832
lat_abst	1.64	0.611066
regulator	1.59	0.630360
wtotelecom~t	1.51	0.660575
logpopu	1.31	0.765143
Mean VIF	2.84	

Table 7-26: Variance Inflation Factors Test – Performance variable 2

Variable	VIF	1/VIF
islands	6.29	0.158903
ibit	5.40	0.185023
loggdppc	4.15	0.240848
ireg	4.04	0.247400
y11	3.60	0.277873
y10	3.44	0.290812
y9	3.41	0.292850
y12	3.34	0.299074
y8	3.32	0.301447
y7	3.25	0.307600
y6	3.23	0.309200
y5	3.11	0.321781
sqrturbanp	3.06	0.327103
y4	2.95	0.338530
y3	2.70	0.369780
y2	2.45	0.407868
iwto	2.37	0.422713
logbit	2.10	0.477216
logcorrupt~e	1.87	0.535253
competition	1.83	0.547921
lat_abst	1.62	0.617946
regulator	1.56	0.641331
wtotelecom~t	1.51	0.663755
logpopu	1.26	0.794055
Mean VIF	2.99	

BIBLIOGRAPHY

Abe T 2006, 'Introduction of Competition in Mobile Phone Networks', Media Release by the Office of the Commissioner, Independent Consumer and Competition Commission – 18 January 2006, Port Moresby.

—. 2007[a], 'Challenges to regulating the utilities', Speech to Port Moresby Chamber of Commerce Inc, Independent Consumer and Competition Commission – 5 October 2007, Port Moresby.

—. 2007[b], 'Time to get the facts straight on mobile competition', Press Statement – 30 July 2007, Independent Consumer and Competition Commission, Port Moresby.

Acemoglu D, Johnson S and Robinson JA 2001, 'The colonial origins of comparative development: an empirical investigation', The American Economic Review, Vol. 91, No. 5, pp. 1369 – 1401.

Adlung R 2007, 'Negotiations on safeguards and subsidies in services: a never-ending story', Journal of International Economic Law, Vol. 10, Issue 2, pp. 235-265.

Aghion P and Schankerman M 1999, 'Competition, entry and the social returns to infrastructure in transition economies', Economics of Transition, Vol. 7, Issue 1, pp. 79-101.

Aisbett E 2007, 'Bilateral investment treaties and foreign direct investment: correlation versus causation', Department of Agricultural and Resource Economics, CUDARE Working Paper 1032 University of California, Berkeley.

—. 2008, 'Investment promotion and protection agreements and regulatory takings: understanding the debate, Crawford School of Economics and Government Policy Briefs 8 - Foreign Direct Investment, The Australian National University.

Aiyar SSA 2008, 'Small states: not handicapped and under-aided, but advantaged and over-aided', Cato Journal, Vol. 28, No. 3, pp. 449-478.

Altinger L and Enders A 1996, 'The scope and depth of GATS commitments', The World Economy, Vol. 19 Issue 3, pp. 307–332.

Alvarion 2006, 'Tonga national operator to cover islands with WiMAX using Alvarion,' Press Release, viewed 09 March 2008, <http://www.alvarion.com/presscenter/pressreleases/8577/>

Amalgamated Telecommunications Holdings Limited 2008, Corporate Information, viewed 26 March 2008, <http://www.ath.com.fj/corporate_info/index.html>

Armstrong HW and Read R 1998, 'Trade and growth in small states: The impact of global trade liberalization', World Economy, Vol. 21, No. 4, pp.563-585.

Armstrong HW and Read R 2006[a], 'Geographical 'handicaps' and small states: some implications for the Pacific from a global perspective', Asia Pacific Viewpoint, Vol. 47, No. 1, pp. 79-92.

Armstrong HW and Read R 2006[b], 'Determinants of economic growth and resilience in small states', (eds) L Briguglio, G Cordina and EJ Kisanga in Building economic resilience of small states, Formatek Publishing, Malta.

Armstrong M and Sappington DEM 2006, 'Regulation, competition, and liberalization', Journal of Economic Literature, Vol. XLIV, pp. 325-366.

Aryeetey E 1994, 'Private investment under uncertainty in Ghana,' World Development, Vol. 22, pp. 1211–21.

Asian Development Bank (ADB) 2008[a], 'Key indicators 2008', viewed 15 June 2008, <www.adb.org/statistics>

—. 2008[b], 'Basic statistics 2008', viewed 15 June 2008, <http://www.adb.org/Statistics/pdf/Basic-Statistics-2008.pdf>

Australian Agency for International Development (AusAID) 2006, 'Pacific 2020 – challenges and opportunities for growth', Commonwealth of Australia, Canberra.

—. 2008[a], 'Pacific economic survey 08 – connecting the region', Commonwealth of Australia, Canberra.

—. 2008[b], 'Telecommunications in the Pacific—background paper for the Pacific economic survey 2008, Commonwealth of Australia, Canberra.

Baldacchino G 2006, 'Innovative development strategies from non-sovereign island jurisdictions? A global review of economic policy and governance practices', World Development , Vol. 34, No. 5, pp.852-867.

Barro RJ, 'Determinants of economic growth: a cross-country empirical study', NBER Working Paper 5698, National Bureau of Economic Research, viewed 22 September 2010, <http://www.nber.org/papers/w5698>

Barro RJ and Gordon DB 1983, 'Rules, discretion and reputation in a model of monetary policy', Journal of Monetary Economics, Vol. 12, pp. 101-121.

Baselala E n.d, 'The Radisson deal', Island Business, viewed 12 October 2009, <http://www.islandsbusiness.com/fiji_business/index_dynamic/containerNameToReplace=MiddleMiddle/focusModuleID=17820/overideSkinName=issueArticle-full.tpl>

Baselala E 2007, 'The Radisson deal—what it means to each telecom player', Island Business', viewed 26 March 2008, <http://www.islandsbusiness.com/fiji_business/index_dynamic/containerNameToReplace=MiddleMiddle/focusModuleID=17820/overideSkinName=issueArticle-full.tpl>

Baudrier A 2001, 'Independent regulation and telecommunications performance in developing countries', Annual ISNIE Conference, Institutions and Governance, Berkeley, downloaded 21 June 2008, <http://www.isnie.org/ISNIE01/Papers01/baudrier.pdf>

Beach WW and Kane T 2008, 'Methodology: measuring the 10 economic freedoms' in '2008 index of economic freedom', downloaded 24 March 2009, <http://www.heritage.org/Index/PDF/2008/Index2008_Chap4.pdf>

Becker G 1983, 'A theory of competition among pressure groups for political influence', Quarterly Journal of Economics, Vol. 98, No. 3, pp. 371-400.

Bertelli AM and Whitford AB 2009, 'Perceiving credible commitments: how independent regulators shape elite perceptions of regulatory quality', British Journal of Political Science, Vol. 39, No. 3, pp. 517-537.

Blake B 2006, 'Regional workshop on gender, conflict, peace and security - a report on Tonga', 15-17 June – Mocambo Hotel, Nadi, Fiji, viewed 1 June 2009, <http://www.forumsec.org/_resources/article/files/Betty%20Blake%20-%20Catholic%20Women's%20League,%20Tonga.pdf>

Blackburn K and Christensen M 1989, 'Monetary policy and policy credibility: theories and evidence', Journal of Economic Literature, Vol. XXVII, pp.1-45.

Bo ED 2006, 'Regulatory capture: a review', Oxford Economic Policy, Vol. 22, No. 2, pp. 203-225.

Bosworth M 2003, 'China's WTO accession: trade and policy implications for Pacific island countries', Pacific Economic Bulletin, Vol. 18, No. 2, pp. 125-136.

—. 2006, 'Tonga's industrial incentives post-WTO accession – WTO compliance and policy implications', Final Report prepared for the Commonwealth Secretariat, ANU.

Bosworth M and Duncan R 2002, 'Facilitating the accession of ESCAP Developing Countries to WTO through regional cooperation', in Current status of the WTO accession process and the experience of ESCAP acceding countries, ESCAP Studies in Trade and Investment 49, UN, New York.

Briguglio L 1995, 'Small island developing states and their economic vulnerabilities,' World Development, Vol. 23, No. 9, pp.1615-1632.

—. 1998, 'Small country size and returns to scale in manufacturing', World Development, Vol. 26, No. 3, pp.507-515.

Briguglio L, Cordina G, Farrugia N and Vella S 2006, 'Conceptualizing and measuring economic resilience', (eds) L Briguglio, G Cordina and EJ Kisanga in Building economic resilience of small states, Formatek Publishing, Malta.

Brunetti A, Kisunko G and Weder B 1998, 'Credibility of rules and economic growth: evidence from a worldwide survey of the private sector', World Bank Economic Review, Vol. 12, No. 3, pp. 353-384.

Bryman A 2006, 'Integrating quantitative and qualitative research: how is it done?' Qualitative Research, Vol. 6, No. 1, pp. 97-113.

Burns P and Riechmann C 2004, 'Regulatory instruments and investment behaviour', Utilities Policy, Vol. 12, pp. 211-219.

Buthe T and Milner HV 2008, 'The politics of foreign direct investment into developing countries: increasing FDI through international trade agreements', American Journal of Political Science, Vol. 52, No. 4, pp. 741-762.

Calderon C and Serven L 2004, 'The effects of infrastructure development on growth and income distribution', World Bank Policy Research Working Paper No. 3400, World Bank, Washington.

Caribbean PressReleases.com 2006, 'Papua New Guinea next for Digicel', viewed 8 May 2008, <http://www.caribbeanpressreleases.com/articles/407/1/Papua-New-Guinea-next-for-Digicel/Launch-set-for-2007.html>

Castillo DE 2007, Process optimization: a statistical approach, Springer, Arlington.

Cellular-news 2008, 'Digicel faces loss of international gateway in Papua New Guinea', viewed 8 May 2008, <http://www.cellular-news.com/story/printer/29660.php>

Chand S 2003, 'An assessment of the proposal for a Pacific economic and political community', Pacific Economic Bulletin, Vol. 18, No. 2, pp. 117-124.

—. 2006, 'Developing resilience through labour mobility in microstates', (eds) L Briguglio, G Cordina and EJ Kisanga in Building economic resilience of small states, Formatek Publishing, Malta.

Chirinko RS and Schaller H 2009, 'The irreversibility premium', Journal of Monetary Economics', Vol. 56, pp. 390-408.

Change.gov 2008, 'Remarks of President-Elect Barack Obama' – as prepared for delivery SEC, CFTC, and Federal Reserve Board Announcements, Tuesday 18 December, Newsroom Blog, downloaded on 13 November 2009, <http://change.gov/newsroom/entry/presidentelect_obama_names_key_regulatory_appointments/>

Cieslik A and Kaniewsk M 2004, 'Telecommunications infrastructure and regional economic development: The case of Poland', Regional Studies, Vol. 38, Issue 6, pp. 713-725.

Commonwealth Secretariat and World Bank 2000, 'Small states: meeting the challenge in the global economy', viewed 27 April 2010, <http://siteresources.worldbank.org/PROJECTS/Resources/meetingchallengeinglobaleconomyl.pdf>

Consumer Council of Fiji 2009, 'Submission to Commerce Commission – review of the Telecommunications pricing determination', 26 February 2009, downloaded on 12 August 2009, <http://consumersfiji.org/Telecommunications_Review(1).pdf>

Cottarelli C and Giannini C 1997, 'Credibility without rules?, IMF Occasional Policy Paper No. 154, December.

Court of Appeal 2000, 'Cable and Wireless (Dominica) Limited vs. Marpin Telecommunications and Broadcasting Company Limited, Privy Council Appeal No. 15, Commonwealth of Dominica, <http://www.privy-council.org.uk/files/other/CABLE~1%20RTF.rtf>

Court of Appeal 2006, Vodafone Fiji Limited vs. The Minister for Information, Communications and media Relations, Civil Appeal No.: ABU0014 of 2006S, Date of Judgment 28th July 2006, Suva.

Crotty M 1998, The foundations of social research: meaning and perspective in the social research, Thousands Oak, London.

Cubbin J and Stern J 2006, 'The impact of regulatory governance and privatization on electricity industry generation capacity in developing countries', The World Economic Review, Vol. 20, No. 1, pp. 115-141.

Cuervo-Cazurra A 2006 ,'Who cares about corruption?', Journal of International Business Studies, Vol. 37, pp. 803-822.

Der G and Everitt B 2002, A handbook of statistical analyses using SAS, 2nd ed., CRC Press, Boca Raton.

Digicel 2007, 'PANGTEL acts illegally – it's business as usual for Digicel', viewed 8 May 2008, <http://www.digicelpng.com/article_printversion.php?aid=10034andpn=in_the_media>

—. 2008[a], 'Amended Telecommunications Act introduces monopoly on the international gateway', viewed 8 May 2008, <http://www.digicelpng.com/about/article.php?aid=10110andpn=in_the_mediaandref_page=about>

—. 2008[b], 'Digicel and Telikom start testing interconnection', viewed 8 May 2008, <http://www.digicelpng.com/about/article_printversion.php?aid=10019andpn=in_the_mediaandref_page=about>

—. 2008[c], 'A monopoly on international communications will mean poorer service and less competition', viewed 8 May 2008, <http://www.digicelpacific.com/en/media-center/press-releases/products-services/ict-policy-not-beneficial-for-competition>

Digicel Group 2009, 'About Digicel', viewed 29 May 2009, <http://www.digicelgroup.com/en/about>

Digicel News 2007, 'PANGTEL acts illegally – it's business as usual for Digicel', viewed 8 May 2008, <http://www.digicelpng.com/about/article_printversion.php?aid=10034andpn=in_the_mediaandref_page=about>

—. 2009, 'Digicel ready for new ICT bill', viewed 25 January 2010, <http://www.digicelpng.com/en/about/news/digicel-welcomes-ict-bill>

Digicel Vanuatu 2008, 'Digicel awarded GSM mobile licence in Vanuatu', Press Release, viewed 10 May 2008, <http://www.digicelvanuatu.com/vanuatu/press_release.html>

Dixit AK 1996, 'The making of economic policy. A transaction-cost politics perspective, MIT Press, Cambridge.

Dixit A and Pindyck R 1994, Investment under uncertainty, Princeton University Press, Princeton.

Downes AS 2006, 'Market reform and resilience building in small developing states', (eds) L Briguglio, G Cordina and EJ Kisanga in Building economic resilience of small states, Formatek Publishing, Malta.

Duncan R 2008, 'Pacific trade issues', Pacific studies series, Asian Development Bank, Manila.

Duncan R and Chand S 2002, 'The economies of the arc of instability', Asian-Pacific Economic Literature, Vol. 16, No.1, pp. 1-9.

Duncan R and McMaster J 2008, 'Impact of ICT on university education in Small Island States: the case of the University of the South Pacific', in EM Favaro (ed.), Small states, small solutions – improving connectivity and increasing the effectiveness of public services, The World Bank , Washington.

Dye T 1976, Policy analysis: what Governments do, why they do it and what difference it makes, The University of Alabama Press, Alabama.

Easterly W and Kraay A 2000, 'Small States, small problems? Income, growth and volatility in Small States', World Development, Vol. 28, No. 11, pp. 2013-2027.

Easterly W and Levine R 2003, 'Tropics, germs, and crops: how endowments influence economic development', Journal of Monetary Economics, Vol. 50, pp. 3-39.

Egger P and Lanz R 2008, 'The determinants of GATS commitment coverage', The World Economy, Vol. 31, Issue 11, pp. 1666-1694

Eilmansberger T 2009, 'Bilateral investment treaties and EU law', Common Market Law Review, Vol. 46, pp. 383-429.

Estache A, Goicoechea A and Manacorda M 2006, 'Telecommunications performance, reforms, and governance', Policy research working paper series 3822, World Bank.

Etzioni A 2009, 'The capture theory of regulations-revisited', Society, Vol. 46, No. 4, pp. 319-323.

Fink C, Mattoo A and Rathindran R 2003, 'An assessment of Telecommunications reform in developing countries', Information Economics and Policy, Vol. 15, pp. 443-466.

Fischer S 1988, 'Rules versus discretion in monetary policy', National Bureau of Economic Research, Working Paper No. 2518, Cambridge.

Fiji Government Online 2007[a], 'Press release', No.1879, 29 November 2007, Fiji Government, Suva.

—. 2007[b], 'Two new board members of the Commerce Commission appointed – Waradi', Press Releases, 23 November, downloaded on 17 August 2009, <http://www.fiji.gov.fj/publish/page_10677.shtml>

—. 2008[a], 'Press release', No.0292, 26 February 2008, Fiji Government, Suva.

—. 2008[b], 'Extra funds for Telecommunications authority', Press Releases, 27 February, downloaded on 12 August 2008, <http://www.fiji.gov.fj/publish/page_11294.shtml>

—. 2009[a], 'Opening statement by Mr Sayed-Khaiyum – Fiji's trade policy review', Press Releases, 26 March, downloaded on 02 August 2009, <http://www.fiji.gov.fj/publish/page_14562.shtml>

—. 2009[b], 'Price control revoked', Press Releases, 16 March, downloaded on 02 September 2009, <http://www.fiji.gov.fj/publish/printer_14479.shtml>

Fijilive 2009, 'Commerce Commission has new chair', Fijilive Online, 27 February, downloaded on 17 August 2009, <http://www.fijilive.com/news/2009/02/27/14025.Fijilive>

Fiji Ministry of Information, Communications and Media Relations 2005, 'Address by Honorable Mrs. Marieta M. Rigamoto', Workshop on Road Map for Telecommunications Sector Reform – 12 December, Southern Cross Hotel, Suva.

Flacher D and Jennequin H 2008, 'Is Telecommunications regulation efficient? An international perspective', Telecommunications Policy, Vol. 32, No. 5, pp. 364-377.

Flyvbjerg B 2006, 'Five misunderstandings about case-study research', Qualitative Inquiry, Vol. 12, No. 2, pp. 219-245.

Frankel JA and Romer D 1999, 'Does trade cause growth?', The American Economic Review, Vol. 89, No. 3, pp. 379-399.

Furlong SR 1997, 'Interest group influence on rule making', Administration and Society, Vol. 29, No. 3, pp. 325-347.

Gallup JL, Sachs JD and Mellinger AD 1999, 'Geography and economic development', International Regional Science Review, Vol. 22, No. 2, pp. 179-232.

Gasmi F, Laffont JJ and Sharkey WW 2000, 'Competition, universal-service and Telecommunications policy in developing countries', Information Economics and Policy, Vol. 12, pp.221-248.

Gay D 2005, 'Vanuatu's suspended accession bid: second thoughts?', in P Gallagher (ed.), Managing the Challenges of WTO Participation', Cambridge University Press, Cambridge.

Garcia-Murillo M and Kuerbis B 2005, 'The effect of institutional constraints on the success of universal service policies: a comparison between Latin America and the world', Telecommunications Policy, Vol. 29, No. 9-10, pp. 779-796.

Gibson J 2007, 'Is remoteness a cause of slow growth in the Pacific? A spatial-econometric analysis', Pacific Economic Bulletin, Vol. 22, No. 1, pp. 83-101.

Gilardi F 2002, 'Policy credibility and delegation to independent regulatory agencies: a comparative empirical analysis', Journal of European Public Policy, Vol. 9, No. 6, pp.873-893.

—. 2005[a], 'The formal independence of independent regulators: A comparison of 17 countries and 7 sectors', Swiss Political Science Review, Vol. 598, pp. 84-101.

—. 2005[b], 'The institutional foundations of regulatory capitalism: The diffusion on independent regulatory agencies in Western Europe', The Annals of the American Academy, Vol. 11, No. 4, pp. 139-167.

Goetschel L 1998, 'The foreign and security policy interests of small states in today's Europe', (ed) L. Goetschel in Small states inside and outside the European Union - interests and policies, Kluwer Academic Publishers, Boston, pp. 13-27.

Government of Papua New Guinea 1996, 'Telikom PNG Limited Act, No. 51, Government of Papua New Guinea, Port Moresby.

—. 2002, 'Telecommunications Industry Act', No. 26, Government of Papua New Guinea, Port Moresby.

—. 2002, 'Independent Consumer and Competition Commission Act, No. 06, Government of Papua New Guinea, Port Moresby.

Government of Samoa 2005, 'Telecommunications Act', No. 20, Government of Samoa, Apia.

—. 2008, 'Telecommunications Amendment', No. 18, Government of Samoa, Apia.

—. 2005, 'Telecommunications Act', Government of Samoa, Apia.

Government of Tonga 2000[a], 'Communications Act 2000', Act 22, Government of Tonga, Nuku'alofa.

—. 2000[b], 'Tonga Communications Corporation Act 2000', Act 21, Government of Tonga, Nuku'alofa.

Government of Vanuatu 1982, 'Telecommunications Act 1982', Government of Vanuatu, Port Vila.

—. 1986, 'Telecommunications Act 1986', Act 2, Government of Vanuatu, Port Vila.

—. 1988, 'Telecommunications Act', Government of Vanuatu, Port Vila.

—. 2007[a], 'Telecommunications Act 2007 – draft', Ministry of Infrastructure and Public Utilities, MGFW draft 2.0 28.02.07, Port Vila.

—. 2007[b], 'Telecommunications policy statement of the Government of Vanuatu – proposal for public consultation', Port Vila.

—. 2007[c], 'Utilities regulatory authority', Act 11, Government of Vanuatu, Port Vila.

—. 2008, 'Vanuatu Interim Telecommunications Regulator's Annual Report', Office of the Interim Telecommunications Regulator, Port Vila.

—. 2009[a], 'Telecommunications and Radiocommunications Regulation Act, No. 30, Government of Vanuatu, Port Vila.

—. 2009[b], 'Digicel now covers 85% of Vanuatu', Press Release, Office of the Vanuatu Telecommunications Regulator, Port Vila, viewed 3 February 2010, <http://www.telecomregulator.gov.vu/attachments/055_Press%20Release%20-%20Digicel%2085percent.pdf>

Government of Western Samoa 1972, 'Post Office Act', Government of Western Samoa, Apia.

Greene WH 2003, Econometric analysis', 5nd ed., Prentice Hall, New Jersey.

Grynberg R 2006, 'A theory of trade and development of small vulnerable states', (ed) R Grynberg in WTO at the margins – small states and the multilateral trading system, University Press, Cambridge.

Grynberg R and Joy RM 2000, 'The accession of Vanuatu to the WTO – lessons for the Multilateral Trading System', Journal of World Trade, Vol. 34, No. 6, pp. 159-173.

Guzman AT 1998, 'Why LDCs sign treaties that hurt them: explaining the popularity of Bilateral Investment Treaties', Virginia Journal of International Law, Vol.38, pp. 639-688.

—. 2005, 'The design of international agreements', The European Journal of International Law, Vol. 16, No. 4, pp. 579-612.

Haggarty L, Shirley MM and Wallsten S 2002, 'Telecommunication reform in Ghana', World Bank Policy Research Working Paper No. 2983, viewed 12 December 2009, <http://papers.ssrn.com/sol3/papers.cfm?abstract_id=636345>

Hausmann R 2001, 'Prisoners of geography', Foreign Policy, Jan-Feb, No. 122, pp. 44-53

Harberger AC 1988, 'Policymaking and economic policy in small island developing countries', in R Dornbusch and FLCH Helmers (eds), The open economy: tools for policymakers in developing countries, Oxford University Press, New York, pp. 249-63.

Helm D 2006, 'Regulatory reform, capture, and the regulatory burden', Oxford Review of Economic Policy, Vol. 22, No. 2, 169-185.

Henao I 2004, 'Country report on Papua New Guinea' – Sub-regional Conference on ICT for Development in Pacific Island Developing Countries, 6 – 9 December 2004, Suva, Fiji.

Henisz W and Zelner B 2001, 'The institutional environment for Telecommunications investment', Journal of Economics and Management Strategy, Vol. 10, pp. 123–147.

Henisz WJ and Zelner BA 2006, 'Interest groups, veto points, and electricity infrastructure deployment', International Organisation, Vol. 60, No. 1, pp. 263-286.

Hernandez AP n.d., 'Mobile phone war of PNG', The National, viewed 14 December 2008, <http://www.thenational.com.pg/073107/w7.htm>

High Court of Fiji 2005, Vodafone vs. The Minister for Information, Communications and media Relations, Civil Action No.: HBC0576, Date of Decision 20th December 2005, Civil Jurisdiction, Suva.

Horscroft V 2006, 'A theory of trade and development of small vulnerable states', (ed) R Grynberg in 'WTO at the margins – small states and the multilateral trading system', University Press, Cambridge.

Independent Consumer and Competition Commission 2007, 'Press Release - Time to get the facts straight on mobile competition', Office of the Commissioner, National Capital District.

—. 2008, 'Notification of amended Government policy on information communications technology', ICCC, Boroko.

International Telecommunications Union 2000, 'Regulatory information', International Telecommunications Union, Geneva.

—. 2004, 'Bula internet: Fiji ICT case study', International Telecommunications Union, Geneva.

—. 2006, 'Telecommunications Report 2006', International Telecommunications Union, Geneva.

—. 2007, 'World Telecommunications ICT Indicators 2007 Database', International Telecommunications Union, Geneva.

Island Business 2007, 'Digicel issue raised with Government', Islands Business Online, viewed 23 May 2009, <http://www.islandsbusiness.com/news/index_dynamic/containerNameToReplace=MiddleMiddle/focusModuleID=130/focusContentID=9935/tableName=mediaRelease/overideSkinName=newsArticle-full.Telikom>

—. 2008, 'Ongoing concern over World Bank/Digicel link – Digicel will kill us', viewed 26 May 2008, <http://www.islandsbusiness.com/archives/islands_business/index_dynamic/containerNameToReplace=MiddleMiddle/focusModuleID=17899/overideSkinName=issueArticle-full.Telikom>

Jankee KC 2006, 'Financial globalization and economic resilience in Mauritius', (eds) L Briguglio, G Cordina and EJ Kisanga in 'Building economic resilience of small states', Formatek Publishing, Malta.

Jayaraman TK 2006, 'Macroeconomic reform and resilience building in small states', (eds) L Briguglio, G Cordina and EJ Kisanga in 'Building economic resilience of small states', Formatek Publishing, Malta.

Joku H 2008, 'Telecommunications: Digicel tightlipped on gateway issue', Islands Business Online, viewed 26 May 2008, <http://www.islandsbusiness.com/islands_business/index_dynamic/containerNameToReplace=MiddleMiddle/focusModuleID=17940/overideSkinName=issueArticle-full.Telikom>

Kaufmann D 1997, 'Corruption: the facts', Foreign Policy, Summer, pp. 114-131.

Keck A and Djiofack-Zebaze C 2009, 'Telecommunications services in Africa: the impact of WTO commitments and unilateral reform on sector performance on sector performance and economic growth', World Development, Vol. 37, No. 5, pp. 919-940.

Kelegai L and Middleton M n.d., ' Conquering the frontier: developing human resources for ICTs in Papua New Guinea', Regional Initiative for Information and Communications Technology Strategies (RIFICTS) Conference, 24th – 26th July, Kuala Lumpur, Malaysia.

Kerner E 2009, 'Why should I believe you? The costs and consequences of Bilateral Investment Treaties', International Studies Quarterly, Vol. 53, pp. 73-102.

Kessides IN, Noll RG & Benjamin NC 2009, 'Regionalizing telecommunications reform in West Africa', World Bank, Policy Research Working Paper 5126, viewed 30 April 2010, <http://vle.worldbank.org/bnpp/files/Regionalizing%20Telecommunications%20Reform.pdf>

Kim S 2007,'Bilateral investment treaties, political risk and foreign direct investment', Asia Pacific Journal of Economics and Business, Vol. 11, No. 1, pp. 6-24.

King G, Keohane RO and Verba S 1994, Designing social inquiry – scientific inference in qualitative research, Princeton University Press, New Jersey.

Knox AD 1967, 'Some economic problems of small countries', in B. Benedict (ed.) Problems of Smaller Territories', Athlone Press, London.

Kolone Vaai 2008, 'The Samoan experience', Presentation for the Pacific Telecommunications Conference, 10-11 July, Apia.

Krippendorff Klaus 1980, Content analysis – an introduction to its methodology, Sage Publications, California.

Kuznets S 1960, 'Economic growth of small nations', in 'Economic consequences of the size of nations - proceedings of a conference held by the International Economic Association', (ed) E. A. G. Robinson, Macmillian and Co. Ltd, London, pp.14-32.

Kydland, F and Prescott EC 1977, 'Rules rather than discretion: the inconsistency of optimal plans', Journal of Political Economy, Vol. 85, No. 3, pp. 473–492.

Lall SV 2007, Infrastructure and regional growth, growth dynamics and policy relevance for India, Annals of Regional Science, Vol. 41, Issue 3, pp. 581-599.

Lam PL and Shiu A 2008, 'Productivity analysis of the Telecommunications sector in China', Telecommunications Policy, Vol. 32, pp. 559-571.

Larmour P 1997, 'Introduction', in P Larmour (ed) 'The governance of common property in the Pacific region', National Centre for Development Studies, Paragon Printers, Canberra.

—. 2005, Foreign flowers: institutional transfer and good governance in the Pacific islands, University of Hawaii Press, Hawaii,

Lattimore R 2003, 'Competition policy and Telecommunications', in A Sidorenko and C Findlay (eds) 'Regulations and market access', Asia Pacific Press, The Australian National University, Canberra.

Lee RC and Findlay C 2005, 'Telecommunications reform in Indonesia: achievements and challenges', Bulletin of Indonesian Economic Studies, Vol. 41, No. 3, pp. 341-365.

Lee SH and Levendis J 2006, 'Creation of a separate Telecommunications regulatory agency: a duration analysis of its time pattern', Contemporary Economic Policy, Vol. 24, No. 3, pp. 407-417.

Legislative Assembly of Samoa 2009, 'Approved estimates of receipts and payments of the Government of Samoa for the financial year ending 30th June 2009', Parliamentary Paper 2008/2009 No.2, Apia.

Lesa MK 2007, 'A load of hogwash – MP attacks SamoaTel and Digicel', Samoa Observer, 11 July 2007, Apia.

Levine ME and Forrence JL 1990, 'Regulatory capture, public interest, and the public agenda: toward a synthesis', Journal of Law, Economics, and Organization, Vol. 6, Special Issue, pp. 167-198.

Levy B and Spiller PT 1994, 'The institutional foundations of regulatory commitment: a comparative analysis of Telecommunications regulation', The Journal of Law, Economics and Organization, Vol. 10, No. 2, pp. 201-246.

Levy B and Spiller PT 1996, 'A framework for resolving the regulatory problem', in B. Levy and P.T. Spiller (Eds), Regulations, Institutions, and Commitment, Oxford University Press, Oxford pp. 1-35.

Li W and Xu LC 2002, 'The political economy of privatization and competition: cross-country evidence from the Telecommunications sector', Journal of Comparative Economics, Vol. 30, pp. 439-462.

Li W, Qiang CZW and Xu LC 2005, 'Regulatory reforms in the Telecommunications sector in developing countries: the role of democracy and private interests', World Development, Vol. 33, No. 8, pp. 1307-1324.

Ligauila P 2009, 'Fiji's military regime expels three foreign journalists as local media protests on', The Associated Press, ABC New International, viewed 31 April 2010, <http://abcnews.go.com/International/wireStory?id=7321322>

Limao N and Olarreaga M 2006, 'Trade preferences to small developing countries and the welfare costs of lost multilateral liberalization', World Bank Economic Review , Vol. 20, No. 2, pp.217-240.

Limao N and Venables AJ 2001, 'Infrastructure, geographical disadvantage, transport costs, and trade', World Bank Economic Review, Vol. 15, No. 3, pp.451-479.

Lodge M and Stirton L 2002, 'Embedding regulatory autonomy in Caribbean Telecommunications, Annals of Public and Cooperative Economics, Vol. 73, No. 4, pp. 667-693.

Lohmann S 1992, 'Optimal commitment in monetary policy: credibility versus flexibility', The American Economic Review, Vol. 82, No. 1, pp. 273-286.

Madden G, Savage SJ and Ng J 2003, 'Asia-Pacific Telecommunications liberalisation and productivity performance', Australian Economic Papers, March, pp. 91-102.

Maiorano F and Stern J 2007, 'Institutions and Telecommunications infrastructure in low and middle-income countries: the case of mobile telephony', Utilities Policy, Vol. 15,

Majone G 1997, Independent agencies and the delegation problem: theoretical and normative dimensions', in Bernard Steuenberg and Frans van Vught (eds), Political Institutions and Public Policy, Kluwer Academic Publishers, Dordrecht, pp. 139-56.

Matangi Tonga 2007, 'Digicel Pacific to acquire TonFon Communications', viewed 28 November 2007, <http://www.matangitonga.to/article/tonganews/business/article_print_tonga_digicel_2>

—. 2008[a], 'Digicel launches Tonga network', viewed 8 May 2008. <http://www.matangitonga.to/article/tonganews/business/digicel_070508_1532.shtml>

—. 2008[b], 'PM, Ministers to step down from public enterprises boards', viewed 28 February 2008, <http://www.matangitonga.to/user?article=article/tonganews/Government/director_workshop_250208_1629.shtml>

Matoto A, '2008, 'Budget speech to the Chamber of Commerce', Tonga-Now, Ministry of Finance, viewed 1 June 2009,

<http://minfo.gov.to/index.php?option=com_contentandview=articleandid=195%3Aspeech-to-the-chamber-of-commerce-25th-june-2008andItemid=398>

Mazmanian DA and Sabatier PA 1980, 'A multivariate model of public policy-making', American Journal of Political Science, Vol. 24, No. 3, pp. 439- 468.

Melody WH 1997, 'Comment- on the meaning and importance of "independence" in Telecommunications reform', Telecommunications Policy, Vol. 21, No. 3, pp. 195-197.

Mihov I and Sibert A 2006, 'Credibility and flexibility with independent monetary policy committees', Journal of Money, Credit and Banking, Vol. 38, No. 1, pp. 23-4.

Monroe AD 2000, Essentials of political research, Westview Press, Colorado

National Gazette 2007, 'Notification of Government policy on Telecommunications – Telecommunications Act 1996', No. G165, Independent Consumer and Competition Commission, Port Moresby.

National Executive Council 2008, 'National Government ICT policy – revising Government policy for ICT sector reform', Papua New Guinea Government, Port Moresby.

Neumayer E and Spess L 2005, 'Do bilateral investment treaties increase foreign direct investment to Developing Countries?', World Dvelopment, Vol. 33, pp. 1567-1585.

Noll RG 1999, 'Telecommunications reform in developing countries', Working Paper 99-10, AEI-Brookings Joint Centre for Regulatory Sudies.

—. 2000, 'Telecommunications reform in developing countries', in AO Krueger (ed.), Economic policy reform The second stage, The University of Chicago Press, Chicago.

'Ofa SV 2008[a], 'General agreement on trade in services (GATS) and WTO accession commitments – the experience of Tonga and Vanuatu', in J Streatfield and S Lacey (eds), New reflections on international trade: essays on agriculture, WTO accession and systemic issues, Cameron May, London.

—. 2008[b], 'The Telecommunications sector in the Pacific: a regulatory policy survey', Pacific Economic Bulletin, Vol. 23, No. 3, pp 69-100.

—. 2009, 'The WTO's telecommunications commitments and the credibility of telecommunications regulatory reforms in small island developing states', Pacific Economic Bulletin, Vol. 24, No. 3, pp. 39-57.

—. 2010, 'Telecommunications reform in Fiji, Samoa and Vanuatu and the credibility problem: the impact of independent regulators', Pacific Economic Bulletin, Vol. 25, No. 1, pp. 96-113.

—. 2011, 'Telecommunications regulatory reforms and the credibility problem: case studies from Papua New Guinea and Tonga', in R Duncan (ed.), *'The Political Economy of Economic Reform in the Pacific',* Asian Development Bank, Manila, 2011.

Olson M 1965, The logic of collective action, Harvard University Press, Cambridge.

Oxfam New Zealand n.d., 'Blood from a stone', Briefing Papers, viewed 1 June 2009, <http://www.oxfam.org/sites/www.oxfam.org/files/blood.pdf>

—. 2005, 'Proposed WTO accession: key issues for Tonga', viewed 1 June 2009, <http://classshares.student.usp.ac.fj/SO310/wto%2520key%2520issues%2520for%2520tonga.pdf>

Pacific Islands Broadcasting Association 2007, 'Digicel issue raised with PNG Government', viewed 8 November 2008, <http://www.highbeam.com/doc/1G1-168306117.html>

Pacific Magazine 2008, 'Digicel awarded licence to operate in Vanuatu', viewed 21 May 2008. <http://www.pacificmagazine.net/news/2008/03/17/digicel-gets-vanuatu-licence?printview=1>

Paine E n.d., 'Delivering improved service sees cash-cow partly sold', Islands Business, viewed 27 March 2010, <http://www.islandsbusiness.com/islands_business/index_dynamic/containerNameToReplace=MiddleMiddle/focusModuleID=18199/overideSkinName=issueArticle-full.tpl>

Painter M and Wong SF 2007, 'The Telecommunications regulatory regimes in Hong Kong and Singapore: when direct state intervention meets indirect policy instrument', The Pacific Review, Vol. 20, No. 2, pp. 173-195.

Papua New Guinea Department of Public Enterprises, Information and Development Co-operation 2006, 'National information and communication technology (ICT) policy – September 2006, Government of Papua New Guinea, Port Moresby.

—. 2007, 'National information and communication technology (ICT) policy – May 2007', Government of Papua New Guinea, Port Moresby.

Papua New Guinea Department of Communications and Information 1994, 'National policy on information and communication of Papua New Guinea', Government of Papua New Guinea, Port Moresby.

—. 2008, ' National Information and Communication Technology (ICT) Policy – April 2008', Government of Papua New Guinea, Port Moresby.

—. 2009, 'National ICT policy: Phase 2 reforms (final report) – March 2009', Government of Papua New Guinea, Port Moresby.

Papua New Guinea Government 2007, 'Refining Government policy for ICT sector reform - September 2007', Attachment 1, Government of Papua New Guinea, Port Moresby.

Papua New Guinea Ministry of Information and Communications Services 1993, 'National policy on information and communication of Papua New Guinea', Government of Papua New Guinea, Port Moresby.

Papua New Guinea Office of the Prime Minister 2005, 'Media release – Progress report to the parliament on Telikom 1995-2005', Government of Papua New Guinea, Port Moresby.

PANGTEL, 'Telecommunications Act 1996 (amendments), viewed 24 March 2008, <http://www.pangtel.gov.pg/Legislation/legislation.htm>

Parliament of Fiji 2006[a], 'Telecommunications Bill 2006 – explanatory note', Attorney Generals Chambers, viewed 26 March 2008 <http://www.parliament.gov.fj/legislative/bills.aspx?billID=318andviewtype=fullandbillnav=bill>

—. 2006[b], 'Telecommunications Bill 2006', Ministry of Information and Communications, viewed 26 March 2008, <http://www.parliament.gov.fj/legislative/bills.aspx?billID=318andviewtype=summaryandbillnav=bill>

Parliament of Samoa 2005, 'Telecommunications Act 2005', Ministry of Communications and Information Technology, viewed 24 March 2008, <http://www.parliament.gov.ws/documents/acts/TELECOMMUNICATIONSMUNICATIONS_ACT_2005_-_Eng.pdf>

Peltzman S 1976, 'Toward a more general theory of regulation', Journal of Law and Economics, Vol. 19, pp. 211-40.

Pindyck RS 1988, 'Irreversible investment, capacity choice, and the value of the firm', American Economic Review, Vol. 78, No. 5, pp. 969-985.

Populations Division 2007, 'World population prospects – the 2006 revision', Department of Economic and Social Affairs, United Nations, New York.

Posner RA 1975, 'The social costs of monopoly and regulation', Journal of Political Economy, Vol. 83, No. 4, pp. 807-827.

Post LA, Raile AN and Raile ED 2008, 'Defining political will', Annual meeting of the National Communication Association 94th Annual Convention, San Diego, CA Online, viewed 1 December 2009, <http://www.allacademic.com/one/www/www/index.php?cmd=www_searchandoffset=0andlimit=5andmulti_search_search_mode=publicationandmulti_search_publication_fulltext_mod=fulltextandtextfield_submit=trueandsearch_module=multi_searchandsearch=Searchandsearch_field=title_idxandfulltext_search=Defining+Political+Will>

Public Service Commission 2008, 'Vacancy – Samoan Telecommunications regulator', Government of Samoa, Official Circular, Special Issue 2008/3, Apia.

Productivity Commission n.d., Inquiry – Review of Telecommunications Specific Competition Regulation, viewed 14 January 2009, <http://www.pc.gov.au/__data/assets/pdf_file/0018/25803/sub046.pdf>

Radio New Zealand International 2006, 'Two mobile operators enter Papua New Guinea market', viewed 26 May 2008, <http://www.rnzi.com/pages/news.php?op=readandid=26574>

Ram R 1997, 'Tropics and economic development: an empirical investigation', World Development, Volume 25, No. 9, pp. 1443-1452.

Republic of Fiji Islands 2009, 'Commerce (amendment) promulgation', Promulgation No. 4 of 2009, Interim Government of the Republic of Fiji Islands, Suva.

Republic of Vanuatu 2006, 'Telecommunications Act 1989', Cap. 206, Consolidated Edition, Government of Vanuatu, Port Vila.

Reuters 2007, 'Digicel acquires Tonga mobile operator TonFon', viewed 18 December 2007, <http://www.reuters.com/article/pressRelease/idUS49930+29-Nov-2007+MW20071129>

—. 2008, 'Digicel awarded GSM mobile licence in Fiji', Reuters, 27 February 2008.

Robinson EAG 1960, 'The size of the nation and the cost of administration', Economic consequences of the size of nations - proceedings of a conference held by the International Economic Association, (ed) EAG Robinson, Macmillian and Co. Ltd, London, pp. 223-239.

Rodrik D 1989, 'Policy uncertainty', National Bureau for Economic Research Working Paper No. W2999, downloaded 21 January 2009, <http://www.nber.org/papers/w2999.pdf?new_window=1>

—. 1991, 'Policy uncertainty and private investment in Developing Countries', Journal of Development Economics, Vol. 36, pp. 229-242.

Rodrik D, Subramanian A and Trebbi F 2004, 'Institutions rule: the primacy of institutions over geography and integration in economic development', Journal of Economic Growth, Vol. 9, pp. 131-165.

Roller LH and Waverman L 2001, 'Telecommunications infrastructure and economic development: a simultaneous, American Economic Review, Vol. 91, No. 4, pp. 909-923.

Ros AJ 1997, 'When, where, and how? Implementing effective Telecommunications competition and regulatory policy', Journal of Project Finance, Vol. 2, No.4, pp. 33-42.

—. 1999, 'Does ownership or competition matter? The effects of Telecommunications reform on network expansion and efficiency', Journal of Regulatory Economics, Vol. 15, pp. 65-92.

Sachs JD 2001, 'Tropical underdevelopment', National Bureau of Economic Research, Working Paper 8119, Cambridge.

Salacuse WJ and Sullivan PN 2005, ' Do bilateral investment treaties really work?: an evaluation of bilateral investment treaties and their grand bargain', Harvard International Law Journal, Vol. 46, pp. 67-130.

Samoa 2005, 'Telecommunications Act 2005', Legislative Assembly of Samoa, Apia. Samoa Office of the Regulator 2006, 'Order of the Regulator – number 2006/4', Government of Samoa, Apia.

—. 2007, 'Order of the Regulator – number 2007/4', Government of Samoa, Apia.

—. 2008, 'Order of the Regulator – Number 2008/03', Government of Samoa, Apia.

SamoaTel 2007, 'SamoaTel leads mobile growth, Digicel sues', Media Release Online, downloaded on 8 September 2009, <http://www.SamoaTel.ws/index.php?option=com_contentandtask=viewandid=30andItemid=68>

Serven L and Solimano A 1993, 'Debt crisis, adjustment policies and capital formation in developing countries: where do we stand?', World Development, Vol. 21, No. 1, pp. 127-140.

Shepsle KA 1991, 'Discretion, institutions, and the problem of Government commitment', in Pierre Bourdieu and James S Coleman (eds), Social theory for a changing society, Westview Press, Boulder, pp. 245-263.

Shiu A and Lam PL 2008, 'Causal relationship between Telecommunications and economic growth in China and its regions', Regional Studies, Vol. 42, No. 5, pp. 705-718.

Shively WP 2005, The craft of political research, Sixth Edition, Prentice Hall, New Jersey.

—. WP 2009, The craft of political research, Seventh Edition, Prentice Hall, New Jersey.

Singh M 2009[a], 'Lack of funds closes Commerce Commission', Fiji Times Online, 28 September 2008, viewed 17 August 2009, < http://www.fijitimes.com/story.aspx?id=102043>

—. M 2009[b], 'Conspiracy: Sweeney claims dismissal linked to inquiry', Fiji Times Online, 3 March 2009, viewed 17 August 2009, <http://www.fijitimes.com.fj/story.aspx?id=115749>

Singleton RA and Straits BC 2005, Approaches to social research, Fourth Edition, Oxford University Press, New York.

Soakai A 2004, 'ICT in Tonga, Presentation for the Sub-Regional Forum on ICTs for Development in Pacific Island Developing Countries', Suva, Fiji.

—. A 2006, 'Tonga's Telecommunications reform begins to bear fruit', Press Release, Prime Minister's Office, Government of Tonga, Nuku'alofa.

Srinivasan TN 1986, 'The costs and benefits of being a small, remote, island, landlocked, or ministate economy', The World Bank Research Observer, Vol. 1, No. 2, pp. 205-218.

Srivastava P 1994, 'Nationalizing to liberalize: credibility in trade liberalization', Journal of International Economics', Vol. 36, No. 3-4, pp. 449-465.

Stern J and Trillas F 2003, 'Independence and discretion in Telecommunications regulation: lessons from independent central banks', Utilities Policy, Vol. 11, No. 4, pp. 191-201.

Streeten P 1993, 'The special problems of small countries', World Development, Vol. 21, No. 2, pp. 197-202.

Stigler GJ 1971, 'The theory of economic regulation', Bell Journal of Economic and Management Science, Vol. 2, No. 1, pp. 3-21.

Stuff.co.nz 2009, 'Samoa rebounds after tsunami', Online Source, downloaded on 30 November 2009, <http://www.stuff.co.nz/travel/pacific-islands/3091595/Samoa-rebounds-after-tsunami>

Supreme Court of Papua New Guinea 2008, 'PacLII Databases – Telikom PNG Ltd v Independent Consumer and Competition Commission [2008] PGSC5; SC906 (28 March 2008', viewed 18 December 2008, <http://www.paclii.org/pg/cases/PGSC/2008/5.html>

Supreme Court of the Republic of Vanuatu 2006, 'Telecommunications Vanuatu Limited vs. The Minister for Infrastructure and Public Utilities', Civil Case No. 205 of 2005, Government of the Republic of Vanuatu, Port Vila.

Supreme Court of Samoa 2008, 'Digicel (Samoa) Ltd v Attorney General [2008]', WSSC 15 (30 March 2008), Apia.

Sutherland E 2009, 'Telecommunications in small island developing states', 37th Research Conference on Communication, Information, and Internet Policy, September 25-27, 2009, George Mason University, School of Law, Arlington, viewed 10 January 2010, <http://70.120.87.161/dev/tprc/images/stories/papers/sutherland_2009.pdf>

Szmrecsanyi B 2006, Morphosyntactic Persistence in Spoken English: a corpus study at the intersection of variations sociolinguistics, psycholingui, Walter de Gruyter Gmbh & Company, KG, Berlin.

Tabureguci D 2007[a], 'Goodbye monopoly hello open market', Fiji's Business Magazine, December 2007, Suva.

—. 2007[b], FINTEL wants more share in local market, Island Business, October Edition, viewed 26 March 2008, <http://www.islandsbusiness.com/archives/islands_business/index_dynamic/containerNameToReplace=MiddleMiddle/focusModuleID=17681/overideSkinName=issueArticle-full.Telikom>

—. 2008, 'PNG's ICT policy under the knife again – NETCO/SERVCO model scrapped?', Island Business, viewed 26 May 2008, <http://www.islandsbusiness.com/archives/islands_business/index_dynamic/containerNameToReplace=MiddleMiddle/focusModuleID=17900/overideSkinName=issueArticle-full.Telikom>

Tashakkori A and Teddlie C 1998, 'Mixed methods – combining qualitative and quantitative approaches', Applied social research series, Vol. 46, Sage Publications, Thousand Oaks.

Telecommunications Fiji Ltd. 2008, 'Corporate Profile', viewed 26 March 2008, <http://www.tfl.com.fj/index.cfm?go=tfl.corporateandid=6A996481-EF1C-2424-CFD1FCEF5627D89Dandcategory=corporate>

Telikom PNG 2009, 'Corporate Information', viewed January 2008, <http://www.Telikompng.com.pg/>

The National 2007[a], 'Pangtel shuts down Digicel', The National Online, viewed 15 May 2009, <http://www.thenational.com.pg/072507/nation2.htm>

—. 2007[b], 'Mobile dissent', viewed 26 May 2008, <http://www.thenational.com.pg/032807/nation1.htm>

—. 2007[c], 'Enter Greencom', viewed 26 May 2008, <http://www.thenational.com.pg/110907/Nation%203.htm>

Thomas Abe 2007[a], 'Challenges to regulating the utilities', Speech to Port Moresby Chamber of Commerce Inc, Independent Consumer and Competition Commission, 5 October 2007, Port Moresby.

—. 2007[b], 'Time to get the facts straight on mobile competition', Press Statement, 30 July 2007, Independent Consumer and Competition Commission, Port Moresby.

Tigre PB 1999, 'The political economy of Latin American Telecommunications: multilateral agreements and national regulatory systems – final draft', Latin American Trade Network, Research Program on International Economic Institutions.

Tobin J and Rose-Ackerman S 2005, 'Foreign direct investment and the business environment in developing countries: the impact of bilateral investment treaties', Yale Law and Economic Research Paper, No. 293, New Haven, CT.

Tonga-NOW 2007, 'Irish Telecommunications group Digicel to buy TONFON', viewed 28 November 2007, <http://www.tonga-now.to/ArticlePreview.aspx?ID+4723andPrint=1>

Tonga Department of Communications 2000, 'Communications policy statement 2000', Prime Minister's Office, Government of Tonga, Nuku'alofa.

—. 2006, 'Annual report 2006', Prime Minister's Office, Government of Tonga, Nuku'alofa.

—. 2008, 'Press release', Government of Tonga, viewed 14 March 2008, <http://www.pmo.gov.to/artman/publish/printer_105.shtml>

Tonga Department of Statistics 2008, Population Census 2006 – Provisional figures, Government of Tonga, Nuku'alofa.

—. 2009, Secondary and Middle Education Enrolments, Government of Tonga, Nuku'alofa.

Tonga Ministry of Education 2007, 'Education Enrolments', Annual Report, Government of Tonga, Nuku'alofa.

Tonga Telecommunications Corporations 2009, Company Information, viewed January 2008, <http://www.tcc.to/>

Tongasat 2008, 'Tongasat', viewed 10 March 2008, <http://www.tongasat.com/>

Tyler M and Bednarczyk S 1993, 'Regulatory institutions and processes in Telecommunications: an alternative study of alternatives', Telecommunications Policy, Vol. 17, pp. 650–676.

'Utoikamanu STT 2006, 'Consumption tax – the Tongan experience', Pacific Islands Report, Pacific Islands Development Program/East-West Centre, viewed 1 June 2009, <http://archives.pireport.org/archive/2007/July/07-27-rp.htm>

United Nations Conference on Trade and Development (UNCTAD) 2000, 'Bilateral investment treaties 1959-1999', United Nations, New York.

United Nations Economic and Social Conference for Asia Pacific (UNESCAP) 2007, 'Statistical yearbook for Asia and the Pacific 2007', viewed 28 January 2010, <http://www.unescap.org/Stat/data/syb2008/index.asp>

Vaai K 2008, 'Presentation on Pacific Telecommunications Conference', National University of Samoa, Apia.

Vakil CN and Brahmananda PR 1960, The problems of developing countries', In EAG Robinson (ed), Economic Consequences of the Size of Nations, MacMillan, London, pp.133-150.

Van Evera S 1997, Guide to methods for students of political science, Cornell University Press, Ithaca.

Vanuatu Daily Post 2008, 'TVL shares given up to benefit rural - PRO', downloaded on 24 August 2009, <http://www.dailypost.vu/ArticleArchives/tabid/56/articleType/ArticleView/articleId/2434/TVL-shares-given-up-to-benefit-rural-PRO.aspx>

Vanuatu Department of Trade 2008, 'Annual report 2007', Government of Vanuatu, Port Vila.

Vanuatu Office of the Interim Telecommunications Regulator 2008[a], 'Vanuatu Telecommunications regulator's annual report', Government of the Republic of Vanuatu, Port Vila.

—. 2008[b], 'Interim report 2008', Vanuatu Office of the Interim Telecommunications Regulator, Port Vila.

Vanuatu Ministry of Infrastructure and Public Utilities 2007, 'Telecommunications (amendment) Act', No. 15, Vanuatu Government, Port Vila.

—. 2008, 'Government grants licence to Digicel', Press Release, No. 2281, Vanuatu Daily Post Port Vila.

—. 2009, 'Telecommunications and Radiocommunications regulation Act 2009', Draft for Consultation purposes only, Vanuatu Government, Port Vila.

Vanuatu National Statistics Office 2009, 'Government Revenue 1995-2008', Vanuatu Government Finance Statistics, Port Vila, <http://www.spc.int/prism/country/VU/stats/ECONOMIC/GFS/gfs-revenue.htm>

Varoudakis A and Rossotto CM 2004, 'Regulatory reform and performance in Telecommunications: unrealized potential in the MENA countries', Telecommunications Policy, Vol. 28, pp. 59-78.

Vodafone Fiji Limited 2009, 'Vodafone welcomes lifting of price control order', Online Source, 16 March, downloaded 17 August 2009,

<http://www2.vodafone.com.fj/pages.cfm/general/about-us/media-releases-1/media-releases-09/march-16-1.html>

Wallsten SJ 2001, 'An econometric analysis of Telecommunications competition, privatization, and regulation in Africa and Latin America', The Journal of Industrial Economics, Vol. XLIX, Issue 1, pp. 0022-1821.

—. 2003, 'Of carts and horses: regulation and privatization in Telecommunications reforms', Policy Reform, Vol. 6, No. 4, pp. 217-231.

—. 2004, 'Privatizing monopolies in developing countries: the real effects of exclusivity periods in Telecommunications', Journal of Regulatory Economics, Vol. 26, No. 3, pp. 303-320.

Waverman L, Meschi M and Fuss M 2005, 'The impact of Telecommunications on economic growth in Developing Countries, The Vodafone Policy Paper Series 2, pp. 10-23.

Weatherhead M 2006, 'Small countries: a survey of the literature', (ed) R Grynberg in WTO at the margins – small states and the multilateral trading system, University Press, Cambridge.

Wei SJ 2000, 'How taxing is corruption on international investors?', The Review of Economics and Statistics, Vol. 82, No. 1, pp. 1.11.

Willie R 2008, 'Government TVL shares used as compensation to end monopoly', Vanuatu Daily Post, Port Vila.

Winters LA and Martins PMG 2006, 'When comparative advantage doesn't matter: business costs in small economies', (ed) R Grynberg in WTO at the margins – small states and the multilateral trading system, University Press, Cambridge.

World Bank 1994, World development report 1994: infrastructure for development, Oxford University Press, London.

—. 2006, The Pacific infrastructure challenge – a review of obstacles and opportunities for improving performance in the Pacific islands, Pacific Islands Country Management Unit, East Asia and Pacific Region.

—. 2008, Telecommunications in the Pacific – background paper for the Pacific Economic Survey 2008, World Bank, Jakarta.

—. 2009, 'Worldwide governance indicators project 2009', World Bank, viewed 28 February 2010, <http://info.worldbank.org/governance/wgi/index.asp>

World Trade Organization 1991, 'WTO's services sectoral classification list', MTN.GNS/W/120, viewed 19 December 2009, <http://www.wto.org/english/tratop_e/serv_e/mtn_gns_w_120_e.doc>

—. 1995, 'Papua New Guinea – schedule of specific commitments', Trade in Services, GATS/SC/118, WTO Secretariat, Geneva.

—. 1997, 'Papua New Guinea – schedule of specific commitments: supplement 1', Trade in Services, GATS/SC/118/Suppl.1, WTO Secretariat, Geneva.

—. 1999, 'Trade policy review: Papua New Guinea – Report by the Secretariat', WT/TPR/S/62, WTO Secretariat, Geneva.

—. 2001, 'Draft report of the working party on the accession of Vanuatu – addendum', Draft Schedule – Vanuatu WT/ACC/VUT/13/Add.2, WTO Secretariat, Geneva.

—. 2002, 'The legal texts – the results of the Uruguay round of multilateral trade negotiations', WTO Secretariat, Geneva.

—. 2005[a], 'Tonga report of the working party on the accession of Tonga – addendum Part II schedule of specific commitments in services – list of article II MFN exemptions, WT/ACC/TON/17/Add.2, Hong Kong.

—. 2005[b], 'Background documents 31st and 32nd Trade Policy Course – Trade in Services (GATS)', WTO Secretariat, Geneva.

—. 2005[c], Report of the working party on the accession of Tonga – Addendum: Part II Schedule of Specific Commitments in Services, WT/ACC/TON/17/Add.2 and WT/MIN(05)/4/Add.2, WTO Secretariat, Geneva.

—. 2006, 'The general agreement on trade in services: an introduction', WTO Secretariat, viewed 17 May 2010, <http://www.wto.org/english/tratop_e/serv_e/gsintr_e.doc>

—. 2008, 'Understanding the WTO', Fourth Edition, World Trade Organisation, Geneva, viewed 27 April 2010, <http://www.wto.org/english/thewto_e/whatis_e/tif_e/understanding_e.pdf>

—. 2009, Online Source – Doha Development Agenda, viewed on 26 November, <http://www.wto.org/english/thewto_e/minist_e/min01_e/mindecl_e.htm#organization>

Worrell D, Codrington H, Craigwell R and Greenidge K 2006, 'Economic resilience with an exchange rate peg: The Barbados experience', (eds) L Briguglio, G Cordina and EJ Kisanga in Building economic resilience of small states, Formatek Publishing, Malta.

Yackee JW 2008, 'Bilateral investment treaties, credible commitment, and the rule of (international) law: do Bilateral investment treaties promote foreign direct investment?', Law and Society Review, Vol. 42, No. 4, pp. 805-832.

Yanow D 2000, Conducting interpretive policy analysis, Thousand Oaks, California.

Yusuf RM 1991, 'Using Telecommunications as a catalyst for growth', Telecommunications Journal, Vol. 58, Issue 7, pp. 443-446.

INDEX